Cultural Politics in International Relations

PAUL SHEERAN
King Alfred's College, Winchester

Ashgate

Aldershot • Burlington USA • Singapore • Sydney

Published by
Ashgate Publishing Limited
Gower House
Croft Road
Aldershot
Hampshire GU11 3HR
England

Ashgate Publishing Company
131 Main Street
Burlington, VT 05401-5600 USA

Ashgate website: http://www.ashgate.com

British Library Cataloguing in Publication Data
Sheeran, Paul
  Cultural politics in international relations
  1.International relations 2.Counterculture - Soviet Union
  3.Soviet Union - Politics and government - 1985-1991
  I.Title
  947'.085

Library of Congress Control Number: 2001091562

ISBN 0 7546 1759 9

Printed in Great Britain by
Antony Rowe Ltd, Chippenham, Wiltshire.

CULTURAL POLITICS IN INTERNATIONAL RELATIONS

For Gill, Jack and Emma

Contents

Preface

Having entered the twenty-first century there is confusion as to what constitutes the content of International Relations.[1] The confidence that was present in the discipline the previous century has taken flight. This is not necessarily the problem it is often perceived to be. Turbulence and storms can sweep away the inadequacy of complacency. Empowered by uncertainty, the struggle for understanding is regenerated.

The resignation of President Boris Yeltsin, on the last day of the twentieth century, as head of the Russian State, and the transfer of power to his Prime Minister, Vladimir Putin, ended the possession of figures that seemingly had a direct influence on the Soviet past.[2] Lenin, Stalin, Khrushchev, Brezhnev, Andropov, Chernenko, Gorbachev and Yeltsin are effectively book-marked, the apparent constructors and de-constructors of a Soviet practice.

The story, however, despite appearances, is not concluded. The process that led to the collapse of the former Soviet Union has not been thoroughly understood. As a result, its repercussions on the vagaries of world politics have not been fully assessed. It is argued in this book that the disintegration of the former Soviet Union presents a radical point in the development of International Relations as a discipline. The work demonstrates how seemingly rigid systems can be undermined and *altered* by internal social pressure.

Is the content of the pages that follow strictly International Relations? At the height of the Cold War it is unlikely that material which referred to activity outside high politics (a collective expression for certain issue areas of crucial importance) would be taken seriously, let alone considered, as a guide to assessing the potential for change in the international system.[3] The asking of such a question highlights the strength of islands of thought in the discipline and the dominance of entrenched positions, a condition arguably propagated by the structural realists in particular.[4]

The loss of authority within the community of International Relations can be traced to the loss in the stability and order between the great powers that prevailed in varying degrees in the later part of the twentieth century, a requirement imposed by the threat of nuclear annihilation. In the environment of a persistent status quo between East and West, a conflagration occurred with apparent spontaneity: the disintegration of the Soviet Union. On closer examination the cautious identification of an incremental and deliberate process seemingly reveals the existence of counter-hegemonic cultural terrorism. Circulated, or so it would appear, in the pre-Gorbachev era, through various methods, rock music included, via the gulag, the kitchen, the illegal gathering, it imploded and exploded on the international stage, destabilising the participants directly. The grand and often chaotic social Russian opera and deviation from it was not autonomous from the Soviet era, but part of it. The spiritual element embedded in Russian life was seemingly crucial in the Soviet change process, a dimension of culture rarely considered in Western analysis of Soviet Studies during the Cold War period.[5]

It was widely assumed by theorists and practitioners of international affairs that the established system of the Soviet Union was a permanent fixture.[6] In the literature of Soviet Studies, reform and technical modifications were considered possible. The potential for widespread transformation was, however, given the uncertainties of the contemporary world politics and the need for order and security to maintain a modicum of stability, deemed unlikely by its contributors.[7] The various actors who were directly involved in the Soviet change process did not however adhere to the script. The *official* protagonists of both East and West appeared to find themselves, along with the 'experts' of international affairs, in the dark wood, alluded to by Dante, where the right road was wholly lost and gone.

The metamorphosis that occurred in the former Soviet Union and its effects on the discipline of International Relations are explicitly and implicitly related. The former, from its beginning, appears with the subliminal skill of the conjurer to have concealed an array of contradictions in its essence, desires and direction. The latter suggestively, but not inaccurately, consciously ignored the existence of the underlying forces prevalent within the system. In particular it ignored the cultural malignancy and the presence of coded criticism (*where secrecy evades censorship to convey a countercharge against the authority responsible for the prohibition*), concentrating instead on the collective capabilities and hegemonic rhetoric of the Soviet Union. In the analysis of the Soviet change process 'indeed, it might be said before anything else that the crises unleashed by the reformation of Soviet society themselves brought on a corresponding crises in the analysis and interpretation of Soviet society'.[8] In this context, the need to consider cultural politics in International Relations is obvious.

The aim of this investigation is to access the apparent failure of the discipline of International Relations to understand change in the former Soviet Union and consider the implications of subsequent change in world politics. In particular, it seems that the discipline of International Relations was limited in adequately conceptualising and acknowledging the role of globalization in the changing nature of international affairs. The development of the former Soviet Union was not adequately examined in its historical context to identify the trends and processes that fundamentally countervailed its ideological and culturally engineered social evolution.[9]

The initial intention of the work is to de-familiarise the narratives, or more specifically, the narrative, which sought to monitor the situation in the former Soviet Union through an examination of the Soviet political structure and key personnel within it. In the light that some events relating to the demise of the Soviet Union have arguably become the content of axiomatic reference, the need to challenge the conventional claims that, on close analysis appear limited and suspect, is pressing. In seeking to understand the generic mixture of episodes which appear, in various degrees, disguised and coded, the *essence* of the Soviet system and its opposing forces are re-evaluated to measure and record social phenomena largely absent from the social-scientific laboratories of Anglo-American International Relations.

The work of the so-called dissidents of International Relations[10] provides a starting point from which to connect with the wide dissension from official Soviet ideology in the tradition of Dostoyevsky and a host of Russian *devils* and renegades. To reiterate, it is a beginning from which the appeal and limit of it will become clear. In regards to the material presented, a move to a theory of pluralism that violates the constraints imposed by the arbitrary discourses *policing* the studies of the former Soviet Union is viewed as necessary to glean results other than those unsatisfactorily arrived at through professional ignorance.

Cultural Politics in International Relations encapsulates an analysis of the structural, material and ideological conditions that were in flux during the eradication of Soviet power and an analysis of the discipline that claimed to understand it. The relatively non-violent disintegration of the former Soviet Union revealed ambiguities that continue to be the content of historical puzzles, the solution of being to ignore them. Nonetheless, key forces can be discerned and measured. It is not the intention within this work to address these in their entirety, but to clarify and connect a few troublesome and related pieces. To stipulate at the outset: the role of alternative-counter culture in undermining the Soviet regime and the failure of International Relations as a discipline in identifying and assessing the power inherent within it highlights the need to recognise indigenous social forces. Therefore, one objective of the book is to illustrate the methods used by dissidents against inflexible structures and circumstances, in whatever form they appear.

Whilst alternative/counter-culture have similar connotations, in this investigation counterculture is perceived to be deliberately at variance with the social norm constructed by Soviet ideology and culture. Alternative culture is counterculture's historic residue: the ideas and attitudes that are critical of a dominant form of social organisation, its conventions and regulations, and the authority which constructs and legitimates it in a particular time-place.

To understand the strategies and effectiveness of alternative/counter-culture in opposing the Soviet regime a thematically directed procedure will be followed to analyse the turbulence that disabled the Soviet system. The method of identifying and analysing related stems is utilised to represent the various ideas, motifs and sentiments that were operational in contributing to change within the composition of Soviet life. The popular argument that contradictions within the Soviet system were not important in contributing to its end is categorically rejected.[11]

The first theme will analyse the protagonists involved in the struggle for power in the Soviet Union. In the ruling hierarchy, each of the following would have connections and commitments, of varying degrees, with either the orthodox communists who sought to maintain the traditional grip of the Party on all important matters, or the reforming communists who attempted to democratise Soviet life. In their respective groupings, but not in a neat taxonomic arrangement, they are as follows:

1. The reformers of socialism led by Gorbachev and the discourse of reform.
2. The Party-state elite (the old Nomenklatura).
3. The traditionalists both within the Party and the state apparatus who sought to resurrect the repressive order before and after Gorbachev.
4. The ideas and agendas voiced by republican interests and the generic emancipation from the communist architects who had 'gone even further than their imperial predecessors in both denying and humiliating the national cultures of the peoples of the Soviet Russian state'.[12] In the context of preserving spiritual faith in an environment of repression, music had been a tool through which it could be maintained in public through coded performance. This will be considered along with spiritual opposition to the regime in its various cultural forms and contexts.

5. The numerous and heterogeneous cultural terrorists who through various methods, both explicit and implicit, resisted institutional representation and ideological dogma. This is conceptualised as arising from the activity of alternative/counter-culture.

The second theme will consider the political actions of *ordinary* people that operated within the environment in which the above political manoeuvrings took place. *Glasnost* (the policy of public frankness and accountability) permeated throughout society during the mid-80s but its effectiveness was apparently viewed cynically throughout all levels of society. In the economic domain, those who experienced the restructuring of the Soviet economy directly displayed a 'sceptical attitude toward perestroika'.[13] Other processors nurturing change seem however prevalent: the lengthy efforts of the dissident movement, the intellectuals, and the ideas and beliefs accelerated by the sixties global counterculture movement, were apparently influencing social possibilities and life chances. Hypocrisy was increasingly challenged, and the system appears to have had difficulty in controlling its veracity. Music, and in particular rock music, literature, film and poetry (long tools of alternative culture), appear present in the rhythms accelerating change from the Soviet Union's revolutionary inception to the primitively envisaged blueprint of Gorbachev, causing re-formulations, varied trajectories and unforeseen consequences. In this context an understanding of the intertextuality of Russian literature and the wide range of dissident forms arising from it is crucial in assessing both the formulae and influence of this activity.

It will be suggested throughout that opposition to the Soviet system evolved from the activities and concerns of alternative/counter-culture. Whilst the dissident movement in its widest sense was not necessarily an ideological or cohesive movement, it was armed with numerous methods of political dissent. At the most fundamental level resistance to the Soviet system in a spiritual sense plausibly re-vitalised civil society and undermined the totalitarian structure. The 'thematic-clues' found in unofficial Soviet rock music (music not endorsed by the Soviet authorities) were a particularly incisive and effective weapon in the fight against the manipulation present in the construction and management of the Soviet reality. In this specific musical form, 'the aesthetic centre of gravity in Russia has always been closer to the word, rather than the tune'.[14] In the absence of organised political parties in opposition to the communists it appears that indigenous unofficial Soviet rock music, imbued with lyrical poetic content, was crucial in the approbation of an alternative view.

The third theme, in the context of moving beyond the simplistic and neat separation between the planned economies of the former Soviet Union and the Eastern Bloc countries and the capitalist West, is the commitment to make clear evolving global interactions.

The address made by Gorbachev to the 27th Congress in 1986 includes the recognition of the emergence of trans-national structures. The speech repeatedly returned to the theme of the emergence of international structures, in particular finance production and knowledge, and their ability to penetrate national structures. The structural modifications, which had affected the international system, were creating demands within the Soviet Union that could not be ignored. Rather than continuing to resist change, both outside and within the Soviet region, Gorbachev proposed to accelerate the reform process. Whilst the discourse of reform appears not to have been unanimous in either content or method, it seems clear that the supposition for change and the need to respond to it was inevitable.

In approaching the complexity of global interaction, the theory inherent throughout this investigation correlates closely with what Arjun Appadurai recognised in the construction of an elementary framework to examine the global cultural economy, the prevalence of disjunctures.[15] Distinguishable phenomena arising from 'the historical, linguistic and political situatedness of different sorts of actors: nation-states, multinationals, diasporic communities, as well as sub-national groupings and movements (whether religious, political or economic), and even intimate face to face groups, such as villages, neighbourhoods and families'.

The hypothesis that International Relations as a discipline failed to grasp the process and implications of the Soviet change is a serious indictment against its ability in its traditional form to adequately study the potential for war and peace between states. Assuming from the material collated that this possibility clearly exists, the investigation seeks to test whether the distinction between the domestic and the international was an anachronism long before it became the topic of scholarly debate.

Each of the three themes overlap. This technique is preferred to a traditional narrative structure, in that the 'stringing-together' of thematic variations is reflexive of the complexity found in the everyday activity of Soviet life, and in the wider environments in which it functioned. It could however be argued that each of the themes could be further reduced and examined in isolation. In understanding, however, both the independent and collective forces that contributed to the collapse of the former Soviet Union, an enforced separation of the inextricably linked social phenomena would not provide adequate material to provide insight, let alone solutions, to the puzzle. In understanding how and why the former Soviet Union disintegrated, and International Relations as a discipline seemingly failed in the prognosis of the possibilities relating to it, the contrived and accidental forces will be juxtaposed to analysis, not to the detriment of academic rigour, but to the enhancement of it.

Chapter One, *Stranger in a Strange Land*, raises the importance of satire and humour as tools of opposition to authority and intransigence. The material goes on to unpack the post-World War II order of International Relations, dominated by superpower rivalry.

In surveying the debris of Soviet past, Chapter Two, *Contested Claims*: *The Uncertainty of Certainty*, considers the explanations that sought to make sense of the Soviet disintegration. It examines the episodic change within the former socialist bloc and highlights the problems associated with a narrow reading of the change process. The political, economic, sociological and technological domains are assessed to make clear the prevalence of pressure occurring within the system from a diverse range of sources, a force seemingly generated by alternative counterculture. The analysis is undertaken with an awareness of other factors than counterculture, such as the role of Mikhail Gorbachev, The Strategic Defence Initiative (SDI), superpower relations, technological change, the impact of international capital and Western consumerism that contributed in varying degrees to change process.

Chapter Three, *Cultural Genocide: The Dialectic of Struggle*, is concerned with the methods utilised by alternative culture from an early stage in the Soviet Union's development. Through an assessment of the historic opposition to Russian autocracy, an impression of prolonged struggle is recognised, a factor in the sustained deviance from the Soviet state. The material in the chapter goes on to consider the tenuous relationship between idealism and violence. The role of the *Nomenklatura* in directing and manipulating all aspects of Soviet bureaucracy is introduced to illustrate a flaw in the official structure.

In assessing social realism and its impact on the construction of the norms and values that prevailed in the evolving official culture, Chapter Four, *The System and the Damage Done*, presents an analysis of the authority of the Communist Party of the Soviet Union (CPSU), and the state bureaucracy. It considers the hierarchical dictates of the ruling elite in implementing and *policing* its control of power through extensive ideological indoctrination.

Chapter Five, *Alternative/Counter-Culture: Coded Change*, is concerned with the opposition to *official* culture that occurred in everyday Soviet life. The chapter illustrates how the *sociability* of counter-culture operated to develop an alternative view, a condition that challenged the legitimacy of Soviet authority. The material deepens the specific role played by alternative/counterculture and its presence in the various arts, but especially in indigenous Soviet rock music, as the most popular art form, in opposing the Soviet regime.

The method through which dissidents resisted the Soviet regime is considered in Chapter Six. *The Meaning of Dissent: From Grumble to Revolution* is fundamentally concerned with identifying the categories of dissidence. The Chapter deepens the examination of the influence of humour and satire, tools adapted to expose the flaws of the Soviet system. The material makes clear the use of humour as a political weapon and its ability to highlight the absurdity of dogma and programs that shape morality in any form. The work goes on to consider the response of the authorities in managing dissent and the countermeasures that were initiated to overcome them, from coded-criticism to non-compliance.

Chapter Seven, *Emancipation and Coded (Dis)chord*, looks at the global explosion of popular music and the indigenous nature of Soviet rock as the most popular form of counterculture. In the absence of an official political opposition, music was one activity that promoted an alternative view. The chapter makes clear the influence of poetry on the lyrics, a condition that appears important in degrading the legitimacy of Soviet ideology. The performance of Soviet rock music, the circulation of recorded materials associated with it and the duplication and circulation of lyrics transcribed in samizdat texts (unofficial publications) is examined to measure its part in the weakening of the Soviet system.

In examining the role of Soviet rock lyrics and the literary dissent of the creative intelligentsia, Chapter Eight, *The Intelligentsia*, deepens the analysis of the coded nature of non-compliance, conveyed by the ability of the intelligentsia to effectively expose and ridicule the Soviet system. With a direct and acute experience of repression, the specific role of the intelligentsia was to reveal the guarded nature of the regime, with its frailties, abnormalities and abuses. In examining the role of Soviet rock lyrics and the literary dissent of the creative intelligentsia an alternative culture is identified, with its roots stretching back to the *honest* representation of Russian life modelled by writers such as Pushkin.

Chapter Nine, *A Weak Utopia*, looks at the effect cultural and economic globalization had on the former Soviet Union and measures the import of a range of materials that the authorities failed to limit. The chapter considers the connections between Soviet political economy, the presence of counterculture, and the range of tensions maturing within the Soviet system. A reflection on the atmosphere in which change occurred, producing the growth of social ambivalence towards all institutions associated with Soviet communism is conveyed both through oral history and published sources.

Chapter Ten, *The Politics of Unreason*, concludes the book and reiterates the author's concern about the limits of structural realism in understanding the range of possibilities produced by the change process. The final comments are explicitly directed at the failure of International Relations as a discipline to recognise the influence of social activity on political change in the domestic and international arenas.

Thanks are due to the following for lending their valuable time to the project: Roy Smith, Joanne Hollows, Stephan Chan, Andrew Williams, Ben Taylor, Chris Farrands, Chris May, Rick Simon, Matthew Paterson, Richard Johnson; Leo Feigin, Seva Novogorodtev, Alexander Kan and the Russian section at the BBC World Service, Bush House, London; Zoltan Ivan at the Hungarian section of the BBC World Service, Bush House, London; Boris Kagarlitsky, William Mader; Victor Sumsky and Professor Khoros at IMEMO Institute of International Relations and World Economy, Russian Academy of Sciences, Moscow; Andrei Kologanov and Alla Pokrovskaya at the Moscow State University, Moscow; Sergei Pantisev, Alexander Griffin, Gwen White and Mohammed Aslam; Rosa Peive, for her hospitality and numerous street directions during my stay in Moscow. Numerous others willingly offered their valuable time to endure interviews, queries, and clarifications in relation to this work. Thanks to Celia Harris, Sue O'Dowd, Gill Beck, Lynne Biltcliffe and Nadja Freeman at King Alfred's. A special mention must go to wife Gill for her on-going support and keen constructive criticism. The mistakes, errors and inaccuracies are purely my responsibility.

Notes

[1] See Steve Smith, Ken Booth and Marysia Zalewski (1996) *International theory: positivism and beyond*, for a collection of excellent essays assessing developments in International Relations.
[2] Vladimar Vladimirovich Putin was born in Leningrad October 7 1952. Putin worked for the KGB between 1975-1991, although there are lots of rumours concerning his activities little of substance is known about the man.
[3] See Evans and Newnham (1992:127), *The Dictionary of World Politics*, for a detailed description of high politics.
[4] Richard K. Ashley, (1986:184), in a seminal attack on structural realism, suggests that 'structural realists assume great powers should prevail'. In understanding the nature of change to and within the system, Ashley exposes the shortcomings of neo-realism/structural realism in recognising the influence of social forces on the change process. 'The key point' he goes on 'is not whether there is an overriding structure or a series of structures but the degree of autonomy for human action'. It is argued in this piece that the key failure of

Soviet Studies, and in particular International Relations, to understand the Soviet change process was an inability to recognise the interaction of human life with the system.

[5] A review of the journal, *Soviet Studies*, between 1979-1989, reveals a lack of analysis outside the Soviet system, Soviet life is only fleetingly alluded to. The presence of dissidents and the methods they adopted to oppose the system is conspicuously absent. Material, however, that points to the presence of an alternative view to Soviet communism within the region can be found in particularly in the articles: by Thomas Oleszczuk (1985) 'An Analysis of Bias in *Samizdat* Sources: A Lithuanian Case Study'; Jim Riordan (1988) 'Soviet Youth: Pioneers of Change'.

[6] Kenneth N. Waltz (1979:95) argued in a key text in International Relations that 'States are the units whose interactions form the structure of international-political systems. They will long remain so. The death rate among states is remarkably low. Few states die; many firms do. Who is likely to be around 100 years from now – the United States, the Soviet Union, France, Egypt, Thailand, and Uganda? Or Ford, IBM, Shell, Unileyer, and Massey-Ferguson? I would bet on states, perhaps even on Uganda'.

[7] The journal, *Soviet Studies*, focused generally on the functional aspects of the system and reported on issues such as wheat yields, Soviet capital stock, income distribution, economic planning etc. *The ABC of Political Science* should be consulted for a full list of contents.

[8] Cushman (1993:26), *Glastnost, Perestroika, and the management of oppositional popular culture in the Soviet Union 1985-1991.*

[9] Ulrich Beck (1997:21) considers *globalization* and *individualization* to be useful in understanding the vagaries and ambiguities of a post-rational Western world. In Beck's opinion, 'the former breaks the horizon of the nation state and its ideology theoretically and politically, and the latter has the same effect on sociology's virtual fixation on the priority of groups and collectives'.

[10] Richard K. Ashley and R.B.J. Walker (1990:267) argue in the 'Special Issue: Speaking the Language of Exile – Dissidence in International Relations' that "what is at stake is nothing less than the question of sovereignty: whether or not this most paradoxical question, alive in all the widening margins of culture, can be taken seriously in international studies today". Without doubt, this is the crux of the matter relating to change in relation to the nature of *altered* States.

[11] Herbet Schiller (1997), 'A Century of Expectations and Preparations for Global Electronic Mastery'. Paper presented at the conference *Electronic Empires*: An international conference organised by the Communication, Culture and Media subject group of the Coventry School of Art and Design, England 28-29 March 1997. Schiller, at one point, seemingly argued that the collapse of the former Soviet Union had little to do with social change within the Soviet Union. It is argued throughout this investigation that this position fundamentally ignores the relevance and consequence of activity resulting from indigenous cultural practises during the Soviet change process.

[12] RFE/RL Studies (1989:5).

[13] Bonnell (1989:311), *Moscow: A view from below.*

[14] Zaitsev, I. (1990:12), *Soviet Rock.*

[15] Appaduria (1990:246), *Disjunctures and difference in the Global Political Economy.*

Introduction

In the controversial article, 'The End of History', Francis Fukuyama celebrated what appeared to be the 'unabashed victory of economic and political liberalism' and the 'triumph of the West, of the Western *idea*'.[1] This idea, which was incomplete in the real or material world, but was perceived by Fukuyama to hold hegemony over all philosophical, political and economic substitutes, a condition that rendered alternatives inconsequential and historically redundant. Fukuyama was writing in a period when seemingly global transformations acutely affected ideologies and the material and structural categories identifiable in most areas of the international system. With reference to a Hegelian reading of history, Fukuyama felt inclined to present a version of change that suggested:

> what we may be witnessing is not just the end of the Cold War, or the passing of a particular period in post-war history, but the end of history as such: that is, the end point in mankind's ideological evolution and the universalisation of Western liberal democracy as the final form of human government.[2]

The passage towards the nirvana of liberal democracy depended, albeit unevenly, on the success of the liberal idea over the programs presented against it. Within the seeming ascendancy of liberal democracy, Fukuyama appeared to ignore all signs counter to the central premise embedded in his work. The view that 'the failure of the French Revolution to bring about the greater portion of its declared ends' a condition which 'marks the end of the French Enlightenment as a movement and a system'[3] was without consequence. The trajectories within pluralism were sacrificed in the construction of an Anglo-American world view, which celebrated the dominance of a universal system founded on a particular common-sense.

The acceptance of liberal ideas has not materialised in Russia in the way that Fukuyama envisioned, although admittedly some doubt was posited at the outset. Nonetheless, the democratic tendencies (loosely conceptualised in the original piece) associated with Gorbachev's policies and *ideals* were not the acceptance of a single liberal ideal but an attempt to deepen a discourse of reform that could be manipulated to serve specific autocratic interests. In identifying other key factors in the change process Fukuyama argued that:

> this phenomenon extends beyond high politics and it can also be seen in the ineluctable spread of consumerist Western culture in such diverse contexts as the peasants' markets and colour television sets now omnipresent through China, the co-operative restaurants and clothing stores opened in the past year in Moscow, the Beethoven piped into Japanese department stores, and the rock music enjoyed alike in Prague, Rangoon, and Tehran.[4]

To a point, the snapshot presented above of the expansive nature of the consumer society had features that could be easily recognised in everyday life. The sweep of American consumerism had in the former Soviet Union however not overcome its association with a system of exploitation and usury, which appears to have soured its appeal although paradoxically not the desire to have an experience of it. The view that Western rock music had a limited affect on directly undermining the Soviet system, particularly when compared with the operation of an indigenous Soviet rock *community*, similarly rebukes the *popular* version of globalization.

The claim of the prevalence of a sustained single world-view has been disrupted by the varied nature of ideas and opinions prevalent throughout Russia, which appear to render observations of a homogenous form of liberal-democracy premature. The resurgence of Religion is particularly noticeable (the Russian Orthodox Church is re-asserting its authority and popularity throughout Russia) and in the political domain, a nexus of atomised forces contend for influence to promote a variety of causes, albeit under familiar banners. Despite anomalies, the intransigence of the political elite in Russia, the end result in the region lends itself to the view that:

> at the end of history it is not necessary that all societies become successful liberal societies, merely that they end their ideological pretensions of representing different and higher forms of human society.[5]

The tenuous nature of Russian affairs makes it doubtful that this situation will continue. The old system collapsed without the construction of a new order: it was not a revolution or a transformation but a desperate scramble to both orchestrate and ignore the vagaries and complexity of change occurring concurrently in a range of sectors and consciousness. It is not the intention of this piece to speculate where Russia may be heading, but to make clear the processes that ended the social coercion that prevailed throughout the former Soviet Union.

In a particularly conservative statement Fukuyama claimed that 'in the post-historical period there will be neither art nor philosophy, just the perpetual care-taking of the museum of human history'.[6] Philosophy may have suffered a loss of credibility in the Soviet Union, but considering its recent effect on the lives of ordinary Russians this is not surprising. In the post-Soviet condition, art has become more radical – Olek Kulik's work being particularly noticeable, to reflect life in the most exact way. It is particularly critical of the corrupt form of economic capitalism that prevails in the important sectors of the Russian economy and the 'loss of identity', which is widely perceived to be both positive and negative.[7]

The key problem with Fukuyama's thesis in regards to this investigation is its lack of concern with an alternative culture, a point of view that can be traced back to the counter-enlightenment, and the emergence of relativist and sceptical traditions opposed to one structure of reality. It is suggested in this piece that the evolutionary process of change within the Soviet Union was seemingly influenced by *liberal* forces opposed to the absurdities and extremes of a rationally organised society, and, to a degree, elements of the Enlightenment conditions espoused by Fukuyama. This appears to have partly been initiated from an experience with the conditions in the Soviet Union: a detailed view of them is presented in the following pages to make clear the multiple direction of the change process.

The celebration discernible in the article found in the journal *National Interest* was replaced with greater pessimism in Fukuyama's book *The End of History and the Last Man*. It presumed to recognise an increasing tone of human inertia and presented a theory that mapped its descent into apathy. The post-Soviet condition of passive social activity prevalent in large Russian cities and towns, a feature recognised in the chapter 'Men without Chests' could be presented as a guide to the trend towards the abolition of serious and *authentic* human conflict. This is contradicted, perhaps, to a degree, by the outbreak of sporadic violence from a variety of sources and attempts to re-introduce *kingdoms* and spheres of influence. If one accepts the master-slave thesis to be an accurate representation of process through which higher forms of the human condition are produced – rather than the continuation of a negative sadomasochistic conflict – then the outcomes which Fukuyama predicts have an element of validity. Nonetheless, this appears to be a crude measure of human behaviour that negates the complexity associated with struggle, achievement and recognition. Ultimately, Fukuyama ignores the liberal renegades who long ago left the wagon trail and directed their arrows against the version of liberalism seemingly omnipresent at the end of history.

Fukuyama's interpretation of the past noted, the need to make clear the complex interdependence between States both materially and in the exchange of ideas is extremely relevant to the development of International Relations and the consideration of the Soviet change process.

In response to globalization, David Marsh and Gerry Stoker have argued that political science needs to seriously re-consider its position in theorising the effects of a range of phenomena arising from the international domain. Correspondingly, the discipline of International Relations should perhaps take 'opportunity to rethink the Great Divide and the analytical schemes which have been deployed to legitimise it'.[8]

The collapse of the former Soviet Union has presented the opportunity for the academic discipline and the practise of International Relations to evaluate the material that constitutes the foundations of its basic assumptions. The intransigent and immovable enemy of the West and the *substance* of the Anglo-American discipline of International Relations had unceremoniously vanished into thin air. The rationale that had sought to understand an uncompromising and antagonistic regime is seemingly redundant. The fundamental tenets of the discipline that appeared deficient in assessing the metamorphosis of the Soviet Union were not however abandoned, but were seemingly re-incorporated into theories which claimed to reflect the supposed post-Soviet realities of the international system. This apparent resistance to accept the damage afflicted on the assumptions and practises of structural realism prompts a reconsideration of its original misdemeanour and further flight from it.

The Madness of Methodology

In the entry to the *Collins Concise Dictionary* methodology is defined as '1. The system of methods and principles used in a particular discipline 2. The branch of philosophy concerned with the science of method'. In making clear the methods adopted to infer the value of likely stories in this piece, the intention will be to recognise the possibilities offered by methodological plurality, with the strict qualification to eradicate ambiguity without sacrificing creativity.

In the twentieth century, the assumptions and methods, which underpinned an understanding of political activity, have had to be re-articulated, re-formulated and extended to reflect the proliferation of interests and issues that encompass forces and actions outside the recognised sites of power. Stoker claims that it is this condition which has forced political science in the 1990s to view the political in a much broader way.   As Gamble puts it: 'the political has come to be defined... to embrace other areas of social life such as gender, race and class. Politics has come to be understood as an aspect of all social relations, rather than an activity centred on the institutions of government'.[9]

The move reflects the post-war revolution in social attitudes and life-styles, a conversion to what Marshall McLuhan called the electronic process and the public revelation, communication and dissimulation of agendas other than those directed and legitimated by authority. The methods that have been constructed to reflect the on-going struggles and nexus of relations inherent in the complexity of social phenomena have not, although of course there are always exceptions, been prepared to depart radically from a common sense view.

Paul Feyerabend, writing in a pivotal decade, the 1960s, in which traditional structures were being challenged by the people they were intended to serve, was however instrumental in exposing the limitations of established methods and the dominance inherent in the science it served. Feyerabend claimed that:

> history is full of 'accidents and conjunctures and curious juxtapositions of events' and it demonstrates to us the 'complexity of human change and the unpredictable character of the ultimate consequence of any given act or decision of men'. Are we really to believe the naïve and simple-minded rules which methodologists take as their guide are capable of accounting for such a 'maze of interactions'?[10]

In opposing Feyeraband's anarchist position, a view that recognises sources of knowledge derived from a diverse range of culturally nominated sites, Paul Tibbets cautions against the move to dismiss completely a methodology founded on scientifically established principles.

> We may say that the denial of a set of universally and necessary principles which are truth-guaranteeing, and the subsequent adoption of fallibilism, do not entail the conclusion that science is less methodologically reliable than alternative methods of inquiry. On the contrary, given its historical record and its self-corrective character, science has a greater likelihood for sorting out the credibility of competing claims to knowledge *over time* than do alternative means of fixing belief.[11]

Tibbets' position may, dogmatically held, lead to an exclusion of social phenomena that is beyond the detection of a scientific method. Seidler suggests that:

the idea that we could discover underlying laws that would explain social relationships was part of the dream of positivism. Too often, however, it discounted people's own experience as 'subjective' and 'anecdotal' when faced with the 'objectivity' of scientific laws. But this is not the only way that we can seek understanding.[12]

The relativistic moral, as considered by D.C.Phillips in *Philosophy, Science and Social Inquiry*, purports that 'all methods are on an equally uncertain footing – so there is no philosophical bar to using non-naturalistic methods', although criticism for doing so is generally intense.[13] Unique phenomena resulting from both observable and imperceptible causes may require ephemeral and intuitive methods to aid clarification. This situation is perhaps far from perfect, but the compulsion to ignore material that is both difficult to observe or considered controversial through the intervention of political considerations should not preclude the recognition of limits in procedures, whether scientific or not.

In a flagrant attempt to justify the restraint, incarceration and disappearance of the *socially dangerous*, the Soviet authorities relied on the interpretation of a rigorous scientific method – a methodology of madness- to eradicate its opposition. In so doing, it legitimated its use of coercion in regulating the debate on the condition of truth and its verification. In a study analysing the abuse of psychiatric practices in the former Soviet Union and the diagnosis of sluggish schizophrenia on healthy subjects it was reported that:

the individual is also deemed to be out of touch with reality and to have an inadequate sense of self-preservation if he does not show himself to be sufficiently aware of the precariousness of his position vis-à-vis the authorities. According to this theory, a healthy, individual with strong convictions could be characterised as schizophrenic and interned in a psychiatric hospital.[14]

In the confines of rational investigation, the madness of method led in this context to:

the idea that engagement in two unrelated activities is a symptom of schizophrenia has given rise to the ironic term, "the da Vinci syndrome" after the great Italian artist and scientist who was the supreme example of the

Renaissance genius.   According to this ludicrous view, many of the most talented people in the world would be certified as insane if they have contributed to more than one single field of endeavour.[15]

Whilst this perhaps produced certain benefits in less totalitarian environments it produced limited space for experimentation and constructed a view of the world confident that its perspective correlated with the observation of it. This appears to have led to reoccurring errors in the mode of representation accorded to social phenomena within its sphere of expertise.

It has been raised that in response to the limitations in understanding change in the Soviet condition a need exists to examine the fundamentals of the International Relations discipline.[16] John Gaddis, Edward Walker, Michael Cox and Thomas Cushman have for example identified flaws in both strategic studies and Sovietology.[17] Gaddis claims that 'the event [end of the cold war] was of such importance that no approach to the study of International Relations claiming both foresight and competence should have failed to see it coming'.[18] In the anticipation of finding a solution to the identification of important social phenomena, Gaddis cautions against the 'jettison of the scientific approach to the study of International Relations'. He goes on to urge that in the light of its failures the discipline should 'make use of all the tools at their disposal in trying to anticipate the future'.[19] Walker, in identifying the failure of Sovietologists to understand the multi-dimensional character of perestroika (particularly its non-economic dimensions), introduces six factors that appear to have undermined clarity.[20]

Whilst insight can be gleaned from this analysis at a systemic level, it fails to consider the coded nature of the evolving cultural forms within the Soviet Union and their effect on the change process. Cox questions the effectiveness of the established tools used by the experts of International Relations and suggests that the shortcomings of Sovietology are related to the dominance of empiricism in the academy and the failure of it in 'examining the large picture historically'.[21] In this view, the emergence of new social forces and processors affecting structural change are not identified. It is this failure to which Cushman refers when he suggests that 'positivism not only freezes social and cultural processors but also does so in categories which are favourable to the bureaucratic state apparatus of modern industrial societies'.[22] Richard Falk in a book review of Rosenau and Czempiel's, *Governance without Government: Order and Change in World Politics* highlights a serious problem associated with the failure of

International Relations to overcome and problematise the heritage of the dominant discourse within its parameters.

In an illuminating section, Falk argues that:

> the volume suffers from a late modernist pretension that the cognitive map of specialists can somehow capture reality. Instead of pausing to wonder about perceptual failures attendant on the inability of the discipline to anticipate the end of the Cold War and the disintegration of the Soviet Union, the undertaking proceeds merrily to announce that the new circumstances of international life warrant reinterpretation, as if the old circumstances had been previously understood. This disciplinary oversight was not a matter of surprise but represented the overnight collapse of the intellectual framework that had guided academicians and policy makers for decades and was expected to last indefinitely.[23]

If there is 'something the matter' with International Relations it needs to be recognised, diagnosed and treated. Its recent and contemporary condition resembles the patient Dr P. in Oliver Sacks' *The man who mistook his wife for a hat*. In a passage that may present an analogy to the operational defects in the discipline of International Relations, Sacks reflects on his most interesting case, a patient who could not make a cognitive judgement, though he was prolific in the production of cognitive hypotheses.

> By a sort of comic and awful analogy, our current cognitive neurology and psychology resembles nothing so much as poor Dr P.! We need the concrete and real, as he did; and we fail to see this, as he failed to it. Our cognitive sciences are themselves suffering from an agnosia essentially similar to Dr P's. Dr P. may therefore serve as a warning and a parable – of what happens to a science which eschews the judgmental, the particular, the personal, and becomes entirely abstract and computational.[24]

Jim George, in the book, *Discourses of Global Politics: A Critical (Re)introduction to International Relations*, picks up on the failure of the realist discourse to understand what it believed it saw and its confidence in rejecting what it did not. George claims that:

> Unable to think and speak outside a primitive logic of (objectified, externalised) reality, it could not question the discursive process that saw a range of alternative perspectives – all articulating facts about Soviet capacity and intent – reduced to an unambiguous, singular narrative of "fact", which gave unity and identity to Western scholars and policy practitioners and a

simple self-affirming meaning to the Cold War...And from this perspective, an internally generated, largely voluntary process of self-destruction by the Soviet people were never part of the predictive agenda.[25]

It has been stated that the theoretical content deemed illuminating in revealing the underlying patterns of change in the former Soviet Union is to a degree dependent on the intellectual steps taken by the dissidents of International Relations. From this *starting point* the expectation is to construct a viable framework from which to assess asymmetrical 'structures of feeling' that are seemingly impregnable to rationalist epistemologies. The propagation is constituent on the connections with the proponents of Russian conceptualism and anti-systemic movements. In this context, the clear assumption that alternative culture was influenced by philosophical factors as well as contingent material and structural circumstances is important in understanding the nature of the oppression and the breaking down of the absolutes of the Soviet system.

The philosophical residue is arguably related to a long intellectual process that has substantial links with the animation of Russian intellectual thought in the 19th century. Isaiah Berlin in the incisive *Russian Thinkers*, compares a passage by Herzen with the *Communist Manifesto*, on a point of clarity between consistent 'dialectics' and 'scientific' socialism, and in so doing highlights, in a passage embroiled with prophetic vision, an inherent fault in the socialist project.

Socialism will develop in all its phases until it reaches its own extremes and absurdities. Then there will again burst forth from the titanic breast of the revolting minority a cry of denial. Once more a mortal battle will be joined in which socialism will occupy the place of today's conservatism, and will be defeated by the coming revolution as yet invisible to us...[26]

The popularity amongst the curious and the cream of the intelligentsia of existential passages gleaned from Ivan Turgenev, Feodor Dostoyevsky, Lev Shestov and Nikolai Berdiaev, and later with the unofficial availability of post-structuralism publications by authors such as Michael Foucault, could not be successfully censored from the Soviet totality. Similarly, the work of Vaclav Havel, and the consistent pluralism recognised in the counter enlightenment thought of Isaiah Berlin, add to the theoretical basis of alternative culture. It must however be recognised that this was by no means universal, and to overstate it as an organising set of principles for the entire opposition movement would be a mistake. It must be assumed that other motivations for resisting the dictates of the Soviet system were present and these will be considered in greater depth later in the investigation.

In looking at the human agents that animated and excited divergent interest groups to accelerate opposition, it appears that the coded criticism inherent in unofficial Soviet rock music and the popular support it attracted was fundamental to the change process. In considering its specific function and assessing the extent to which it undermined Soviet authority, the issue of how change is achieved outside the institutions of the state is raised.

The theme of a genealogy of dissent from authority is widened throughout the text with reference to creative and historic forms of non-compliance and satire: Aristophanes jovial criticism of Socrates, Francois Rabelais comic genius to ridicule dogmatic faith and religious education, Bulat Okudzjava's lampooning of the Soviet ideologues through the performance of folk songs add substance to the claim that satire and humour can make (and made) effective political weapons.

Theoretical Framework [s]: Breaking the Silence of Pluralism

The material presented in this piece problematises and raises the apparent weakness and inadequacy of mainstream International Relations theory, conceptualised as realism and its later embodiment in neo-realism, to understand and include content that reflects the wide influence of social phenomena on the change process. In this sense, the potential of a variety of actors to induce change within the international system is sacrificed in favour of an examination of systems and units that neglect the human material.[27]

The view to which the following pages are sympathetic regards a form of liberalism embedded in pluralism that is sceptical of universalisation and an uncritical notion of progress founded on reason. It is a position dubious of the separation of phenomena into neat and confining either/or categories: recognising complexity, divisions and unanimity as potential occurrences at various historical and spatial junctures. Boris Pasternak commented in *Doctor Zhivago* that it is only in bad novels that people are divided into two camps and have nothing to do with each other. In real life, everything gets mixed up. It is assumed in this investigation that the function of pluralism and its consistent antecedents offers insight into the multiplicity of interpretations concerning the Soviet change process, a feature that is relevant to theories that reflect on the practise and possibilities of international relations.

In the essay *The growing relevance of pluralism?* Richard Little considered the resurgence of liberalism and its early development within the discipline of International Relations, before the breakdown of the League of Nations, and the neo-liberal revival in the 1970s, in the light of interdependence and increased trans-national links.   In the piece, Little dismisses the potential of pluralism to be 'the dominant perspective on international relations by the end of the twentieth century'.[28] Nonetheless, Little accepts that little work has been undertaken to expose the nuances of a pluralist position and its value to the International Relations discipline, certainly not its historic development.   Despite this, the author recognises a split within pluralism and presents a brief but limited review of its observable trajectories. The view offered by Rosenau,[29] which refers to the potential of individuals to transform society, is one example, elsewhere 'individuals are seen as a consequence to be much more sceptical of authority making it increasingly difficult for states to maintain their autonomy'.[30] On the other hand, a strand of pluralism 'eschewing grand theory, has become preoccupied with the question of how the international system can be governed in the absence of a hegemonic state'. It is suggested in this piece that the former does not go far enough in challenging the fundamental tenets of realism (recognised by Falk above) and the latter is too similar to neo-realism to be critical and unreflexive of its general and fundamental pretensions.   Correspondingly, this version of neo-liberalism generally fails to acknowledge the negative consequences, through manipulation of a single liberal view, of the activities associated with large and aggressive business practise (generally American) on the democratic process.

The form of pluralism that this piece adopts to make clear the complexity associated with the Soviet change process is the liberalism of the counter-enlightenment: the sceptics and the relativists that have relevance to both post-modernism and liberalism.   It returns to the tensions inherent in the strict application of Enlightenment thought.   It begins with an endorsement of the view that:

> pluralism…leaves room for contingence, liberty, novelty, and gives complete liberty of action to the empirical method, which can be greatly extended.   It accepts unity where it finds it, but it does not attempt to force the vast diversity of events and things into a single rational mould.[31]

It is within the *material* alluded to above, with its genesis, or more accurately, its modern articulation, in the *reaction* against the

Enlightenment that this work finds its theoretical compass to map the evolutionary process of change in the former Soviet Union. It clearly has relevance to the pluralism exposed by strands of the Russian intelligentsia, a move to a theory that could present International Relations with added insight into the value of cultural currency and appreciation of the social change process in whatever form it manifests. Graeme Garrard has argued that the Counter-Enlightenment thought of Isaiah Berlin is a key exponent of this form.

> Berlin is presented here as not only objecting to the Enlightenment, but objecting to it *because* he is a liberal. This is because he believes that the Enlightenment aspiration to organise society rationally in accordance with a universal conception of truth is incompatible with its belief in individual freedom, which is the core value of liberalism. Berlin's liberalism is based on a rejection of Enlightenment monism in the name of pluralism, which identifies with the Counter-Enlightenment. Thus, while liberalism and Enlightenment share a common concern for individual freedom, only the former is able consistently to uphold this value in practise.[32]

Berlin traces reaction to the progressive French thinkers, and the persistence of an alternative doctrine back to:

> The Greek sophists, Protagoras, Antiphon and Critias, that beliefs involving value judgements, and the institutions founded upon them, rested not on discoveries of objective and unalternable natural facts, but on human opinion, which was variable and differed between different societies and at different times; that moral and political values, and in particular justice and social relations in general, rested on fluctuating human opinion.[33]

In the Soviet context, the desire to 'live within the truth', was seemingly not romanticism or the founding point of a grand and universal theory, but a concrete strategy to reflect an attitude of being. This is a condition that may encompass anarchism and nihilism: constructed in response to specific cultural demands, arising from the position of authority, its opposition and one's relation to it.

The aim in this investigation is not to construct a lofty theory to compensate Little's claim that 'pluralism does no more than provide a critique of various approaches to political science, without offering a coherent alternative'. On the contrary, reference to it, through a reflection on the Soviet change process, and its wider connotations, to the study of International Relations, posits only that sufficient doubt exists to the legitimacy of derogatory claims directed at pluralism. It is suggested that further investigation into the origins and evolving nature of the Counter-Enlightenment theses, which are varied and complex, is required to assess its potential value in contributing to the development of International Relations.

Further Considerations on Method and its Application

Oral history is a device that records the interpretation of particular events through the memories of people who experienced them. It is a method often used in situations where there is a need to uncover concealed layers of social phenomena. The technique has been used in this work to elucidate particular impressions of Soviet ideology, its nature, and perceptions of its malfunction and modes of opposition. There is however a degree of inaccuracy in this method. The respondents may have reported a particular event inaccurately or misconstrued its meaning. Nonetheless, in this case, due to the inherent falsity of Soviet data and publications, and a desire to avoid the replication of the apparent errors in the Soviet evaluation resulting from a crude quantitative analysis, oral history remains a useful tool in collating information that may otherwise not be forthcoming. Intensive cross-references and subsequent clarifications overcome the shortcomings that may relate to it. Where opposing views are unable to be reconciled, evidence of each opinion is presented. Therefore, the conjecture can be tenuously rejected or accepted, concomitant with any additional material which may or may not come to light.

The nucleus of the interviews was undertaken in Moscow (many of which lasted several hours). The initial expectation that good quality overseas contacts would not be available in Moscow was unfounded. A special mention must go to Zoltan Ivan, Hungarian Section of the BBC World Service, for enabling me to draw on his extensive contacts, many of which were involved in the Soviet change process. Interviews outside Russia were conducted throughout the late 1990s and continued up to January 2001. Interviews were recorded on a Sony Walkman and transcribed in part using a Sanyo memo-transcriber. All the interviews were conducted in English. Where requests were made for an interview not to be recorded, mental notes were written up immediately afterwards.

The in-depth open and structured interviews (cited in detail throughout the text with the interviewees named in the footnotes) have carefully been cross-referenced to reveal the divergence and convergence between them. The interviews were mainly conducted in Moscow and London with:

members of the former Soviet counter-culture, many of whom experienced intimidation, imprisonment and exile; Komsomol youth; members of the CPSU; the Russian intelligentsia; Soviet rock insiders; record producers and organisers of Soviet rock performances; broadcasters to the former Soviet Union; academics at the Moscow State University, Russia Academy of Sciences, and Moscow's Higher Business School, and the Sakharov Museum and Archive centre; and *ordinary* citizens from Bulgaria, Romania, Russia, Hungary, Poland and the Czech Republic.

The detailed interviews are complimented with established methods of enquiry, and in particular secondary desk research that may or may not introduce different readings into the dialogue. In this context, the ability to operate follow up checks in the attempt to clear up ambiguities and confusion on specific points is extremely valuable. Many of the original interviews have been updated through continued communications with the interviewees through letters, fax, telephone and electronic mail. The use of E-mail has been particularly useful. More informal than a letter, it quickly establishes the forum of a discussion, which can be returned to and developed without excessive cost. This has allowed the further clarification of material coming to light after the initial face to face interviews have taken place, a facilitation which has arguably allowed for incisive disclosures to be gleaned and assessed, and enabled new material to be included up to the point of publication.

For the non-Russian speaker, Moscow is a relatively easy city to get around. The Metro is excellent and the lines are clearly set out on maps and can be followed without difficulty. English is not a neutral language in Russia, but the interviewees in Moscow could communicate in English. An effort was made however, to clarify that questions and answers had been understood.

Along with the interviews and the secondary research a journal/diary was used during the visit to Moscow to keep a record of direct experiences. These are perhaps trivial observations, notes of the sounds, smells and tastes etc., but nonetheless valuable in contributing to an impression of the atmosphere, even after its flight. A large number of photographs were also taken in Moscow, especially in the Arbat area. Whilst these are not presented in the investigation they have served the purpose of adding a visual text to complement direct observation and literary descriptions.

Whilst the range of interviewees present in this investigation were affected by Soviet communism and its transformation, a limitation of the interviews should be recognised. A comprehensive taxonomy of the range of microscopic political agents operative throughout Soviet life was not possible. Activists, in the general sense, held meetings in apartments, parks, function rooms and street corners, and as a result of the dangers associated with such gatherings, only a small circle would be familiar with their existence and agendas. Nonetheless, their presence will be assumed and where possible additional material will be added.

The political and economic centre of the former Soviet Union, and its spheres of direct influence, is designated in this piece as Moscow. If 'Russia was the central actor in the destruction of the USSR'[34] then Moscow appears to have been the location were the implosion of chaotic and ordered forces resulted in ideological, material and structural change, which rippled throughout the Soviet world as a whole. Three decades ago, the former member of the American Embassy in Moscow described the importance of the capital in holding both the reigns and majority of wealth and power in the region.

> Here the old trade routes, the railways, the waterways and the lines of communication come together to form a giant nerve centre. From here originate the couriers of the Communist party, the telegrams and telephone calls, the newspapers and broadcasts which direct and guide the whole Communist Empire.[35]

Little on this point changed up to the collapse of the former Soviet Union. The apparent focus on Moscow however is not to dismiss or ignore the continuities, differences and struggles that took place in all parts of the former Soviet Union. The trajectories, dissolution and (con)fusion of the peoples of *Rus*, their 'relations' with each other, and the shadow cast by the uneven flight of power exercised by the vagaries and whims of the former revolutionary vanguard of the CPSU is present throughout the pages that follow.

Notes

[1] Fukuyama (1989:3), *The End of History.*
[2] *Ibid* (1989:4).
[3] Berlin (1955:24), *The counter-enlightenment.*
[4] *Op cit* (1989:3).
[5] *Ibid* (1989:13).
[6] *Ibid* (1989:18).
[7] The Guardian Newspaper (1999:17), Friday March 12.
[8] Clark (1998:480), *Beyond the Great Divide: globalization and the theory of international relations.*

[9] Stoker (1995:5), *Theory and methods in political science.*

[10] Feyerabend, (1966:17), *Against Method.*

[11] Tibbets (1977:268), *Feyerabend's "Against Method" The case for methodological pluralism.*

[12] Seidler (1994:171), *Recovering the Self.*

[13] Phillips (1993 [1987]:49), *Philosophy, Science and Social Inquiry.*

[14] Gersman (1984:55), *Psychiatric Abuse in the Soviet Union.*

[15] *Ibid* (1984:55).

[16] See Robert Keohane (ed.), *Neorealism and its Critics*; Steve Smith, Ken Booth & Marysia Zalewski.

[17] It is worth looking at Richard K. Betts (1997) 'Should Strategic Studies Survive', in World Politics A Journal of International Relations, Volume 50, Number 1, for a broad review of the problems associated with the discipline and a consideration of the strategies which may overcome them. See William C. Wohlforth's (1998) 'Reality Check: revising theories of International Politics in response to the end of the cold war' also in the *Journal of World Politics*, Vol.50, which is valuable in considering the proposition that 'science should learn from surprise'.

[18] Gaddis (1992:6), *The end of the Cold War.*

[19] *Ibid* (1992:59), *The end of the Cold War.*

[20] Walker (1993:321), *Sovietology and Perestroika: A post-mortem.*

[21] Cox (1994: 89,91), *The end of the USSR and the collapse of the Soviet Union.*

[22] Cushman (1993:29), *Glasnost, Perestroika, and the management of oppositional culture in the former Soviet Union 1985-1991.*

[23] Falk (1993:544), *Book Review.*

[24] Sacks (1985:19), *The man who mistook his wife for a hat.*

[25] George (1984:224), *Discourses of Global Politics.*

[26] Berlin (1978:98), *Russian Thinkers.*

[27] See Hollis and Smith's chapter 'The Growth of the Discipline' in the book, *Explaining and Understanding International Relations*, for an overview of the various paradigms relevant to the practise of international relations.

[28] Little (1996:67), *The growing relevance of pluralism?*

[29] See Rosenau's *Turbulence in World Politics.*

[30] *Op Cit* (1996:80).

[31] Dewey (1994:51), *The development of American Pragmatism.*

[32] Garrard (1997:282), *The Counter-Enlightenment liberalism of Isaiah Berlin.*

[33] Berlin (1955:2), *The Counter-Enlightenment.*

[34] Sakwa (1993:37), *Russian Politics and Society.*

[35] Thayer (1960:3), *Russia.*

1   Stranger in a Strange Land

Russia is replete with likely stories, the contents of them being in part an 'ironic or tragic juxtaposition with *real life*' in a particular and damaging form.[1] Some have been translated and made familiar by international publication. Others remain the possession of smaller, but no less important, circles. They are nostalgically mused over and appreciated or rejected. Many of these insights have never been told or written down: the autobiographies of ghosts erased from the blueprints and processors of utopia. An extraordinary story is the concern of this investigation: the power of the spoken word and its claim to noble intentions.[2] With words come censorship:

> Kharms noted in the 1930s 'I know four kinds of word machines: poems, prayers, songs and spells'. It is not too much to suggest that the obsessive attention paid by the Soviet authorities to verbal expression was derived from a deep-seated fear of the word's magic power.[3]

During the tenure of the Soviet regime, the poet was continually the victim of tyranny and died with an aid to his death. Under the preceding dynasty, Alexander Pushkin (1799-1837),[4] an icon for subsequent Russian authors and poets, was no stranger to intimidation and exile. Undermining French hegemony in both language and literature, Pushkin elevated the importance of the Russian language and popularised the role of the poet in resisting authority. In this particular piece the poet in Soviet society is alluded to as member of the creative intelligentsia, a black market operator, a political prisoner, a non-compliant comrade, a rock musician, a comedian – each unique and different, but sharing the prose of deviance.

To understand the importance of poetry to ordinary Russians is to realise its power, its special place in the nation's tragic history, and the repeated exertions that would silence it.

> All the tyrants of Russia have always feared poets as their most dangerous political enemies. They feared Pushkin, then Lermontov, then Nekrasov.[5]

Murrey's observations on the *Rise of the Greek Epic*, drew attention to the role of poets who were:

> in the habit of claiming not only divine sources of inspiration, but also divine sources of knowledge – divine guarantors of the truth and of their stories.[6]

In Soviet life, truth was synonymous with authority. If poetry and 'its non-linguistic artefacts (a vase, a sculpture, or melody) can indeed represent or describe [and indeed] may also celebrate, praise, mourn, and present alternative worlds'[7] – it is dangerous to the totalitarian order. In defence of system, creative activity that led to the consideration of a non-Soviet world-view was censured, attacked and where possible eliminated.

What actually occurred in the Soviet phase of Russian history was more complex and multi-dimensional than the impression presented by the recognised opponents of socialism. For example, along with the *deviant* views of alternative culture embedded in Soviet society, the development of socialism had been tainted by a treacherous, and perhaps necessary, sleight of hand. Beyond both the ideological rhetoric, and the neutralisation of the intellectuals and bourgeoisie, one finds that a privileged few were not eliminated but coerced and offered incentives other than the promises of communism to construct the Soviet paradise.

In a particularly incisive passage, Vladimir Bukovsky argues that 'it is more just to judge a country by its prisons than by its monuments'.[8]   The recommendation assists in the examination of the human cost associated with the decision taken in 1947 by the Supreme Soviet who decreed that Moscow's skyline should be embellished by eight skyscrapers festooned with swags and statures, giant clocks and extended towers rising to the heavens.   Eight such buildings (of which seven were raised), grouped around the colossal (but never built) Palace of Soviets, required the physical toil of multi-national slave labour, and the skilled direction of an elite of designers, engineers technicians in the construction of the project. The majority of the former returned to unmarked cemeteries or the gulag, whilst the latter received material rewards and new projects on which to procure opportunities.

In considering the role of popular fiction in the Soviet Union during the Stalinist regime, Vera S. Dunham throws light on the paradoxes that were an inherent feature of Soviet society from its earliest conception. In identifying the encouragement of the regime to the *Meshchanstvo*, who served the regime allowing its knowledge, in most cases technical, to be used in the demands of modernisation in exchange for material rewards, the exploitation and the hierarchy of classes present in Tsarist rule was not eradicated but concealed from the populace.[9]   The separation of labour and the value accorded to it continued throughout the Soviet period.

In the literature of the era, Dunham makes clear, with echoes of Orwell, the:

> tacit endorsement of the move from public concerns to private concerns, seen in the pronoun shift from "we" to "I", in the shift from the collective to the family, from self sacrifice to self-gratification, from proletarian austerity to middle-class comfort, from egalitarianism to social stratification, as evidence of bourgeoisie activity within the Soviet Union.[10]

Whilst it reflected a dissension from Soviet ideology, it was isolated and therefore enjoyed relative autonomy from the construction and 'policing' of an official culture.   On pragmatic grounds it was not allowed to exist. Nonetheless, the identification of it caused resentment and tension in various levels of Soviet life.   The official response was to ridicule and deny the existence of it.

> As far as communist project pretended to be a classless society any "meshchanstvo"- petty bourgeois did not have a right to exist and this work was commonly used to describe narrow mindedness, vulgarity and philistinism, which was not fair of course. Even in Gorky's play "Meshchane" if one could disengage himself from the communist rhetoric like "the master who is working" and so on, he will see a normal family with strong traditional values and unlimited parental love and misunderstanding between parents and children. A few decades later Andrei Platonov wrote in his short story when the young lady in her conversation with her Father spoke scornfully about them, he told her: "They were very nice ladies indeed, you should learn a lot to be like them". Or something like that, quotation by memory.[11]

The values, which were allowed unofficially to function within communism, could not, despite crude attempts, be conveniently ringed off. Although society was forcibly atomised, the circulation of ideas and evidence of material well-being could not be completely disguised.   The widened existence of it, however, was not particularly visible, certainly within the early days of the ascendancy of socialism.

> The key point here is the communist preoccupation with the Russian fidelity of the ideas of communism and "meshchanstvo" gets them distracted from. Remember Mayakovsky's negative attitude towards "meshchanstvo".   He wrote about "meshchanstvo" as the way toward capitalism and so on. But, on the other hand, there is a negative thing of "meshchanstvo" – the capitalist consumerism.[12]

Whilst the regime on pragmatic grounds accepted and allowed the existence of meshchanstvo, the meschanin themselves appeared able to further their aspirations by working within the legitimate mechanism of the regime. Although society was expected by the revolutionary vanguard to be regulated by the strict administration of Marxist-Leninist ideas, it appears that ideology was not the only motive for social action. It would seem that less high-minded concerns were often the spur for direct involvement with the system.

> I don't see anything wrong with being "meshchanin" or "obyvatel", really. I consider them as a driving force of progress. Both my grandparents were "meshchane" – NEP men. If one of them decided to give up everything and become a worker, a "hegemon" in order to provide a higher education for his seven children another hesitated and went into exile, and my Father had to become a worker himself to enter university. So what? It has nothing to do with their world perception no matter what sense *commis* [communist ideologues] put in this word.[13]

Reflecting elsewhere on private idiosyncrasies, Boym reveals the complexity, paradoxes and irony, features that were prevalent in the everyday social reality of the Soviet State.[14] Recovered from neglect are stories of items that history often ignores or fails to record: lacquer boxes, gramophones, and bad movies.[15] In commenting on the widening of historical subject matter, particularly in the early Soviet context, Steve Smith highlights the importance of such inclusions:

> The importance of this broadening of historical concern is to undermine taken-for-granted assumption about what is and is not significant about the Russian Revolution, and to reveal how the apparently marginal, when set in relation to other phenomena, can lay bare the unacknowledged working of larger systems of power.[16]

How items of 'value' were obtained through various networks throws light on the complex operation of the official Soviet economy and methods adopted to overcome its limitations. The networks of *blat*: 'the use of personal networks and informal contacts to obtain goods and services in short supply and to find a way around formal procedures',[17] supplanted money as the facilitator, and mechanism, of necessary exchange. Its existence throughout society and its connections with the governmental bureaucracy allowed it semi-official status. Outside the *blat* circulation of goods and services existed the prevalence of the illegal economy, and the wider unofficial trans-national networks that supplied it. The lack of tools and reliable data to measure the degree of this activity, other than the surprising number of Russian millionaires in the post-Soviet condition operating in the import and export trade arguably accounts for the inadequate assessment of this aspect of the Soviet economy.[18]

Quirkiness may reside in all human relationships, but its characteristics are often not recorded; too frivolous are they for the censors of history. In the Soviet condition, however, attention to contradictory and elusive details should not be flagrantly dismissed or ignored. In *Alice in Wonderland*, by Lewis Carol, a child follows a rabbit down a hole and enters an irrational world, a Wonderland that has pejoratively been used to describe the incomprehensibility that was once the Soviet Union.[19] Within the mirage, where the architects, planners and administrators 'freed' and enslaved by the directions of modernity attempted, regardless of human cost, to construct a kingdom of reason on earth. Philosophy inevitably played a crucial role in the construction of it and despite fundamental flaws partially succeeded in its objectives.

The material above has alluded only to a brief selection of contradictions inherent in Soviet life. For Western observers, the once grey monolithic impression of Soviet conditions is perhaps increasingly unsatisfactory, a snap-shot at a time when obtaining a reliable insight was extremely difficult. The realisation of rich creative worlds functioning within the Soviet universe require further insight and illumination, the need to reassess its nature is not merely an academic exercise, but a process that may shed light on the future opposition to authority in whatever form that power takes.

A Cautionary Note

The outsider perhaps cannot, however, hope to thoroughly understand the 'living through' of indigenous conditions that are the home to the alien.[20] Is it not difficult, for the 'confined', for those on the inside, to 'step out' and observe with dispassion, the view of the inside as it appears from the outside? Without doubt 'it is hard to understand this country from the outside, but is it any easier for the Russians themselves (the West calls all 'Russians', from Moldavians to Eskimoes) to grasp what is going on'?[21] Can the character of the confinement – with its baggage, its propaganda and its 'truth', be disengaged from its rituals and adopt an intrinsically efficacious neutral position? Do not both positions share similar handicaps that should not be dismissed but noted? To the observer of strange lands is it not the indigenous strangeness, the site grudgingly open to the stranger – a condition that may in varying degrees be unconsciously concealed behind a common veil – that is the potential site of enlightenment and clarity? Do not both share similar but different starting points? Should coincidences and shared histories not be considered?[22] Are 'we' not, whoever 'we' may be, victims or beneficiaries of similarities as well as differences? The common denominator may be one of error. Its recognition and re-articulation through either verbal communication or physical practise, despite the apparent existence of cultural and linguistic variations, links human societies closely.[23]

A considered hesitation should be noted in the observation of past interpretations and the current reformulation of Soviet life. It is in regards to the question of processors and the apparent direction of them. Randomness, chaotic interventions or consequences, and accidents should arguably not be eradicated from social enquiry, but exposed and considered in detail to ascertain the potential for intransigence, reversion or dialectical acceleration. This has relevance in the monitoring of outcomes and considering possibilities, which may avoid inaccurate assumptions and predictions. Interventions and underlying causes are important to the directions of social trends, so much so that:

> Even in cases in which the agents' habitus are perfectly harmonised and the interlocking of actions and reactions is totally predictable *from outside*, uncertainty remains as to the outcome of the interaction as long as the sequence has not been completed: the passage from the highest probability to absolute certainty is a quantitative leap which is not appropriate to numerical gap.[24]

Through the prospect of nuclear annihilation, the Soviet experiment, its ramifications and its global consequences, potentially affected every living being. Therefore, regardless of nationality and 'place' in the world, everyone has the right to comment on and investigate it. As one prominent Russian intellectual put it:

> it is to be very much desired that the world has not simply followed the "Russian drama" through curiosity, but has drawn from it some lessons. In this sense our crisis and our struggle do not only affect ourselves, just as the sufferings of the third world and the conflict of political forces in western countries are not only of national but global significance.[25]

Early Considerations

High politics has a reputation of being intolerant of ideas that attempt to *understand* a situation. How the disruption occurred in the Soviet, which agents were part of the process and in what context activism was seemingly repressed so a *realistic* sense could be made of the situation is the raison d'être of this modest piece.

In the context outlined above, it would appear that the coded content of Soviet rock music and its potential to evolve and *terrorise* Soviet authority and undermine the system in which it operated, was not deemed important by mainstream International Relations and Soviet Studies theorists and practitioners. A likely explanation may be that it was not either understood by investigators or considered relevant in understanding the strength and longevity of a presumed superpower.

The text below provides an example of insight gleaned from a textual source that would be deemed unconventional by the conservative nature of the International Relations discipline, the sleeve notes to a record by the Russian musician Sergey Kuryokhin. It is however a piece that is crucial to a period of international relations that failed to recognise the generators of change.

> My life experience tells me that future students of Soviet culture will be using these notes as a source of information. It is high time to let them know that the West was duped into believing that it was President Gorbachev or later on Yeltzen who dismantled communism and brought democratic changes to the Russian people. What nonsense! Soviet communism would have collapsed without them even sooner. Only when they saw that the process was irreversible these so-called democrats jumped on the bandwagon. It was first and foremost rock musicians who won the hearts and the minds of the younger generations, and they should be given the credit for the colossal changes in that society.[26]

The direction of analysis concerned with Soviet State and Party personnel, policy formulation and the Soviet rhetoric at Party congresses, conferences and meetings gave little idea of the subtle pressure forcing change. It is contended within these pages that change within the former Soviet Union can only be understood within the Soviet region itself. The insight however, gleaned from the former apparatchiks or State officials who employed their energies in maintaining the system, is arguably limited. The prevalence of extensive deception and corruption within the official Soviet structure and the continued misrepresentation of it, by the aforementioned agents, is seemingly a viable explanation in defending this position. Insight into the Soviet change process may lie elsewhere. For example:

> One concert of Boris Grebenshchikov with his rock group "Aquarium", or Viktor Tzoi, or "Zvuli Mu", or a rock programme by Seva Novgorodsev on

BBC Wavelength, was more important than a hundred speeches of the illiterate president who was trying to keep afloat his sinking boat.[27]

The arguments that have been constructed by authors such as Theda Skocpol, particularly in *States and Social Revolutions*, which suggests influence of the correlation between inter-state conflict and social revolution on revolutions, are, whilst valuable, not conducive to understanding the change process within the former Soviet Union.[28]   It is argued in this piece that the need to recognise the underlying rhythms of change, which contributed crucially to the weakness of the Soviet State, the operation of the ideology of the CSPU and the indigenous opposition to it, precludes in importance the conflicts between State protagonists.

In the initial stages of the investigation, the intention was to assess the effects of popular music (primarily produced in the West), and the emergence of a global counter-culture movement on the aspirations and expectations of an increasingly visible and confident Soviet youth, the assumption being that the influence of Western popular culture had a significant effect on political change within the former Soviet Union. The political consequences of Western influences on Soviet youth would, or so it seemed, provide a basis from which to measure the part played by popular music in the transformation of the Soviet condition. On the one hand it did: contributing to the mythical image of the West.

The interest in popular music and youth culture, in the context of Soviet transformation, has been considered elsewhere. Timothy Ryback, Thomas Cushman, Sabrina Ramet and Hilary Pilkington have, from various disciplinary starting points, considered the part played by popular culture in Soviet society. In the light of findings identified in the undertaking of the work, this element will be examined with the view that it was Soviet rock, with its specific poetic content, and not Western popular music, which appeared instrumental in undermining Soviet culture and ideology. The adoption of Western cultural forms, prompted seemingly by the music of the 1960s, appears to have substantially added to the development of a Soviet counterculture. Nonetheless, whilst it appears that Western rock was overwhelming Soviet attempts of cultural isolation and working class purity, it was the dissident content of coded Soviet lyrics that caused the most damage to the longevity of the Soviet system.

The modification alluded to above places the emphasis on the belligerence active within the system: between its ideological composition and deviance from it, at its most damaging and destructive, the revealing science of the poet. This is a position which may or may not attempt to change the system, but contrives psychologically, and where possible physically, to vacate or make derogatory comment on it. This, indeed, is the essence of alternative culture, not necessarily escapism, but exile within the home.

The Soviet authorities directed extensive resources to limit the dispersion of subversive ideas and beliefs, particularly those associated with the development and popularisation of the avant-garde, progressive and popular rock music, through surveillance, repression and the arrest of open defiance. Its failure on the one hand to control the popularity of Western rock among Soviet citizens or adequately regulate the illegal economy that circulated it, crossing unofficial and official boundaries and borders, conceals the seriousness that the authorities accorded it. On the other, the lengths the authorities went to in scrutinising the content of Soviet rock lyrics indicates where the regime believed itself to be most vulnerable to extensive subversion and cultural terrorism.

The Challenge of Change

The actual complexity associated with the increasing integration of trans-national social relations and the impact of the world economy, on circulating specific cultural commodities, and its derogatory effects on the communist states which sought to remain autonomous from it was realised in the reforming discourse of the Soviet hierarchy from the mid-1980s. A departure from the confident rhetoric that had accompanied the decades before Gorbachev was arguably a response to the deep social and economic problems, which were becoming increasingly obvious to all members of Soviet society.

Almost twenty years before the Party congress in 1986 Brezhnev had declared:

> In the course of the last 50 years absolutely everything has changed in the life of the people. We have built a totally new world, a world of new, socialist relations, a world of the new, socialist man. The spiritual horizon of Soviet people have broadened out immensely; their morals and their attitude to work, society and each other have changed. Renewed and remade by socialism, our country stands before all mankind in all its might and grandeur, in all the brilliance of the talent of its superb people.[29]

The *brilliance* of the Brezhnev era had arguably dazzled only the most opportunistic and corrupt members of the old Nomenklatura system. The various arts, innovation of all kinds, and social creativity stagnated under the regime's efforts to control all aspects of society. The rhetoric could no longer disguise the reality of the world ordinary people experienced and in which they lived.

In an opening address delivered by Mikhail Gorbachev, General Secretary of the CPSU Central Committee, to the 27th Party Congress on February 25 1986, the tension between routine and change was of central importance. On the one hand, an attempt was made to re-vitalise the Marxist-Leninist dream. On the other, it recognised, albeit superficially, the actually occurring problems within it. This bold departure from the silence that had been a feature of the Soviet system, inspired by fear and ignorance, signalled a thaw in the rigid discourse that had prevailed since the late 1960s. Gorbachev drew attention to the material and structural developments effectively outside the total control of modern states and the necessity of finding fresh approaches to dealing with them. Recognising the demands emanating from an integrated world, and responding to the material and ideological regression affecting all areas of Soviet life, Gorbachev, in a crucial speech set out an agenda, which recognised the need for change:

> The 27th Congress of the CPSU has gathered at a critical turning point in the life of the country and the contemporary world as a whole. We are beginning our work with a deep understanding of our responsibility to the Party and the Soviet people. It is our task to elaborate a broad conception, in the Leninist way, of the times we are living in, and to work out a realistic, well thought-out programme of action that would organically blend the grandeur of our aims with our capabilities, and the Party plans with the hopes and aspirations of every person. The resolutions of the 27th Congress will determine both the character and the rate of our movement towards a qualitatively new state of the Soviet socialist society for years and decades ahead.[30]

Commenting on increasing complex independence, Gorbachev went on:

> New economic, political, scientific, technical, internal and international factors are beginning to operate. The interconnection between states and between peoples is increasing. And all this is setting new, especially exacting demands upon every state, whether it is a matter for foreign policy, economic and social activity, or the spiritual image of society.[31]

In urging the acceptance of measured change to the Congress, Gorbachev remained firmly committed to maintaining the authority of the Party. The split, however, with the traditionalists in the Party and their supporters throughout the state apparatus was in regards to the degree of change. Commenting on the obstacles to the demands for change in the economic sphere, Gorbachev makes the intention for movement clear when he suggests:

> In this work we must not be stopped by long established ideas, let alone by prejudices. If, for example, it is necessary and justifiable to apply economic standards instead of targets that are set down as directives, this does not mean a retreat from the principles of planned guidance but only a change in its methods.[32]

By the time of Gorbachev's famous speech, the ideal of a universal communist paradise had not been rejected but suspended. From an early stage in the construction of socialism, pragmatism had undermined idealism. Lenin appears to have viewed contact with the West as a necessary evil to facilitate the rebuilding of the Soviet military industry, through access to credits and technology.

Despite the claim by Lenin that trade with the capitalist powers would lead to their eventual capitulation to the demands of the social revolution it was widely believed, for example, that 'the trade agreement between England and Soviet Russia' set a dangerous president. This was a condition that raised the concern that 'it [was] not international communism that stands to gain by this agreement, but capitalism and imperialism'.[33] In this context, the claim or strategy of socialism in one country was clearly flawed. More contracts continued between the socialist bloc and the non-communist world. In the unofficial economy a nexus of channels operated to connect agents with operators within and outside the former Soviet Union.

Tony Cliff, Carl Levison, Grant Hammond, and Andrew Williams have provided detailed pieces to illustrate that the Soviet Union was not economically isolated from the West. In subsequent chapters, economic relations between the East and West, and the import of commodities with an overt cultural content (records, cassettes) will be analysed to inspect the claim that trans-national channels were penetrating – with and without bureaucratic authorisation – the Soviet arena. What is important at this point is that the claim that the Soviet economy was somehow isolated and autonomous from the international economy is clearly unsustainable in the light of the evidence.

It has been claimed that *something happened* during the 1970s that induced the technological retardation of the USSR.[34] The situation appears to have fundamentally been compounded by changes in the organisation of management and production in the West: a concomitant feature of both integrated production systems and the uneven dissimulation of knowledge.

For example, the appearance of a technical and information revolution accelerated by the need by both states in the industrialised world and business organisations to respond to the damaging effects of the 1970s oil crisis.   This appears to have led to a radical reassessment and transformation of the Fordist and Taylorist theories that widely underpinned practices of management, working methods and modes of production. The re-structuring of Western industries had consequences for the exports (oil, gas) of the Soviet Union and the methods (for example, metallurgy) that produced them.

The failure by the Soviet Union to adopt new technologies and management practises appears to have been a key factor in the deterioration in the quality of its products and services. Using countertrade and barter, and limited transactions in hard currency, the Soviet Union had been able to obtain new technology and key resources from Western markets.   The de-nationalisation of many multi-nationals through intensive cross border activity and strategic alliances allowed many of the politically inspired restrictions on trade in the region to be overcome or by-passed. Difficulties deepened, however, when the value of the abundant key resources in the Soviet Union and the value of its exports deteriorated and the value of imports, along with the technical knowledge to operate and service them, increased.

East West/West East

The breakdown of the post World War II Bretton Woods 'order' and the appearance of visible cracks in the progression of Soviet communism, which can (at least) be read as parallel and related stories, demonstrated the relevance of international political economy and the value of understanding the various nuances of culture to the discipline of International Relations.

The outbreak of the Second World War in 1939 with its subsequent carnage and human suffering dealt a bitter blow to the desires and methods of the idealists that had been in vogue since The Treaty of Versailles.[35] International Relations became imbued with a revived realism. E.H. Carr's well-known *The Twenty Years Crisis* and Hans Morganthau's *Politics amongst Nations: the Struggle for Power and Peace*, and the contributions made by Chatham House, and in particular Martin Wight, reflected the pessimistic turn in the discipline.

In the economic domain, 'the endorsement of capital controls at Bretton Woods thus partly reflected the decision to sacrifice financial liberalism in the interests of creating a stable exchange system and liberal trading order'.[36] The residual tension in world affairs, the 'successful' use of the atom bomb, and the prevalent global disparity of wealth led the increasing crop of independent political entities to concentrate on methods to strengthen and maintain national security.

The economic assistance in the post-war recovery of Europe, provided by the United States in the form of Marshall Plan, and the various economic and political inducements in the Asia-Pacific region, were facilitated by its undisputed hegemonic position vis-à-vis the rest of the world. The dispersion of loans, credits, technical knowledge, and expertise of all kinds had the dual effect of countering the expansion of communism and virtually guaranteeing the ability of foreign markets to absorb the exports of the United State's numerous production facilities. With the development of a Soviet nuclear capability 'the cold war would take precedence, with its politico-strategic orientation serving to effect nearly every aspect of the study of International Relations'.[37] The world was divided between two ideologically separate *East-West* powers. Interests other than those directly related to the distribution of power capabilities were deemed subservient and were largely ignored.

In the context of superpower rivalry, an Anglo-American bias has, since World War II, dominated the field.[38] The emphasis on an empirical version of realism that focuses upon the recurring struggles between states in an arena of international anarchy has been central to both studies and practise. The works of Thucydides (c 460-399 B.C.), Machiavelli (1513), Hobbes (1651), Carr (1939), Morganthau (1946), Bull (1977), Waltz (1979) Buzan (1991), contribute to a paradigm of political realism that is operational wherever the affairs of men are present. Realism, in its *modern* form, as defined by John Vasquez, contains three central and immovable assumptions. Nations are the most important actors. There is a clear distinction between domestic and international politics. The overriding focus of International Relations in the twentieth century was the study of institutions (the State in its modern guise) and relations between them. The need to regulate, legitimate, and govern power and peace being its raison d'être.

The process of de-colonisation that followed World War II led to the creation of a substantial number of independent states within the international system. Whilst the political and economic ties were tenuously severed between newly independent states and the European powers that had colonised them, the imported cultural residue remained to complicate indigenous development and successful autonomy. Frantz Fanon's classic texts, *The Wretched of the Earth* and *Black Skins, White Masks*, reveal the depths of the colonial legacy and the difficulties associated with attempts to overcome them.

The newly independent states of this period experienced severe problems in sustaining growth, optimism being only a part of social, economic and institutional recuperation. Following de-colonisation, the development of such states was dependent partly on the vagaries of the cold war. Ali Mazrui suggests that 'much of the foreign aid to the Third World since World War II has been inspired by ideological and strategic rivalry between East and West'.[39] In what became accepted Western foreign economic policy 'it was assumed that foreign aid helped to protect the security interests of the United States in far-flung corners of the world'. In comparison 'Soviet aid to the Third World has often been even more blatantly strategic'.

The cost of the United States military engagement in Vietnam and the progressive policies of Lyndon Johnson, which attempted to eradicate poverty without raising taxes, threatened the institutional order that had been introduced following World War II. The counter-hegemonic success of OPEC, the proliferation of a management and technical revolution spearheaded by resource scarce Japan, and the modifications to the circulation of capital, fundamentally altered the composition of interlocking but relatively autonomous structures. In effect, a series of related incidents destabilised the established post-war economic order and redistributed in part the loci of power within states to the demands of *the markets*. In comparison to the socialist bloc 'the superiority of the Western economies lay not in their immunity to these systemic challenges, but in their ability to overcome them'.[40] This was not achieved however, without macro and micro difficulties and widespread domestic resistance.

The gradual abandonment of the principles and ties to the system of the Bretton Woods by the United States led to an increasing study of interdependence and a revitalised international political economy. The resulting uncertainty produced structural adjustments and modifications to institutions to reflect the increasing complexity that accompanied technical revolution and pressures to accommodate market de-regulation. The state was viewed as one of many influential actors operational in the international arena. In the early 1970s John Burton and Robert Keohane were, in particular, involved in gleaning the degree of interaction between agents and structures, which had deepened exponentially, in the period of economic growth between 1945 and 1965.

During this period of intense structural change International Relations may have been affected by interdependence in two possible ways:

There is, firstly, the connection that the growth of empirical interdependence has exposed serious shortcomings in the intellectual armoury of traditional students of international relations. Contemporary interdependence, it would be argued, involves processes and subjects that lie outside the competence of such analysts. New features of the world have to be addressed and a new conception of the international realm deployed. Of equal import is the second argument that modern notions of interdependence occasion a basic change of view about all international relations, past and present.[41]

The renewed interest in international political economy from the 1970s led also to an awareness of its limitations in a world increasingly dominated by corporate brands and consumer markets. The animation of integrated capital markets, the explosion in the service sectors, and the changing nature of change, notwithstanding its sophistication and ambiguities, generated the need for political and economic flexibility.

The eclecticism in academe that has accompanied complex interdependence and globalization has in part attempted to move beyond the confines of neat prescriptions, and recognise – not ignore – the problems of separating economics, politics and socio-cultural phenomena in an integrated world increasingly premised on the uneven but conscious totalizing experience.

Autonomy in political and economic affairs was by the early 1980s seemingly becoming increasingly difficult, if not impossible. The Soviet Union in particular was finding itself exposed through its reliance on coal and steel production (declining industries in the West). In the absence of a management and technical revolution that addressed the limitations of scientific management and investment, the Soviet economy and its satellites found it a repeatedly arduous task, despite a political will, to initiate reform that could adequately build on the growth that had been previously possible. In regards to the Soviet Union, Czechoslovakia, Hungary, East Germany, Poland and Romania:

> no matter what their relative prosperity, however, the 1970s deepened the difficulties of each CMEA economy. A fundamental contradiction ensured their vulnerability. In each case party leaders embarked on a staunch effort to save or resurrect as much centralised planning as possible. But this strategy could only work in isolation from the West. Yet at the time, each country became involved with world markets, if only be virtue of the Western loans they contacted to give central planning a new lease on life.[42]

At the end of the 1970s, following the second oil crisis resulting from the revolution in Iran, another problem surfaced. As a consequence of the investment of petrodollars in Western banks and their subsequent recycle to the developing world, when the price of oil decreased and the interest rates in the developed world increased, the banks suddenly became exposed to the risk of the widespread default on loans. In the developed world, the debt crisis was largely resolved through the efforts of industrialised states and the nexus of international institutions that serve their particular interests. In the developing world, the burden of debt continued to be a serious impediment to growth.

Throughout the 1980s, the policies of Ronald Reagan and Margaret Thatcher resulted in years of radical political and economic change. The interweaving of capital markets that had occurred in the late 1970s accelerated and highlighted the potential for a new international financial disorder. Employing a mix of ideas derived from Friedrich List, F.von Hayek and Milton Friedman, the world economy moved towards a return to the laissez-faire economics that had caused the disruption in the early part of the twentieth century. Correspondingly, a revived and rigid new right in the political sphere advocated strong measures in removing impediments that interfered in *the markets*, regardless of their utility, and introduced laws to substantially limit the power of labour. In the international arena, deviation from the dominant model and the ideas and beliefs that underpin it, resulted in financial penalties, trading difficulties and a derogatory credit rating.

Whilst communism remains represented in-kind in China, North Korea and Cuba, its potential as global revolutionary force, certainly in its institutionalised form, has with the collapse of Soviet communism terminally waned. In the absence of the cold war confrontation and the potential major conflict some argue that the 'future of International Affairs will be dull: endless meetings about legal and technical issues among lawyers and technocrats'.[43] The wider content of this investigation suggests that this is not necessarily so.

The above is not intended to signal an in-depth analysis of the comparative advantage apparently enjoyed by the West, particularly from the 1980s, and how this fundamentally weakened the Soviet System (although some references will of course be made). The aim, more modestly, is to highlight the connections, of which there appear to be many, between economic and cultural transactions, and measure the influence of them within the specific context of the investigation.

It has been explicitly claimed that the role of music in the former Soviet Union has not been thoroughly understood, particularly by practitioners and theorists of International Relations, and its part in the demise of Soviet communism is at best vague. Its ability to evade censorship and undermine the authority of the dominant reality demonstrates the importance of cultural politics in International Relations.

The cultural inspired activity alluded to above is relatively absent from the *serious* affairs of strategic studies and Sovietology. Michael Cox, Jim George and John Lewis Gaddis have argued that failure of the discipline of International Relations to predict the disintegration of the former Soviet Union, exposed its epistemological, ontological and methodological limitations and flaws, which had, and continue to have, serious repercussions for policy making and international security. If the essence and rhythms of change are not understood within and between states then a response that aims to manage or at least control the worst manifestations of it, is determined not by critical analysis and reflection but by chance.

Whilst resisting a move to posit the concept of globalization as a central theory of International Relations, in preference of an allusion to globalization as a process, the book recognises the influence of external factors on culture.

The collapse of the former Soviet Union and the method through which it declined suggest that the content of International Relations as a academic discipline is paradoxically parochial (it is overwhelmingly concerned with a Western landscape) and biased in its epistemology and method. The pages that follow provide an indictment of this shortcoming.

Notes

[1] Milner-Gulland (1997:165), *The Russians*.

[2] If words were not so powerful, it would seem that there would be no need for the imposition of literary censorship. Vaclav Havel, reflected, when receiving the Peace Prize of the German Bookseller's Association, on the 'mysterious powers of words in human history'. Quoted in Simon Lee's (1990) *The Cost of Free Speech*.

[3] *Op Cit* (1997:170), *The Russians*.

[4] Gleb Struve in *Russian Stories* argues that while a great many Russians may still argue about the relative merits of Tolstoy and Dostoevsky, or of Gogol or Turgenev, they are practically at one in looking upon Pushkin as the national genius of Russia.

[5] Reavey (1968:xi), *The New Russian Poets*.

[6] Popper (1969), *Conjectures and Refutations*.

[7] Hepburn (1995:691), *Poetry*.

[8] Bulkovsky (1976:26), *To build a castle*.

[9] Boris Pasternak's translators Max Hayward and Manya Harari in a relevant foot-note to Doctor Zhivago (1971:315) offer a distinction to Obyvatel; Meshchanin: neither word has it exact equivalent in English. Obyvatel means literally a man who lives in a place with the implication that he takes no responsible part in its affairs (whatever class he belongs to). Meshchanin is closer to "petit bourgeosis".

[10] Dunham (1990,1976), *In Stalin's Time*.

[11] Eccly (1999), 'Meschanstvo Fallout', *Russia Today Discussion*, on-line posting. Available at:www.Russiatoday. (May 3 1999).

[12] Golovkin87 (1999), 'Meschanstvo Fallout', *Russia Today Discussion*, on-line posting. Available at: www.Russiatoday (May 4 1999).

[13] Eccly (1999), 'Meschanstvo Fallout' Russia Today Discussion, on-line posting. Available at: www.RussiaToday (May 5 1999).

[14] Boym (1994), *Commonplaces: Mythologies of everyday life in Russia*.

[15] See also Arjun Appadurai's (1996:86), *The Social Life of Things*.

[16] Smith (1994:564), *Writing the history of the Russian Revolution after the fall of communism*.

[17] Ledeneva (1998:6), *Russia's Economy of Favours*.

[18] See Olga Kryshtanovskaya (1992:185-195), 'The New Business Elite' for a consideration of this issue. Whilst it is difficult to reach a definitive number of Russian millionaires due to the nature of the numerous financial irregularities in Russia, pieces such as Kryshtanovskaya's indicate that there has been a definite increase in the number of millionaires within Russia both willing and able to be recognised as such.

[19] See Thayer (1961), *Russia*.

[20] Some rituals will be incommensurable to critical observation. Strategies such as in-depth field research, and more specifically ethnography, can be applied to overcome some of the difficulties. It must be noted however that nuances appear, particularly in emerging cultural forms, and perhaps can only be identified by actors nurtured within them.

[21] *Op cit* (1978:51), *To build a castle*.

[22] British links with important figures and events in modern Russian history are numerous. Marx's regular visits to the British library are legendary. Marx's remains lie in Highgate cemetery in North London. Engels comments on activities in industrial life in Manchester are equally well known. Lenin and key figures in the revolutionary movement spent many hours working out political strategies in a room not far away from London's King's Cross station.

[23] In Phillips (1987:27), *Philosophy, Science, and Social Enquiry*, the author suggests that 'something like a community of rationality is shared by all men, but recognised or fostered by different societies in varying degrees (none being perfect)'.

[24] Bourdieu (1977:9), *Outline of a Theory of Practise*.

[25] Kagarlitsky (1990,x), *The dialectic of change*.

[26] Alex Kan (1997), passage from the sleeve notes to Sergey Kuryokhin's *Divine Madness*, 4-CD box set. CD LR 813-816 Leo Records.

[27] *Ibid* (1997), *Divine Madness*.

[28] See 'Revolutions and the International' reviewed by Fred Halliday (1995) in *Millennium Journal of International Studies*.

[29] Extract from a speech made by Brezhnev at the joint jubilee meeting of the Central Committee of the CPSU. Novosti Press Agency, Moscow (1967:40).

[30] Gorbachev (1986:5), *Political Report of the CPSU Central Committee to the 27th Party Congress*, Novosti Press Agency Publishing House.

[31] *Ibid* (1986:10).

[32] *Ibid* (1986:49).

[33] Gramsci (1979:27), *Selections from the Political Writings 1921-1926*.

[34] Castells (1998:28), *End of Millennium*.

[35] International Relations following the Great War developed the prevailing objective of promoting international peace and security. The League of Nations was established in 1920 under a convenant of 26 articles forming part of the Versailles Treaty. Two important texts

to the study of International Relations are *The League of Nations and the Rule of Law* by Alfred Zimmern and Georg Schwarzenberger's *The League of Nations and World Order*.

[36] Hellenier (1991:164), *From Bretton Woods to Global Finance: A world turned upside down*.

[37] Olson and Groom (1991:104), *International Relations Theory Then and Now*.

[38] See Stephan Chan's (1994), 'Beyond the north-west: Africa and the east' for an introduction to the world beyond the Anglo-American conception in Groom & Light (1994) *Contemporary International Relations: A Guide to Theory*.

[39] Mazrui (1991:4), *Culture in World Politics*.

[40] Maier (1991:39), *The Collapse of Communism: approaches for a future history*.

[41] Jones (1994:12), *Interdependence on Trial*.

[42] *Op cit* (1991:43), *The Collapse of Communism*.

[43] Cooper (1990), 'Can we give peace a chance?' *The Guardian* (March 20 1999).

2 Contested Claims:
The Uncertainty of Certainty

The end of the cold war was a defining moment in the turbulent history of East-West relations.[1] The prevailing atmosphere within the Socialist bloc at the end of the Brezhnev era region appeared to be rigidly opposed to change. The idea 'that the citizens of East Berlin would a decade later be passing freely through the Brandeburg Gate' from when Cruise and Pershing missiles were first deployed in West Germany, would be 'no less fantastical than Alice's climbing through the looking glass'.[2]

Clearly, the nature of change had changed. A condition seemingly prompted by affiliated, though not necessarily explicit, episodes that occurred in progressive stages. The propelling force, in part, generated by the sporadic acts of defiance initiated by alternative/counter-culture, produced effects, some surprising, that confounded observers both within the Soviet system and from afar. What is alluded to in the pages below is a reflection on the visible versions of Soviet decline. Less superficial social phenomena, which seemingly violated and shifted dramatically the Soviet story, in subtle and crippling ways, will be considered in-depth in the chapters that follow.

East of Eden

The social unrest throughout Eastern Europe in 1989, which demonstrated the desire of the indigenous majority to seize the initiative from the on-going presence of pervasive social control, was the result of personal choice, economic and political incompetence, and accident. It should be kept in mind that communism had initially occupied the hearts and minds of Russians, whilst to Eastern Europeans, it influenced (on occasion by direct force) the organisation of their land and lives.

The smiles of George Bush, Mikhail Gorbachev and Helmut Kohl, circulated by the various global media to mark the tenth anniversary of the end of the Berlin Wall, were distant from the spiritual pressure that overwhelmed the political leadership in the East, and surprised the dignitaries in the West. It was not a revolution inspired by the leaders of governments, they were part of the process of change but they did not inspire it.

The fundamental assumption by the Western powers that the USSR would never withdraw from its entrenched position in Eastern Europe 'explains why Soviet studies failed to predict the most important strategic development in the post-war period'.[3] Clearly there is a need to discern the process through which the Soviet influence on Eastern Europe ended in the way that it did. This arguably cannot be disassociated from the perceived need to reassert legitimacy in the CPSU, a condition that correlated with its organic incapacity to transform itself and manage the wide demands placed on it.

The move to allow the eastern bloc to establish greater autonomy over its future and lessen its ideological links with Soviet communism appears complex and contradictory. Within the Eastern bloc states the widening activities and popularity of political dissidents was linked to regional destabilisation. Discontent was prevalent amongst ordinary citizens. In response, an optimistic attempt by the Soviet regime to orchestrate their return to the shelter of communism was initiated. It also sent a clear message to the international community that the efforts to reform Soviet communism were not purely a rhetorical exercise but contained tangible policies that the West would view positively. The leadership would, if necessary, in the belief that increased credits and technology transfer could be obtained, take difficult and militarily unpopular decisions, to initiate reform. It appears however that it was not expected that the states of Eastern Europe would seek an immediate return to the 'common heritage' of Western Europe, and the citizens of them would pre-empt such a course.[4] The result that the wall was breached was accidental – it was not part of Kremlin policy.

The political motivation for improved relations with the West was the will to nurture an environment in which communism would be able to escape its recognised cul-de-sac. The discourse active within the Kremlin was constructed to encourage reform. In the early stages however 'the only reform that they could afford [was] a return to détente as it used to be in the 1970s, that is, a one-way street which [would] allow them to enjoy Western technology and cheap credits while preserving their system intact'.[5] Whilst the consequences of this action led to a radically different conclusion to that which had been envisaged, the program to revolutionise the Soviet economy was far from revolutionary. The period of détente with the West may have allowed access to Western credits and technology, but it did not address the fundamental difficulties that impaired the full development of the economy.

The reforming elements within the Soviet system recognised the need to re-structure, but within a Marxist-Leninist conception. The residue of Stalinism espoused in the rhetoric of Erich Honecker and Nicolae Ceausescu was incompatible with the version of reform favoured, but not unanimously, in the Kremlin. It was perceived to be too rigid, and removed from the realities of modernisation. In removing the threat of Red Army or Warsaw Pact intervention by refusing to sanction the use of force to crush mass demonstrations, the 'Sinatra Doctrine' effectively pulled the carpet from East European communism'.[6] Without the coercion from the centre, the periphery could not establish the level of consistent fear, which had previously been secured through prolonged psychological and physical repression.

Honecker, in office since 1976, continued to remain aloof from the reforms taking pace in the Soviet Union, but deepened trade outside the communist bloc. East Germany sought industrial investment and expertise from the West, and 'the level of trade between [East and West Germany] more than trebled from 1974 to 1989, to reach a total of 28 billion DM a year'.[7] Honecker however remained stoical in his ideas and beliefs, using the vast mechanism of the hated *Stasi* to contain all forms of dissent. The uncompromising position maintained by Honecker complicated relations with the Kremlin, and led the reformers of perestroika and glasnost to review the necessity and benefits of the *friendship*.

The animated consumer society that functioned on the other side of the wall, largely from West German television, was widely known to young East Germans. The advertising boards of Western brands could easily be viewed, and jokes, snipes and pervasive malcontent permeated in direct contrast to the official presentation of communist life. The consumerism available in the near West was important, but this factor alone does not account for the rapid metamorphosis that occurred in the former socialist bloc, nor does it explain the presence of embedded dissident social forces in East Germany. In this light it would appear that 'social formations do not just fall because they are irrational or technically inferior. Their technical inefficiency merely makes them vulnerable in the face of pressures that more often do not arise from extrinsic sources, are but obliquely related to management troubles, and rarely address themselves directly to the issue of the system's technical ineptitude'.[8]

The antagonism, coded criticism and embedded dissent towards the authorities that had been prevalent in the occupied states of Eastern Europe had, following the announcement by Gerasimov, which essentially gave permission for non-compliance with the authorities, moved from the underground and the kitchen to demonstrable public expression. A force formulated from the long struggles of the religious networks, particularly Catholicism in Poland and the Lutheran church in East Germany, alternative/counter-culture, political dissent, and ethnic traditions, appeared ready and largely able to counter the measures which had been imposed to limit spontaneous acts of deviance.

The 'Catholic Church in Poland provided powerful alternative channels of communication and the Protestant church in East Germany provided similar, if not quite as potent, bonds of community'.[9] Outside the Socialist bloc, the Polish diaspora maintained a variety of links with the homeland to support opposition to the regime. The occupation of Polish land by the Russians, and the cruelty they had inflicted on the Polish people following the atrocities incurred by the Nazis, was met with on-going resistance.

> The church was naturally dead against the communists. Many Polish women practising their religion were sent to Siberia. The nuns were in particular persecuted. There was universal opposition to the Russians. You must remember one thing. Poland first had to deal with the Germans, then the Russian regime. Poles opposed both.[10]

The church provided both a network of communication and a site that maintained a coded community. It implicitly encouraged acts of deviance, and organised self-help systems outside the control of the authorities. Nevertheless:

> People denounced religion to become party members. Many, however, continued to practice their beliefs in private (as did many that did not join the Party). The Pope John Paul II [Cardinal Karol Wojtyla, Archbishop of Cracow] gave the Poles hope. Here, suddenly, we had an international figure whom by his nationality forced people to look beyond the regime.[11]

Brezhnev, Suslov and Andropov grew increasingly concerned by the widening and open deviance within Poland and sought to introduce strategies that would limit the spread of opposition growing throughout East Europe. By 1981, 9.5 million workers had joined the independent trade union (Solidarity). Solidarity was crucial to the change process in Poland. In response to the increasing demand to establish a non-communist government from various sectors in Poland, some extremely desperate measures were considered by the Central Committee to limit the social turbulence. The most famous being the alleged attempt on the life of the Pope masterminded by the KGB.

> The rationale of the attack was based on the Soviets' conviction that the Pope's support for Lech Walesa and the unprecedented Solidarity movement threatened the Soviets' continued control of the Polish State. The open letter from the Pope declaring his determination to go to Poland, if necessary, to resist Soviet armed intervention, raised the stakes.[12]

The KGB was allegedly given instructions to instigate an assassination of the Pope.   The secret police used their contacts throughout the communist world to recruit and aid an assassin.

> In this instance the trial of attribution was so indistinct that the initial assertions that Agca was a "right-wing" fanatic" or a "Muslim fundamentalist" deflected the world press and served the Soviet interest.   The assassin's control was exercised by the KGB through the successive echelons of Bulgarians, right wing Turks, and religious fundamentalists, ensuring that no Soviet tell-tales would emerge and that any reaction or reprisal would be confused.[13]

Throughout Eastern Europe, the opposition to occupation by a foreign power had, by the late 1980s, deepened with the activities of a younger generation demanding greater autonomy over their life choices. Repeated expressions of open deviance were reported and recorded, and to a degree dealt with through arrests and expulsions. In East Germany specifically, the desire for change was not a spontaneous response to the arrival of Gorbachev and the effects of the reforms, it had progressed and widened in the previous two decades. Gorbachev may have been simply a succession of sparks that led to the fire. From the late sixties:

> The East German dissidents were a small and a scattered minority, and many writers among them were practising communists and proud of it. They did not challenge the Communist monopoly of power, but only sought to expose its worst abuses…and they were powerfully reinforced by popular actors, singers and 'rock' musicians who used satire as a weapon.[14]

Similarly in the Soviet Union, unofficial rock music appears to have been fundamental in attracting and circulating dissent throughout Eastern Europe, and popularising a set of ideas and opinions that could not be organised in an official political party.

In the context of Eastern Europe more specifically, rock music played a role in reinforcing the steady growth in the demand for freedom and in providing outlets through which alternative political ideas could be expressed and nurtured.[15]

Whilst there were signs that by the mid-eighties change was inevitable, the success of it to improve or remove the system was by no means guaranteed. It seemed:

that even when democrats are convinced that they have the majority of the population behind them, they may have reason to believe that the outcome is problematic because of the potential power of repression from internal and external mercenaries, better armed and more ruthless than the supporter of revolution.[16]

Despite the physical strength of the state, vis-à-vis the *people*, military intervention on the scale of the 1956 and 1968 invasions in Hungary and Czechoslovakia would be politically unacceptable to democratic institutions active in a global economic environment. Following the debacle in Afghanistan, Gorbachev intended to reap the benefits from increased technology transfer and financial credits in return for oil and gas exports through improved relations with the West. Policies that would threaten the success of the strategy were initially resisted. The concern was to secure the longevity of the Soviet Union.

The desire to give socialism a human face goes back to the idealism of the 1920s. Gorbachev appears to have been influenced by the optimism that accompanied Khrushchev's early reforms, and the actions of Dubcek. These reforms were however limited. Andrei Kolganov, Professor at the Moscow State University, suggests:

The program of de-Stalinisation that followed Stalin's death was limited. It, however, accompanied the incredible progress in science, education and engineering, change in all sectors in fact. By the mid-sixties, the developments in technology slowed. Civil society, if it can be called that, quietly retreated.[17]

In Czechoslovakia, the numerous reports that comment on the 1960s atmosphere of optimism were seemingly typical of the decade. Change appeared tangible. 'Dubcek, besides being a Slovak nationalist, was an economic reformer, in government relatively humane and in economics relatively liberal: the sort of communist who makes other communists look particularly tyrannical and incompetent'.[18] The optimism that had flourished throughout the Soviet region and the reforms that were gradually being implemented during the thaw were dramatically altered by the Soviet suppression of the Prague spring. The thaw was decidedly over, and the aspirations of the generation were forced underground. The repercussion of the action led to a revitalisation of coded criticism against the authorities. In the late sixties, 'the general feeling amongst the people was anger and shock. When the Russians invaded there was a lot of antagonism against the soldiers. A lot of people were arrested and some lost their jobs'.[19]

The ideas that were associated with Dubcek and the Prague Spring were relevant to the reforms that would follow later in the Soviet Union. The aim of Alexander Dubcek, First Secretary, Slovak Communist Party, 1968-69 and Czech political leader had been to present socialism with a human face. Gorbachev at the time however did not appear initially to deviate from the traditional progression expected by the *Nomenklatura* and the Party. His fellow students at the Moscow State University went on to make different choices:

> His [Gorbachev's] roommate, a Czechoslovak named Zdenek Mlynar, went on to become one of the leaders of the 1968 Prague Spring [acting as top advisor to Dubcek during most of the crisis]. Another of his classmates, a Ukrainian named Levko Lukyanenko, used his legal training to draft a brief that argued that the Ukraine had a constitutional right to secede [formally withdraw] from the Union of Soviet Socialist Republics. That argument earned him a fifteen-year prison term. In 1976, shortly after his release, Lukyanenko joined the Ukrainian Helsinki Watch Group. For that he got another fifteen-year prison term. Another of Gorbachev's classmates, Lev Yudovich, later defended dissidents at trials.[20]

Gorbachev's progression through the state apparatus and party are clearly stated in the sleeve notes to the book *Perestroika*. It is the standard route to the higher echelons of Soviet power. There is little evidence that Gorbachev risked association with radicals or the intelligentsia. Gorbachev may have had sympathy with the social idealists, the promises of social improvement found in the former President's writings. The concept of commune democracy, espoused by Marx and Lenin, is a theme Gorbachev repeatedly refers to. Richard Sakwa, in a succinct and incisive essay has reflected on the problems and the ambiguities inherent in the theory of commune democracy. Sakwa puts forward its importance in explaining many of the contradictions in the reform process.[21] The early reforms that Gorbachev introduced were seemingly however an extension of the policies considered by Andropov at an earlier stage in response to the threat of social and political disintegration.

The intention by Gorbachev to re-introduce a *social* form of managed socialism should not be dismissed outright, but it should be recognised in the context that the reforming movement sought to maintain power and not devolve it. What resulted from the increasing tensions throughout the Soviet State and its satellites was a pragmatic, but flawed response, that sought to address the problems without a clear idea how to do it.

It should, in a military context, be mentioned that the costs associated with maintaining a large Soviet ground presence in East European states was increasingly burdensome and raised a number of issues relating to strategic interests and financial priorities of the Soviet Union.

> Central to this argument is that the pressures of domestic, regional and global factors have increasingly meant declining Soviet returns in both economic and security spheres. Thus, although the Soviet Union was the obvious regional hegemon, the maintenance of its dominance in fact contributes to its weakness as a national economy, relative to the domestic capitalist states.[22]

The result of Soviet interference in Poland had led to a situation where private business, except in Polish agriculture, was illegal. In the early days of Soviet interference in Poland 'private business had been wiped out in Eastern Europe due to high taxes'. In industry, 'most people hated the Russians and didn't work very hard'.[23]

The pressures that contributed to change in Eastern Europe were multifarious, and can only be understood in the wider Soviet change process, which had developed over a number of years. It was not planned that Eastern Europe would be allowed to separate from the socialist bloc. In the period that social forces in Eastern Europe challenged the *possession* associated with Soviet influence, the Soviet system was experiencing material, ideological and structural turbulence, which both limited and directed its relations in International Affairs. The protest in the East could not, without widespread repression, be contained. The leadership in Moscow did not want to be associated at that point with a policy that would cause international indignation, particularly when the inward investment was becoming crucial to economic regeneration. In the circumstances, the leadership was crippled in its decision-making through the poverty of alternatives. In the context of change in Eastern Europe for East Europeans, whose lands had been occupied and people defiled 'Gorbachev, deserves some credit'.[24] It was 'he who opened the door'.[25] Even though it was accidental is of little consequence to the people in this region.

The Counter-Reformation

By the early 1980s, the Soviet system stagnated. Within its structures, imbued with lies and incompetence, it continued without either direction or belief. The rhetoric of the Party and the propaganda of the press attempted to present a caricature of reality; an activity that was increasingly ridiculed by those who had most experience of it – the people who engaged with it daily.

To limit the decay in ideological direction and material development, a gradual realisation took hold: reform should be initiated in sectors most affected by deterioration in quality and performance. Whilst Brezhnev lived, it was not considered prudent by Politburo members to raise matters which suggested the Soviet system was explicitly failing in its objectives.

In understanding how the discourse of reform became acceptable to the Party vanguard, the pressures arising from both international and domestic sites need to be considered and related to the experiences of card-carrying communists and non-communists in the Soviet Union. It must be recalled that 'throughout Soviet history, deception has always been the [Soviet] state's most formidable weapon'.[26] In this context it appears that the perceptions of each 'major' western state, in relation to the Soviet Union, miscalculated the nature and strength of the leadership. The fault seems to have been propagated by the belief that each State identified similar characteristics in policy, 'we can do business together' rather than specific codes of conduct produced by historical and cultural experience.

The leaders of the Soviet Union, America and Britain, their selection, and subsequent actions, throw light on how International Relations during the Soviet era were constructed and often misunderstood. The British class system guaranteed that the selection of its leaders would overwhelmingly be determined by privilege, particularly education (elite schools/universities) of future candidates. American leaders were selected on their ability to utilise and monopolise on wealth and celebrity (a businessman or an actor could attain high office). In the Soviet Union, selection to the hierarchy of Soviet power resulted from progress through institutionalised social development.

One of the main attractions of Komsomol membership [was] the prospect of its leading, eventually, to membership of the Communist Party. It [was] extremely difficult to become a communist in the Soviet Union; so particular [was] the Party that all members and candidate members (probationers) total only four and half per cent of the population. Political respectability is not enough; the aspiring member [had] to prove his worth in work, study, and in voluntary effort of some kind for the common good. Even this judging by the numbers, [was] not enough, but for anyone who [sought] to climb the ladder of influence, a good record of active service work in the Pioneers and the Komsomol [was] the best start he [could] have.[27]

The policies adopted by the United States under the guidance of the former administration of President Ronald Reagan, particularly in the second term, have been used to explain the defeat of the communist opposition. The prevalent view, held by the Anglo-American strategic studies community, is expressed in the work of Samuel F. Wells. Wells argues that the increasing costs associated with ever increasing military expenditures during the Reagan years resulted in the failure of the Soviet Union to maintain economic and military parity with the United States. The costs, in particular, associated with research and development, deployment and maintenance, of increasingly sophisticated weaponry, and the training of technically able operators, could not be met by industry and the technical institutes within the Soviet Union.

Reagan's term as President of the United States was both important and paradoxical to the changing nature of international affairs, predominately constructed on the ideological and material differences existing in the East-West duality. In the book *Diplomacy*, Henry Kissinger, presents an insight into the contrary nature of ideas and beliefs of the former President. In recognising Reagan's numerous biblical references to the Armageddon and the rhetoric of anti-communism, the foreign policy of this period is imbued with the arrogance of righteousness and a fear of apocalyptic responsibility. Despite playing 'hardball' with the communists, Reagan did not want to be responsible for nuclear annihilation. Kissinger claims that the historical conditions were kind to the President's dreams and visions: a decade earlier, he would have seemed too militant, a decade later, too one-track.[28] Reagan's policies nonetheless found popular support with the electorate in the United States, and the strategic *successes* in the international arena added to an antagonistic foreign policy that resulted in accumulating casualties, particularly in Latin America.

A tough military policy and a commitment to accelerate the technical development of how modern warfare would be conducted created tensions with Reagan's spiritual convictions. Nevertheless, the Strategic Defence

Initiative (SDI) announced publicly in March 1983 on the one hand accelerated the negative rhetoric prevalent in the discourse of the East-West protagonists, but on the other it allowed reflection on and communication about sensitive points that otherwise may not have been discussed. The development of the defence initiate, and in particular the on-going investment provided by the Pentagon to fund research and development of military hardware and software led the Soviet Union to seriously review its military capabilities.

The Soviet Union's vast Military-Industry Complex (MIC)[29] consumed resources that could otherwise have been directed to meeting the wider needs of its citizens. The widespread corruption and technical stagnation prevalent in the military-industry and non-military complexes, coupled with the incompetence prevalent throughout the Soviet bureaucracy undermined the military strategic plan. The requirement, however urgent, to review military strategy and the method associated with its realisation did not appear to include an option to a superior technical force without engagement with it.

Despite moderate objections, the view expounded by Wells, is repeatedly cited as the motivation for Soviet leaders to reassess their system.[30] SDI undoubtedly concerned the Soviet military establishment. It also affected the rest of the world. In the United States public reaction was mixed and many scientific experts doubted the ability of SDI to be a realisable and operational system in the short term. The United States had become increasingly unsympathetic and belligerent to the concerns of its allies. The British Conservative Government under the leadership of Margaret Thatcher continued to comply with the Americans on most points. This was conditional on the 'special relationship' between the two leaders, and a concern with the potential strength of a united Germany in relation to British interests.

The Campaign for Nuclear Disarmament (CND), the women of Greenham Common, and green groups in Continental Europe were increasingly influencing or being reflected in the discourse within political circles, which questioned the wisdom of SDI and added to the unease in Europe with American foreign policy. Whilst it could be argued that this is exactly what the propaganda exported from the Soviet Union was intended to achieve (evidence exists concerning the influence of communist cells within these organisations),[31] the opposition to SDI was not confined to narrow circles. The doubts concerning the nuclear arms race, made public in Britain following the peace protest at Greenham Common, moved similarly beyond rock fans at the annual Glastonbury rock festival, and were increasingly echoed in all sectors of society.

SDI accelerated the rhetoric against the warmongering of the capitalist imperialists but on pragmatic grounds it encouraged both sides to reconsider the nuclear issue. It appears that the view held by Hough stipulating SDI as a motor for the fundamental reassessment of foreign and military policy inside the Kremlin can be widely supported. It did not however lead directly to the rapid demise of the Soviet Union. The Soviet leadership had received a shock, and required a period of reflection and restructuring before addressing and responding directly to the full implication of it.

It would be naïve to suggest that an altruistic nature prevailed on the issue of nuclear weapons in the Kremlin. Nevertheless, Gorbachev's position on the nuclear issue appeared to be related in part to the intellectual debate on the issue that had agitated many dissidents decades before, such as Sakharov in the 1960s. The similarities with Sakharov's 1968 *Progress, Coexistence and Intellectual Freedom* and Gorbachev's 1987 address to the CPSU Congress deserve comparison. The fears of *hot* international relations and responses to it are clearly back on the agenda. In a passage written by Sakharov, the author states that:

Two kinds of attempts are being made to portray thermonuclear war as an "ordinary" political act in the eyes of public opinion. One is the concept of the "paper tiger", the concept of the irresponsible Maoist adventurists. The other is the strategic doctrine of escalation worked out by scientific and military circles in the United States. Without minimising the seriousness of the challenge inherent in that doctrine, we will just note that the political strategy of peaceful coexistence is an effective counterweight to the doctrine.[32]

In the extract from two decades later, Gorbachev reflects on the 'myth of the communist threat' and the 'imperialist countries own aggressiveness' and suggests:

that is why it is not easy at all, in the current circumstances, to predict the future of the relations between the socialist and the capitalist countries, the USSR and USA. The decisive factors here will be the correlation of forces on the world scene, the growth and activity of the peace potential and its capability of effectively repulsing the threat of nuclear war. Much will depend, too, on the degree of realism that Western circles will show in assessing the situation. But it is unfortunate when not only the eyesight but also the soul of politicians is blind. With nuclear war being totally unacceptable, peaceful coexistence rather than confrontation of the systems should be the rule in inter-state relations.[33]

Gorbachev, in a passage worthy of a dissident, although other narratives are clearly at work, tells the 27th Congress:

> But the complexity and acuteness of this moment in history makes it increasingly vital to outlaw nuclear weapons, destroy them and other weapons of mass annihilation completely, and improve international relations.[34]

In recognising the demands to reform the Soviet military, what other factors may have been crucial in undermining the capabilities of the Soviet Union? A view combining the military and economic dimension suggests that:

> In the 1980s, leaders of the communist regimes found themselves under heavy stress in many ways at once. They felt themselves to be threatened from abroad by an American government that had become increasingly bellicose, and was spending heavily on armaments – even what appeared to be first strike nuclear weapons, designed to "decapitate" command and control systems in the Soviet Union. At the same time, ageing socialist economies were unable to maintain earlier rates of economic growth, and their citizens were demanding higher standards of living.[35]

The economic problems that affected the former Soviet Union, particularly from the early 1980s, were serious and wide ranging. Placed in their historical context however, they were not beyond reform and in some sectors growth was maintained. The former Soviet Union was endowed with numerous natural resources and a 'technically minded and resourceful population'.[36] It is a mistake to undermine the achievements of so many of the Soviet people who clearly believed that they were constructing a better future.

An increasing burden on the Soviet regime was maintaining the service that supplied citizens with their basic needs – the foundation of the *social contract*. The reliance on the:

> annual reduction in prices for a wide range of goods, the free supply of natural gas and heating to all households, and the almost free urban public transport were perceived by the population as legitimate and effective steps to the realisation of socialist ideas. They were so popular that none of the subsequent

leaders, from Khrushchev to Gorbachev, made any attempts to radically reverse this practice.[37]

The demands on the Soviet State, in both production and supply, appear to have been increasingly unsustainable without substantial investment, but politically immovable. To meet the costs associated with the vast social provision of goods and services would perhaps be, for any large economy, difficult to maintain in a competitive global economy. Nonetheless the provision of basic services at a nominal rate softened, particularly in the eyes of the older generation, the shortages in other less important commodities. Political dissent on this issue was suspended paradoxically through the operation of self-interest.

Despite evidence to the contrary, the Sovietologists were sceptical about the collapse of the Soviet economy. From 1917, its economic collapse had on several occasions been prematurely predicted. Elsewhere David Kotz with Fred Weir have offered a detailed and persuasive argument that although the economies of the Soviet Union and its satellites were experiencing serious structural and material difficulties, the evidence that they imploded purely by a capitulation to capitalist en mass cannot be sustained. A serious problem that re-occurs in an analysis of the Soviet economy 'lies in the evidence that Soviet State socialism produced rapid economic development for sixty years before succumbing'. Whilst it did encounter increasing economic difficulties in the 1970s and 1980s, it continued to yield economic growth, although at a reduced rate, through to the end of the 1980s.[38]

The command economy had, before the end of Brezhnev's tenure in high office, resulted in what had become widely known as developed stagnation. Industry, in all but the most privileged of sectors, had difficulty in obtaining quality resources of all kinds. Apathy and theft were prevalent in the work place. The apparatchiks in the burgeoning bureaucracy of Brezhnev's *empire* succeeded in stifling the creativity that tenuously flourished during the *thaw* period. Coercion, corruption and widespread bureaucratic incompetence resulted in the collective loss in material and ideological development. The Brezhnev 'era of stagnation' was however for some people in some regions of the Soviet Union an '"era of boom", since it institutionalised corruption and so enabled market exchange to flourish'.[39] For the majority of people however, it was an era of diminishing possibilities and absolute boredom. As Kan remarks, 'it was the hypocrisy of the Brezhnev era that finished off support in communism completely'.[40]

Trouble in Paradise

Brezhnev died on November 10, 1982, and controls were immediately implemented to maintain order and security in Moscow. Minister of Defence Ustinov recommended, Yuri Vladimirovich Andropov (1914-84) be elected General Secretary of the Party's Central Committee, a position that he would take up before becoming state president in 1983. It was not expected, however, that Andropov would assume the leadership. Therefore, the period was fraught with nervous manoeuvrings, which correlated with the increasing conflict of interests within the Politburo over how the Party should continue to be run. Chernenko had appeared to be in the best position to follow Brezhnev. Gorbachev, Gromyko and Ustinov were 'all loyal to Brezhnev, but their loyalty did not extend to his protégés'.[41] Andropov, under his leadership, would support Gorbachev in establishing and elevating his position within the politburo. 'It was against this background that Mikhail Gorbachev emerged as the nominal second in command and a potential successor; thus, Gorbachev came to be closely identified with the reform faction'.[42] Despite support for Chernenko, it was grudgingly felt that a moderate change from the policies that had been introduced during the Brezhnev era was required to address the material and deep social problems occurring throughout the Soviet Union. 'Andropov's fifteen months in power witnessed a vigorous attempt to reform both the economy and what could be called the structure of social relations'.[43]

Konstantin Ustinovich Chernenko (1911-85), a former close friend of Brezhnev, succeeded Andropov in February 1984 as General Secretary of the Communist Party. 'In Moscow's kitchens, people were arguing about how long Chernenko could survive',[44] and if Grigoriy Romanov would then continue the slide back to a Brezhnev style rule. 'Chernenko's year in power, in fact, differed little from the preceding years. Rhetoric about the "struggle against corruption" persisted in the mass media, but the campaign ceased to affect even middle level officials'.[45]

The structure of the international post-war world economy had been realigned during the 1970s. Integrated markets and communication links led to the widespread but uneven dispersion of information and knowledge. The 1980s continued the technological advances in computing and the spread of the various media, the ownership of a personal computer becoming for ordinary people in the rich industrialised countries as accessible as owning a television set. Whilst it appeared that the conservative Romanov would succeed Chernenko, the political, economic and social climate demanded a more flexible approach if the elite were to prolong the influence it enjoyed in all aspects of Soviet life. 'Those five years [1982-1987] saw more changes in the USSR than just the succession of four General Secretaries. The social situation altered, with the emergence of a new generation for whom changes were just as natural as 'stability' had been for their predecessors'.[46]

It was in a general atmosphere of adjustment, in part prompted by the inquisitiveness and recklessness of youth, that the need was recognised to address the social and material problems that prevailed throughout the Socialist bloc. The social unrest and difficult international trading conditions benefited the reforming discourse prevailing in the Kremlin. Mikhail Gorbachev (1931-) followed Chernenko, and assumed leadership as the General Secretary of Communist Party in 1985. Unlike Khrushchev who had initiated reforms to avoid a legitimisation crisis between the rulers and the ruled, Gorbachev initially continued the reforms stated by Andropov to reverse the economic stagnation that enveloped the country. When these proved to be insufficient, more extensive measures were considered and implemented, which were compounded by statistical data, corrupted by severe doctoring, to placate the macro and micro economic difficulties and guard against the loss of privileges associated with official posts.

The exponential rise in complaints to the Central Committee and the general discord that circulated throughout society led to the revival of *glasnost*. The reforms affected both communist ideology and the composition of government. In the former, the early reforms appeared to encourage the role of CPSU to be 'one of genuine 'guidance' rather than dominance'.[47] In the latter, efforts were made to overcome the resistance to change in the various ministries through fresh appointments and transfers in personal.

Man of the Year

Mikhail Gorbachev has been described as a 'nice, complex, but ultimately frustratingly paradoxical figure'.[48] In an assessment of his character the pendulum swings unendingly between idealist and pragmatist. In the West, a *personality*, to Russians, a troubled Lear, apparently impervious to the caution that nothing comes of nothing. From conversations with Russians and a review of the literature relating to this interesting figure, a profile of Gorbachev emerges as a contradictory political animal. He is accorded a grand vision, although tenuously, one that both took up the democratic ideas proposed by the dissident's decades earlier. Another view suggests Gorbachev was a figure who had little visionary zeal, and merely responded pragmatically to pressures as they appeared. He has been presented as a buffoon, whose constant stream of words and pronouncements failed to benefit the country, the Party or *the people*.

> Gorbachev did not have the economic ideas or tools to make his ideas real. He was warned that economic reform *perestroika* should be implemented before the political reform *glasnost.* Gorbachev did not listen and the resulting chaos is still obvious.[49]

The view in the West that Gorbachev was an intellectual was not widely accepted in the Soviet Union. A former Professor of Linguistics at the Russian Academy of Sciences suggests:

> Gorbachev was a bumbling fool. You only had to listen to his speeches made in Russian to understand that the man did not even finish his sentences. If he deviated from his script he spoke nonsense. How we used to laugh at his broadcasts. Really, they were very funny. The West may have been duped to believe that he was something of an intellectual ...ha, ha. If that is so, then the credit lies with the skill of his interpreter.[50]

The failings of Gorbachev can be explained by his reliance on a vision and not a deeply thought out strategic project that addressed the embedded structural difficulties. The fundamental need to revitalise the democratic element of socialism and expunge the negative aspects of Soviet ideology clouded the need to address all aspects of the political economy. Kagarlitsky claims Gorbachev had 'nothing that [could] be called a project. It [was] a loose set of political and economic improvisations', which reflected the re-generation of Leninist project rather than a radical actualisation of it.[51] Gorbachev was responsible for leading a process of reform and not a revolution.

In international affairs, the superpowers were in dispute over regional disputes. Paul Hirst has noted that 'when Mikhail Gorbachev came to power in 1985 the West was still involved in the second Cold War that began with the invasion of Afghanistan in 1979'.[52] In the early days of his rule speculation rather than substance prevailed concerning the qualities of the new leader. There was little to suggest that anything radical had occurred in the transition. Gorbachev had joined the communist party in 1952.

He was only 21 and a second year student at Moscow University when he joined the communist party. This alone indicates a more than average zeal and desire to serve the authorities. Particularly so, if we bear in mind, that this was in 1952 – a year of great purges and the last political campaign of the Stalin era: the campaign against "cosmopolitans", Jews and intellectuals.[53]

To become a Party member it was necessary to demonstrate a regular progression through the official institutions regulated by the Party. The process would be:

... as a youngster, you joined the pioneers without question. Not to do so would immediately draw attention to the child's parents or guardians. At 14, you joined Komsomol and most at this stage went along with what was demanded. Later, you became a party member. This was very difficult. The easiest way for ordinary people to gain membership to the communist party was to become a soldier.[54]

Once a member of the Communist party it was possible, but not guaranteed, to progress through the ranks of the Nomenklatura. On becoming a communist member one behaved differently, and remained publicly aloof from non-members. In the light that all 'appointments of all kinds and school entrance were determined by the Nomenklatura system',[55] it was crucial to forge influential contacts amongst the Nomenklatura that could be of use in progressing within the Party-state system. Gorbachev did not deviate from this procedure.

Whilst few reforms were hinted at or introduced in the early period, a change in style from the stolid traditionalist position was evident from the reforming rhetoric that increasingly appeared in state controlled publications. The *essence* of reform was however clearly recognised; change could not be suspended indefinitely. The 'doublethink' discernible throughout the Soviet region could be identified, but uncertainly confounded the succession of events.

The major achievement of these early 'reformers', despite their defeat, was to demonstrate that Soviet politics was not marked by the choicelessness that is sometimes assumed. There were alternatives not only to the Stalinist administration system but also to the conditions that prepared the way for its emergence under Lenin. The consolidation of Soviet authoritarianism was not the result of some primordial Russian problem or even relative underdevelopment; it was the consequence of political stratagems and beliefs.[56]

In seeking to agitate the debate relating to ideology and correspondingly overcome the resistance to change that prevailed in production and knowledge structures, Gorbachev encouraged the creative intelligentsia to reflect and comment critically on the regime. Following the directives announced by Gorbachev at the twenty-seventh Congress dissent entered the mainstream. This 'created the political, ideological, and psychological conditions' for a sharp turn.[57] Filmmakers for example were able to make explicit references to political, economic and social shortcomings of the Soviet system. Elsewhere in the various media, factions were encouraged to criticise – to create movement. The forces from below were given momentum to express their frustrations publicly. The ferocity and method alternative/counter-culture to ridicule and defy the regime shocked the establishment, forcing it to react further than it would have done without the provocation. It could, perhaps, understand the demands and the desires of the *occupied* states in seeking to rebuke the presence of the *occupiers*. The apparent repudiation of the Soviet regime from a large contingent of Russians, however, in all sectors of society, and not just from the celebrity dissidents, came as a surprise.

The degree of transparency that had accompanied the reforms could be tested following the disaster on the 26th April 1986 at the Chernobyl power station. The authorities, and the media orchestrated by *Pravda*, claimed that the suppression of information was to limit immediate panic in Chernobyl and the surrounding region. The delay in announcing the full implications of the accident directed suspicions towards the leadership. It was widely believed that 'the news of the Chernobyl nuclear disaster got out only because of its effects on foreign nations'.[58] If the Swedish scientists had not identified the radioactive particles and clouds moving across Northern Europe, the delay in announcing the disaster to the International community may have been further delayed or, more likely, hushed up completely. The affair severely damaged Gorbachev's democratic credentials.

The surrounding region of Chernobyl was an example of the inequality inherent within Soviet society. The account that the Party elite near Chernobyl were prescribed iodine whilst ordinary people received neither information nor medication was a scandal that the Soviet people became gradually aware of.[59] It was a stark example of the difference between the ordinary Russian and the power of the apparatchik.

Chernobyl was an important point in Soviet history. It posed questions about the effectiveness and professionalism of the Soviet nuclear industry. It had been a benchmark for the military industry sector and its failure undermined further the confidence in the system. The apartments near the Chernobyl complex had been specially built, with better shops and facilities, to provide for the families of the specialists who worked at the plant.[60]   The explosion itself, the reaction of the authorities, and the emergency procedure that followed, pointed to the ingrained incompetence of the regime and its leading members. The incident at Chernobyl provided ammunition to representatives from groups of environmentalists, scientists and reformers in the struggle for change.

> The slow response of the Soviet leadership to the Chernobyl disaster was a trigger for the first popular political movement to span the USSR.   These environmental movements mobilised broad coalitions around opposition to vast projects of dam building in Siberia.   Together with nationalist movements in the Soviet 'near abroad', it was these mass ecological movements, far more than intellectual dissent, that were the real internal catalysts for the Soviet collapse.[61]

Whilst Chernobyl activated the 'mass' ecological movements, and general criticism of the authorities, it should not be missed out that they evolved from a long tradition of intellectual dissent within the Soviet Union. These *groups* had previously considered a range of issues such as the negative aspects of the nuclear arms race, nuclear industry, industrial modernisation and *Westernization*, of which the theoretical import of communism had been a part.   Within orthodox political channels, despite being tempered by the demands of modernisation, ecological concerns within Russia have a long history.

The Defective Plan

In response to the difficulties resulting from the oil crisis in the late 1970s, Fordism, the system of mass production of standardised goods employing semi-skilled workers using specialised equipment gave way to new forms of organisation and practice in the West that can be called post-Fordist methods.[62]   The use of technology in the development of flexible automation achieved economies of scale without large and costly process associated with methods of Fordist assembly.   Japan and the United States, adjusting and manipulating the process through a concomitant management revolution accumulated vast profits and expanded the operations of multinational companies capable of acting logistically in global markets. Despite the general view that the Soviet economy was not driven by the imperatives of capital accumulation, the failure of the Soviet Union to maintain its industrial *competitiveness* was largely the result of 'the fact that Russia missed out on the management revolution that occurred in the West'.[63]

Gorbachev acknowledged the seriousness of the problems facing Soviet industry and attempted to convey the potential consequences of not decisively acting to manage and limit them. The Soviet Union depended on the credits raised from its exports to import technology, specialist goods, and hard currency. In some professions and sectors, the Soviet Union lacked the technical skills and the rapid learning curves required by an internationally competitive environment, particularly in advanced technology. This led to a corresponding fall in imports, causing shortages of a range of goods and services. The consequence of this development to the socialist bloc was that when the international labour value, particular in unskilled and semi-skilled sectors collapsed, its labour value become a burden and not the asset it had been in preceding years.

> Under the old regime land had no value. Human labour was seen as the agency for creating value. Since land and environmental resources were the produce of nature rather than human effort they were viewed as free goods.[64]

The change in the international production structure by the early 1980s and the loss in the importance of the need for mass labour created new demands in both capitalist and socialist economies. In the Soviet Union, the quality of goods and services deteriorated and production failed to remain in any sense competitive with production in the West. Without investment, re-training, and a re-vitalisation of strategic planning, it would be impossible to maintain the level of imports and exports that had cushioned the ruling elite from the everyday social and material hardships pervasively present in Soviet life.

Gorbachev had some understanding of the degree of apathy prevalent throughout industry and its potential to cause structural damage. By encouraging criticism of the worst manifestations of Nomenklatura inactivity, Gorbachev believed that the processes through which poor performance was allowed to continue without responsible intervention would be made clear and the decline halted. At conference, he made clear the problem.

> And though efforts have been made of late, we have not succeeded in wholly remedying the situation. The output of industrial and agricultural goods fell for

the 11th five-year plan period. There are serious lags in engineering, the oil and coal industries, electrical engineering, in ferrous metals and chemical industries, and in capital construction. Neither have the targets been met for the main indicators of efficiency and the improvement of the people's standard of living.[65]

In an attack on the stagnation and failure of management, Gorbachev continued in the address with a veiled attack on the elements of the old guard of the Nomenklatura, who were accused of sacrificing the needs of reform to their personal interests.

It is hard, however, to understand those who adopt a wait-and-see policy or who, like the Gogol Character that thought up all kinds of fanciful ideas, do not actually do anything or change anything. There will be no reconciliation with the stand taken by functionaries of this kind. We will simply have to part ways with them. All the more so do we have to part ways with those who hope that everything will settle down and return to the old lines. That will not happen. Comrades![66]

The atmosphere in industry had become extremely negative. Workers, disillusioned by the rhetoric of both the Party and the unions operated mechanically giving little thought to the quality of the work that they produced.

Working conditions were not very good. It was a classical thing, what was not glued down was stolen, and that was the way of living. People would go to work, have a cup of coffee, talk for two hours and then start looking round. My father did it – everybody did it? Our house was repaired with everything stolen from the factory. A saw, a box of nails, whatever, things you would require. But that was the way because you knew that your bosses would possibly let you, particularly if you were a member of the communist party they are agreeing with the system. Their houses, their dachas were built and repaired by pilfering from the factory. But, so what? After all, they say it all belongs to us. You know we should all have the chance to take the part in what we want.[67]

The restructuring that occurred in the large state industries did not reproduce the methods utilised in the Western management revolution but were the implementation of a moderate set of reforms intended to limit the explicit negligence prevalent in Soviet industry. The intention was to improve the operation of scientific management through incremental reforms not fundamentally revolutionise its key principles.

The crisis that prompted the reforms cannot be purely explained by 'the transition towards the information society'.[68] A mechanical view does not take account of pressure originating from non-technically motivated indigenous phenomena: coded activity that was seemingly in existence throughout the Soviet system. Whilst it appears accurate to suggest that the information revolution created structural turbulence and accelerated the dissimulation of cultural codes and practises, it did not fundamentally transform the production of ideas, which appear, in the Soviet condition, localised and imbued with historical struggle.

Whilst management, unions and workers were no doubt aware of the failure throughout industry, the resistance to radical industrial reform was evident by the response of workers and the community as a whole.

> Industry had to reform in the 1980s. New technology and the changing organisation of production outside the former Soviet Union made the desire for change in the resource starved industries acute. This did not mean, however, that the organisation of industry inside the former Soviet Union capitulated to organisational models in the West. Large companies did not get rid of employees (like many businesses in the West). Industry maintained a commitment to keep workers; companies are part of the community. A tenuous, but nonetheless community interest over self-interest...one that dismisses and continues to ignore the range of pressures and organisational methods present in a competitive market economy.[69]

In the context of subsidies, welfare networks and work associations, workers throughout the Soviet Union had relative security. A reliance on it helped in maintaining the apathy and indifference that prevailed in large sectors of Soviet life. To a point:

> Many people thought the regime was all right. If you didn't actively support it and were quiet about it, you got a job even if you didn't work hard. Education and welfare were adequately provided for. If you followed the rules, you kept out from trouble.[70]

The degree to which ordinary citizens received a basic provision to subsist is important. It should not be ignored that the harsh winters claimed a number of lives every year, and it would be far worse without the embedded social provision. On the one hand:

> a factory or office worker received extremely low compensation, by international standards, for his work. But this low monetary compensation was

supplemented with in-kind perquisites, for instance, the use of apartments for life, free heating and natural gas, hot water, kindergartens and nurseries, schools and so forth, as well as the cutting of prices for food products and industrial goods – the so-called prime necessities.[71]

Although many workers received help to procure the essentials, the apathy and disillusionment that prevailed throughout factories and work places in the Soviet Union and East Europe could not either be controlled or eradicated. The negative aspects of a relatively free working ethic had become ingrained in Soviet culture.

Workers stole from the factories. You got paid if you worked hard or not – although a lot of effort went into the appearance of work most people hardly work at all. Managers lied about production targets. If they weren't met, they would doctor the figures. Failure to meet targets would result in the manager in question or entire management level being removed. The central planning concept was undermined at level by fabrication and deceit. It was the culture it nurtured.[72]

A manager or a local official could expect other perks than those deemed outside authority. Members of the *Nomenklatura*, 'received considerably higher in-kind compensation in the form of superior apartments, dachas, personal cars, access to special medical clinics, special food rations, and so forth'.[73] Without doubt 'the good jobs went to party members'.[74] They avoided the difficulties prevalent in the lives of ordinary citizens.

We didn't starve, but we didn't live well. Life could be all right if you obeyed the rules. The bosses and the top authorities though, they lived like gods. They were careful to disguise their wealth and now [post-Soviet era] they happily display it. Good capitalists![75]

Incentives and propaganda were regularly offered to workers through the maintenance and indoctrination of ideology. The workers themselves had little or no actual representation. Their grievances and suggestions were monitored and considered but were, unless they questioned the authority of the Party, rarely acted on. The unions were in this context a function of the Party. The repeated visits by the Party officials and union members attempted to motivate and educate the ordinary worker. Nonetheless:

> Politics was not a big deal for the ordinary worker. When the communist ideologue came to the factory the workers pretended to listen and the speaker pretended to say something that they might want to hear. Workers were apathetic. When the system is obviously not working and people are living through it, it is very difficult to convince them that the opposite is the case.[76]

In the mines of Siberia, the miners increasingly displayed a rebellious nature to the concern of both the Party and union officials. Gorbachev unlike Brezhnev was not however inclined to use force against the miners. A report on foreign radio that force was being used to stop strikes would undermine the intention of glasnost. It has been stated that Gorbachev could ill afford the wrath of the press in the international media, a development that could potentially damage access to Western credit and technology. Other less obvious methods of persuasion were adopted in negotiations with the miners, generally in the guise of promises and lies.

In recognising the Communist Party's weakness in eradicating resistance, which was becoming increasingly open and combative, the Unions began to distance themselves from their close relationship with the Party. Where possible, the unions adopted a position of independence, and attempted to re-instate their legitimacy with their members.

The ideology that had evolved from Marxist-Leninism was however not absent from the organisation of every day life. It had not capitulated under the reforms or taken flight from the political contest but continued in regulating the life opportunities of people within the former Soviet Union. Despite an atmosphere conducive to change:

> it does not matter that no one believes in communist dogma nowadays. In their everyday life the Soviet people may perceive it as a nuisance, or as a source of numerous jokes shared equally by the people and their rulers. But at the end of the day, the Communist Party is still in firm control of every aspect of Soviet life, and communist ideology is never challenged within the Party.[77]

The serious threats to the Party seemingly come from outside it. The failure of the system to address the needs of ordinary people was made stark with the daily experience of disillusion. The intelligentsia had become familiar with the rhetoric of the authorities and ridiculed it using a variety of forms, many of which were copied and distributed through illegal methods to a population keenly interested in material that circulated through unofficial channels. The reforms highlighted and accentuated the complaints that had been embedded in Soviet society and formed the material on which creative opposition excelled.

Management of the system continued in an ad hoc manner and illustrated the failure of the Soviet planners. The defeat of *perestroika* and glasnost in regenerating the economy, and the resistance of a popular acceptance of 'transparent' socialism, signalled the end of the reforms in the manner they had been conducted. By 1988 greater independence was demanded by the republics. The People's Deputies had provided the forum for separatist forces to publicise their cause. The demands led to bloodshed. The bumbling response by Gorbachev, which appeared little more than considered amnesia, to the actions by the *Spetsnaz* (special forces) in Vilnius, Lithuania, established a precedence on which to build their demands and gauge the reality of democracy occurring within the Soviet Union. In the final days of Soviet communism, the fragmentation in both territory and ideas proliferated and swept it aside.

The role of alternative/counter-culture in undermining the ideology of the regime is largely, and deliberately, absent from the material presented above. It is not part of the official story. Its part in weakening the Soviet system will be considered in depth in subsequent chapters.

The events alluded to above were not autonomous from the processors encouraging them. In failing to represent the contribution and influence of alternative/counter-culture, International Relations as a discipline is guilty of a selective reading of contemporary history.

Notes

[1] Kissinger (1996:794) has cited Gorbachev's 1989 visit to Finland and the announcement made by his spokesman, Gerasimov that Moscow had adopted the "Sinatra Doctrine" in Eastern Europe, has a vital turning point in Soviet foreign policy and history. 'You know the Frank Sinatra song, *I did it my way*?' said Gerasimov, 'Hungary and Poland are doing it their way'.

[2] Soper (1990:4), *Troubled Pleasures*.

[3] Cox (1994:93), *The end of the USSR and the collapse of communism*.

[4] Meny (1987:3) suggests 'the European democracies possess in common ideas and institutions, which are peculiar to them as a group and so unite them. These may be listed under four main headings: the affirmation of pluralism, the specific mechanisms that allow expression of choice, the organisation of balanced institutions with limited powers, and the subordination of the public authorities to higher rules (constitutionalism)'.

[5] Bukovsky (1987:175), *Soviet Hypocrisy and Western Gullibility*.

[6] Held (1996:276), *Models of Democracy*.

[7] Ardagh (1991:415), *Germany and Germans*.

[8] Bauman (1991:192), *Communism: A post-mortem*.

[9] Coser (1990:182), *The intellectuals and Soviet reform*.

[10] Henry Marchewicz (1998), Polish World War II war veteran. Interviewed (23 January 1998).

[11] Joanna Eccles (1998), Polish citizen from Warsaw. Joanna grew up in Warsaw during the 1960s and left Poland in the early 1980s. Interviewed (8 February 1998).

[12] Corson and Crowley (1986:380), *The new KGB: engine of Soviet power.*

[13] *Ibid* (1986:380).

[14] Beamish and Hadley (1979:166), *The Kremlin's Dilemma.*

[15] Ramet (1995:234), *Social currents in Eastern Europe.*

[16] Hook (1987:110), *Paradoxes of Freedom.*

[17] Andrei Kolganov (1998) Academician at the Moscow State University. Interviewed in Moscow (April 1998).

[18] Calvocoressi (1991:245), *World Politics since 1945.*

[19] Nirmalendran, A. Teacher, Karlovy Vary, West Bohemian Region, former Czecholovakia.

[20] Alexeyena and Goldberg (1990:32), *The Thaw Generation.*

[21] Sakwa (1989), Commune Democracy and Gorbachev's reforms.

[22] Gill, S. and Law, D. (1988:321), *The Global Political Economy.*

[23] *Op cit* Eccles.

[24] Zoltan Ivan (1998) Broadcaster for the BBC World Service, Hungarian Section. Discussion (March 1998).

[25] *Op cit* Eccles.

[26] *Op cit* (1986:395), *The new KGB.*

[27] Grant (1964: 72,73), *Soviet Education.*

[28] Kissinger (1994:802), *Diplomacy.*

[29] Ogonyok (1991:8) estimates the Military Industry Complex (MIC) directly employed 14.5m persons, almost 10 per cent of the total labour force in the USSR. Inputs to defence controlled industries and military R&D institutes from other sectors of Soviet Industry were estimated at R480b, or 52 per cent of GNP (73 per cent of NMP). The Army, KGB, Police and enterprise of the MIC are estimated by the same source to consume 60 per cent of all fuel output and 60 per cent of all metal ores. See Filatotchev, et al, (1992:518). Given the particularly secret nature of the MIC in the Soviet Union the assumption that the above figures are conservative estimate must be considered.

[30] See Suganami (1997:460), *Narratives of War Origins and Endings: A note on the end of the Cold War.*

[31] See Bukovsky's *Soviet Hypocrisy and Western Gullibility.*

[32] Sakharov (1974:65,66), *Sakharov speaks.*

[33] Gorbachev (1986:16), *Political Report.*

[34] *Ibid* (1986:16).

[35] Hackett-Fischer's (1996) book, *The Great Wave*, provides an interesting account of the price revolutions throughout the twentieth century.

[36] See David Kotz with Fred Weir (1997), *Revolution from Above*, on this point for a range of statistical evidence.

[37] Medvedev (1986:87), *Gorbachev.*

[38] *Op cit* (1997:18), *Revolution from above.*

[39] Gray (1997:142), *False Dawn.*

[40] Alex Kan (1998), Broadcaster/Writer interviewed 13 December 1999.

[41] *Op cit* (1986:11), *Gorbachev.*

[42] Winston (1991:130), *Soviet Power.*

[43] Sakwa (1990:27), *Gorbachev and his reforms 1985-1990.*

[44] Kagarlitsky (1988:vii), *The Thinking Reed.*

[45] Heller and Nekrich (1986:727), *Utopia in Power.*

[46] *Op cit* (1988:viii), *The Thinking Reed.*

[47] Hill (1998:33), *Gorbachev and CPSU.*

[48] Boris Kagarlitsky (1998) Writer and leading member of Moscow Popular Front. Interviewed (April 1998).

[49] Andrei Kolgonov (1998) Academician at the Moscow State University. Interviewed (April 1998).

[50] Leo Feigin (1999), Writer, Broadcaster, Record Producer and Promoter. Former Professor of Linguistics at the Russian Academy of Sciences. Interviewed (January 1999). In support of this view, Peter Rutland (1998:33) has argued that 'it is hard to find anybody fluent in Russian who has heard Gorbachev speak and come away in awe of his intellectual abilities'.

[51] Kagarlitsky (1990:361).

[52] Hirst (1991:225), *The state, civil society and the collapse of communism.*

[53] Bukovsky (1987:173), *To Choose Freedom.*

[54] Alexander Kan (1999), Broadcaster and author. Interviewed (February 1999).

[55] *Ibid* (1999) Kan.

[56] Sakwa (1990:32), *Gorbachev and his reforms 1985-1990.*

[57] Lawton (1989:26), *Toward a new freedom.*

[58] Hook (1997:4), *Paradoxes of Freedom.*

[59] BBC Television, *The Second Revolution: The Battle for Glasnost.*

[60] See Tony Parker (1987), Russian Voices, for incisive comment on the local and social issues relating to the Chernobyl incident.

[61] *Op cit* (1999:149), *False Dawn.*

[62] Bernard (1994:216), 'Post-Fordism, Transnational Production, and the Changing Global Political Economy'. See also Mark Rupert's, *Producing Hegemony: the politics of mass production and the American global power.*

[63] Victor Sumsky (1998), Leading researcher at the Institute of World Economy and International Relations, The Russian Academy of Science. Interviewed April 1998.

[64] Kellett (1999:28), *Poland's scramble for Modernisation.*

[65] *Op cit* (1986:30), Political Report.

[66] *Ibid* (1986:49).

[67] *Op cit*, Nirmakendran.

[68] Castells (1998:7), *End of Millennium.*

[69] *Op cit*, Andrei Kolognov.

[70] K.Ciepka (1998), Club Secretary, The Polish Catholic Centre, interviewed (6 July 1998). Lived under Soviet occupation for some three years prior to 1950.

[71] *Op cit*, Medvedev.

[72] Anthony Aszabo (1998), Romanian citizen. Interviewed 4 February 1998.

[73] *Op cit*, Medvedev, 90.

[74] *Op cit*, Eccles.

[75] *Op cit*, Ciepka.

[76] *Op cit*, Aszabio.

[77] Bukovksy (1987), *To build a Castle.*

3 Cultural Genocide: The Dialectic of Struggle

The need to reflect on the early Soviet past is undertaken to enable a clear identification of the initial deviance from the Soviet system. The exclusion of social material: non communists, religious minorities, foreigners, deemed unsuitable identifies a number of human agents who were disposed to formulating an opposing view to the harshly enforced doctrine of Soviet communism. The wider necessity to consider both the motivation and appearance of opposition to the Soviet *idea* exposes the relationship between idealism and violence, the institutionalisation of communism and fear, and the role of the *Nomenklatura* in directing and manipulating all aspects of Soviet bureaucracy.

Revolution and Change

The pain, suffering and despair that was a re-occurring feature of everyday life in the sub-continent of northern Eurasia during the twentieth century is only recently open to an accurate account.[1] What began as a desire to liberate an exploited class from appalling poverty and cultural genocide in 1917, resulted in a system that ultimately failed to achieve and maintain its goal (the emancipation of slave labour from its historical chains and the realisation of a sustainable socialist society).

In the years preceding the revolution of 1917 the resentment, hatred and vilification of autocratic and bourgeois elite had become increasingly intense. With the deterioration of the already appalling living and working conditions, representations were repeatedly made to the Tsar to address the numerous social difficulties. Whilst wealth creation was beginning to result from gradual industrialisation, little was done to overcome the appalling conditions in which ordinary people were expected to subsist.

The strike in January 1905 at the Putilov engineering works in St. Petersburg was followed four days later by a march containing the workers and their families. The intention was to hand a petition into the Tsar requesting the introduction of basic civil rights and improved working conditions. Before the opportunity of presenting their grievances, the Imperial Guard checked the protesters, opening fire on the unarmed masses, killing nearly one hundred protesters. The day, remembered as 'Bloody Sunday', ended the psychological hegemony and physical hold of the Tsar over the Russian people.[2]

Sergei Eisenstein (1924), in the film Strike (*Stachka*), captured the heroic and brutal clash between workers with their employers and the police, during a factory strike; a record that is not purely propaganda. The antagonism between the workers and the bourgeoisie was increasingly violent, leading to street disturbances and arrests. Pasternak's book *Doctor Zhivago* captures the tension of this period, and illustrates the range of ideas that were being circulated.

History, the strikers believed, could be only changed by radical individual effort. It was the responsibility of the urban workers to destroy the bonds that restricted them from taking a full part in the organisation and management of society.[3]

Bulavka suggests that:

> the crucial thing to note here is that they did not just adapt to the new social circumstances around them, they themselves *formed, created* and, to put it simply, *made* these new social relations into something materially real in all domains of the life – from the economic to the social and the cultural; a reality which gave full credence to the basis of social creativity.[4]

The attitude which made the urban proletariat conducive to seeking redress from the Tsarist regime was not a result of biological necessity but a response to the cultural distance between the proletariat and the bourgeoisie, the severe hardships the workers had to endure and the uncertainly produced by the war. In the best industrial plants, which were few:

> many workers were lodged in vast dormitories, barrack like, with rooms for forty workers, and in Kamorka, each family marked out a space with blankets and sheets. Beds were simple planks. In the dormitories men slept on plank shelves in tiers going up to the ceiling.[5]

The daily combat with shortages and the cold fuelled a defiant condition. A sense of frustration and hatred exaggerated by the oft-whimsical nature of the Russian hierarchy, who were ostentatious in their display of wealth and manners. In the broad conditions of poverty and social segregation, the circulation of libertarian ideas from Western Europe communicated by active revolutionaries, who were monitored and infiltrated by the Tsar's secret police (*Okhrana*), found a fertile reception in the worst of industrial plants. The demands of the workers to be represented in worker's councils gathered momentum.   The response alternated between concessions and threats. The resistance to widespread reform and the intensive repression of political activists sapped the efforts of the revolutionaries, who either fled to Western Europe or moved underground. The criticism towards Tsarism did not however dissipate.

> The origin of these ideas, needless to say predate the Bolsheviks, and can really be seen as the heroic, and as a rule tragic, endeavour not only of the people of Russia, but the whole of humanity, tearing itself free from the necessities and obligations of Tsarism.[6]

The ability of the Bolsheviks to assume power was a remarkable feat of ingenuity and physical effort.   Other than a passionate belief in radical philosophy and the Marxist rejection of capitalist relations, Lenin and Trotsky had galvanised a force capable of countervailing the popularity of the *pluralists*, who were incapacitated by internal disagreements over policy and programs, and later collapsed without serious resistance. It was not certain however that Lenin's plans would be successful.   The revolutionaries had been spread throughout Europe and were far from trusted amongst the *ordinary* Russians from whom they sought support. As a social force, it was akin to a situation whereby:

> an elite consisting of some of the most active, energetic, enterprising and disciplined members of society that emigrates abroad and assimilates the culture and historical experiences of the most advanced countries of the West, without however losing the most essential characteristics of its own nationality, that is to say without breaking its sentimental and historical links with its own people. Having thus performed its intellectual apprenticeship it returns to its own country and compels the people to an enforced awakening, skipping historical stages in the process.[7]

Despite Lenin's animation, the revolutionary forces that were unleashed in Russia were seemingly not the result of a particular individual action (although particular individuals were obviously influential). The views and aspirations of the social forces that contributed to the revolution were not a harmonious movement but a discriminating kaleidoscope of interest groups that grasped the initiative presented by the historical circumstances. [8]

A view, widely held by the urban workers, demonstrated that 'the proletarian revolution was to eradicate the inequalities built into bourgeois society. But how was socialism itself to define the notion of equality so as not to violate the domain of personal freedoms'?[9] The experience of everyday life, its abuses, its violence could not be expunged from the ideology of the Bolshevik-Soldier.

Nonetheless, in the heady days of the revolution, despite being affected by appalling conditions and difficulties of all kinds, optimism was not stifled. After the fires of the political revolution in October 1917, and the separation between church and state, there now began to emerge the flames of the Cultural Revolution which was to dominate the 1920s and early 1930s. Bulavka's account recalls that:

> the social openness towards culture at this time, and the individuals self-awareness of it, occurred not only because it was turned into a working instrument of the revolutionary masses as part of their desire to create a new life and civilisation. The maelstrom of revolutionary events also gave birth to a revolutionary mass with an acute need to comprehend as fully as possible the ideas which were emerging, to understand their proper interests in all of this, and to link all this together in the best way possible. To parallel their emergence as a new subject of historical actions, artistic culture now took on the form of a true, meaningful ideology; a philosophy of proper cultural interests and needs.[10]

The policies that had been introduced during the early part of the civil war were taken in extremely difficult conditions; survival in its most basic form was a prominent concern. 'The Bolshevik regime was moving towards liberalisation – the New Economic Policy and the cessation of the Red Terror proved that is was so – and what was necessary was to halt the momentum of the civil war'.[11] It appeared briefly that the proletariat was willing to make further sacrifices in the construction of an egalitarian society. It was a period when the hopes released by the success of the revolution appeared attainable.

The Soviet Union was established on December 30, 1922. In the immediate aftermath of the Great War and a protracted civil war 'the regime encountered a prolonged armed resistance at least until 1928, and that entire period, beginning with the October revolution can be more properly considered the period of formation'.[12] The methods of war communism adopted by the Bolshevik leadership to force victory from the grips of defeat were successful, but not without a high human cost. A report composed in the Volga records the horrors of the 1921 famine, blamed in part on the communist strategy and methods in relation to the rural economy.

> Here in the old Tsarist day's nobles had built villas and laid out fine gardens for their pleasure in the summer months. Now those houses were filled with refugees from the famine, dying of hunger and disease, and across the snow came small children, hand in hand, who had walked a long way from staving villages where their parents were already dead. Like frozen birds many of them died in the snow.[13]

The creativity that had been released by the revolution was not however totally stifled and despite the harsh conditions of everyday life hope in an improvement in social fortunes had not been abandoned. Few mechanical devices worked in the region and pure muscle was the tool of restructuring. It was, however, the increasing hold of the Stalinist bureaucracy and its effectiveness in dislodging the 'processes of social creativity' which damaged the wide aspirations of an inclusive culture that recognised the value of selfless social contribution to the construction of a fair and just multinational society.[14] The artificial creation of, and keen obedience to, the Soviet new man seemingly undermined the emancipatory and creative development of the revolution, and placed gradually a totalitarian roof over the populations of *Rus*.

The outcome of this process was the creation of an inward looking revolutionary elite, whose focus was on management and security rather than on achieving the goals of social regeneration and equality. Walter Benjamin's classic *Moscow Diary*, dealing with his two-month stay in Moscow from December 6, 1926 to the end of January 1927 captures the concerns amongst literati community relating to the creative direction of the revolution. It was obvious that the institutionalisation of communism instilled discipline at the expense of creativity. The effort to construct a homogenous Soviet culture was ruthlessly initiated, and the mistakes of Spartan mentality were extensively repeated.

> The Party denied the free will of the individual – and at the same time it exacted his willing self-sacrifice. It denied his capacity to choose between two alternatives – and the same time it demanded that he should constantly choose the right one. It denied his power to distinguish between good and evil – and at

the same time it spoke pathetically of guilt and treachery. The individual stood under the sign of economic fatality, a wheel in a clockwork which had been wound up for all eternity and could not be stopped or influenced – and the Party demanded that the wheel should revolt against the clockwork and change its course. There was somewhere an error in the calculation; the equation did not work out.[15]

In a collection of letters smuggled out of the Soviet Union through the network of cultural and religious links to the West in 1930s, the contributors tell of their accounts as slaves in the Soviet timber camps, and call on the world for assistance. In one such letter, dated 1 October 1933, 'V' in the North of Russia writes:

> Dear Mrs .-
> It is now four months since we were deported from our home in "C", to the cold north. Food supplies are very bad here, especially in the case of large families, such as ours, for my salary is not enough for three children and my wife. Therefore, I beseech you for the children's sake to send food, more especially as we were taken away quite unexpectedly and against our will.
> Grateful thanks in advance _____.[16]

The result of the well-known attacks on the intelligentsia, the kulaks and any suspicious act was a society enveloped by fear. The proletariat was not exempt from suspicion and retribution. It was the *ordinary* men, women and children who were forced into the labour camps, starving and diseased, to be the slave-fodder of industrialisation. The paradox inherent in the ascension of Stalin's power is evident in its need to develop and modernise. Dunham has exposed the *contract* of the 'Big Deal', an alliance with the rapidly growing managerial 'middle class' (the *Meshchanstvo*) consisting of engineers, managers, and administrators. It was they who received rewards from the regime for their co-operation, which was crucial to the reconstruction of the country and Stalin's grip on power.

A Question of Manners

The residue of French hegemony that dominated the Russian upper classes, and particularly the language up to and beyond the counter-hegemonic intervention made by Puskin, ironically continued to affect Soviet cultural life. The idea that history is not influenced by the cultural residue that formulated it is mistaken. Prompted by Golovkin's comments on Madame

Bovary, a clear identification is made with the potrebitelskoie (trans.consumerist values) of the *meshchanstvo* and the French society of the Flaubert century, 'which was also a bit potrebitelskoie', a similarity that was far from expunged in Soviet life. In acknowledgement, Bovary provides a good example.

> It is a brilliant comparison Katherina and Madame Bovary! Yes, both of them belong to this class, although Katherina is a greater character than Emma of course. Remember Emma's excitement: "Oh, I have a lover"! Very shallow feelings, really narrow-minded and she did not take proper care of her child either [a strong indictment in Russia] and was consumed by the consumption of goods, men, whatever. And Katherina belongs to this class only socially, mentally and spiritually she has nothing to do with it.[17]

The connections between the *Meshchanstvo* and the evolving Nomenklatura system that increasingly became institutionalised with the approval of the Soviet leadership established the continuity of power in the Soviet hierarchy. The evolving system that paradoxically undermined the continuation of direct authority was not conducive to the ideological development of egalitarian society. The mode of rule that furthered the opportunities and careers of its extensive but exclusive members would be a path leading nowhere.

It was evident in the 1930s, when, Stalin had consolidated his hold on political power 'that membership of the communist party was crucial not only to a successful administrative career but also to attaining almost any form of upward social mobility'.[18] It also provided a degree of physical security from the secret police. Paradoxically, it was the ordinary worker who had yet to grapple with the demands of literacy who suffered most in the probationary periods of acceptance to the communist party and career possibilities. Whilst levels of literacy and the access to education rapidly improved, resulting in a well educated working class, 'workers and peasants were consistently under represented throughout the Party's history and the university educated were over represented. Periodic attempts were made to recruit members from under-represented groups; during the Khrushchev and Brezhnev eras, for example, more recruits were sought from women and ethnic minorities, with varying degrees of success'.[19]

The differences between the *meshchanstvo* and members of the *nomenklatura* are not wide. There are however schisms that require clarification.

In Russia, people who became *Nomenklatura* understand very well the abyss between them and the rest of the population and they want only one thing: to get maximum of welfare, benefits and money. Every *Nomenklatura* member has numerous relatives and children and he does his best to remain "okolo kormushki"(trans. near to the source, close contact). I don't think they even now know about the difference between meshchanstvo and consumerism. We can say that the *Nomenklatura* are infected with consumerism but consumerism means consumption of commodities and there are some of *Nomenklatura* who simply get money to their bank accounts without consuming too much because their aim is to accumulate and not spend.[20]

The socialisation of the property and opulence of the former Tsars was rapidly commandeered by the vanguard of the revolution. Party members could be found in Moscow's best restaurants and hotels, such as the Hotel Metropole, located near the Kremlin, eating elaborate meals and enjoying the decadence denied to the majority of comrades struggling to subsist in a country ravaged by civil war and famine. The elite lived in comfort and enjoyed dachas outside the city. Money itself may have been limited, but the wealth accrued by other means was boundless.

The wealth of the new rich did not consist only of fine houses, furniture, cars, servants, special facilities for the theatre, special shops, Black sea rest homes; nor only in the untrammelled power – the power to take over an orphanage for private use, or 'expropriate' a non-party member's dog, nor even the enjoyment of virtual immunity from prosecution for civil crime. There was also the intangible but delightful pleasure of belonging to a chic elite, with its precisely gauged hierarchy of ranks. There were uniforms, titles, and the relative size of Stalin's portrait hanging in the office or home indicated valued status. Gradually, too, this new bourgeoisie was transforming itself into a hereditary class.[21]

Before the outbreak of the Second World War, the Soviet version of communism appeared to be rapidly losing its legitimacy. It was increasingly obvious to the ordinary comrades and citizens how the ruling elite lived. The degree of ideological flight is virtually impossible to measure accurately but rumours relating to the corruption of the regime and Stalin's repeated purges were circulating amongst the population. The reports of terror in the army, orchestrated by the Red commissars, under instruction from the Kremlin, was instrumental in alienating the army from the Party, despite its continued loyalty to the Soviet State. The offensive strategy in the Great Patriotic War may indicate Stalin's awareness of the need to simulate patriotism to compensate the loss of popular support. Between 1938 to 1945, it appeared that Stalin lived in a fear of internal collapse of the Soviet regime. The concern was:

> similar to the suddenness which engulfed the Provisional Government of Kerensky in 1917. Such likelihood may have seemed remote, so debilitated was the population at large and so great were the police resources of the Soviet state. But the point is not the validity of such a fear, but its existence and the reactions that it provoked.[22]

The drive to modernise had before the war been the key objective of the regime. Stalin's foreign slaves, incarcerated within the Soviet Union during the conflict and the Russian civil war were made up of Germans, Czechs, Americans, British and numerous other nationalities either forgotten or ignored by their governments. The slaves were forced to work, under the dictum of the 're-education of delinquents through hard work', in horrendous conditions in the rich mines scattered throughout the Soviet Union.

The failure to maintain social inclusion:

> led directly to the beginning of dictatorship, the suppression of all-non socialist parties and news media. When there was economic ruin and much popular discontent, the end of the civil war suppressed all parties except the Communist Party. At the time, as a "temporary" measure (and all of these measures were said to be temporary at the time) factions within the Communist Party were banned. Eventually, this meant the ouster and even execution of all factions except that of Stalin.[23]

Rosa Luxembourg (who actively supported the Russian Revolution) warned in a fraternal criticism of the Bolsheviks in 1918 that 'without general elections, without free struggle of opinions, life dies out in every public institution, becomes a mere semblance of life, in which only the bureaucracy remains an active element'.[24] Robin Blick in the book *The Seeds of Evil* claims Lenin had been unconcerned with the life of the Soviet *people*: power was the pleasure of pleasures. The iron laws of Soviet socialism had taken precedence over the emancipation of the working class. The vanguard of the revolution had led them into the iron cage and closed the door.

The *Nomenklatura*: the Chameleon Class

The material above reflects on how the emergence of a culture of emancipation was deadened by institutionalisation and the force of Bolshevik-Soldier mentality. In absence of open debate and the free exchange of ideas without fear and retribution, the expression of doubt in the Bolshevik project and its methods was given vent through the various arts. Later, it would be Soviet rock music, which continued the tradition of dissent, embroiled in an array of coded forms.

The split between the Party, State and *the people* appears to have taken place gradually. It was an uneven progression that weakened the Soviet system. The early fragmentation of ideas and interests not unified in the attainment of a specific and collective goal: the realisation of a communist world – disrupted the attainment of it. In its place, nurtured a personal strategy of self-interest, not an uncommon feature of Soviet life.

The revolutionary vanguard had by Lenin's death established an institutionalised form that demanded compliance.

> The Russian Revolution of 1917 was intended to fulfil the egalitarian Marxist dream of establishing a communist society. By the early 1920s, however a small group had seized political power and had established a professional class known as the *Nomenklatura*.[25]

With the widening demands of managing and administering all aspects of Soviet life, it grew from its centralised base to regional posts charged with regulating local areas.

> The essence of this order has been the attempt to consciously manage every area of socially relevant activity, outside a closely circumscribed private sphere, through an array of hierarchically structured formal organisations, all co-ordinated and directed at the centre and at successively lower levels by the apparatus of the communist party.[26]

The *Nomenklatura* was established to administer the directives set out by the Party. The administration of the system was part of an extensive bureaucracy that gradually separated from the ideology of the Party in an implicit form, its cadres sought to glean, where available, opportunities and benefits from a system it was set up to manage. It was:

originally rooted in the small size of the Bolshevik party. Even by the 1930s, Communists represented only 3 percent of the Soviet population. Faced with the problem of administering a huge territory, the Bolsheviks created a mechanism of centralised control over personal decisions to ensure all members of the Party were available for nation-wide assignment at the will of the authorities.[27]

The rigidity of the system, embedded with cronyism, festered at an early stage. In the recruitment and establishment of practice, creativity was expelled; a condition that seemingly destabilised the development of socialism before halting it completely. Without responsibility and accountability abuse proliferated in all areas of the system. The bureaucracy:

> took the opposite form to that envisaged by Marx when he [Stalin] sought to imagine the lineaments of a socialist society; far from basing itself on the direct exorcise of power by the masses through a network of institutions of democratic self government, 'existing socialism' involved an unprecedented centralisation of power – economic, political and cultural – in the hands of the *Nomenklatura*, as the ruling class of top bureaucrats and managers was known...the conclusion that the Soviet Union and its like constituted no kind of socialism but some sought of class society seems unavoidable. But what kind of class society?[28]

The *Nomenklatura* appears not to be a class in the traditional 'class sense'. It has features common to it, but it also encapsulates trajectories from it. Chameleon-like it:

> goes further: it denies its own existence. Both in theory and practise, the controlling class tries to pass itself off as part of the administrative machine such as exists in every country in the world.[29]

The *Nomenklatura* undertook the task of managing the everyday details that pervaded the exchanges within the mechanical system. Its knowledge of the administrational structure allowed it to accumulate privileges that could not be accessed through other means.

> The "leading" posts in the Soviet economic, political and cultural bureaucracy – includes not only the Party's own apparatus but also positions in industry, parliaments, police, military, foreign affairs, science and culture. The list would also include chief engineers, head physicians and head teachers. Even

collective farmers and manual workers acting as (unpaid) Party secretaries or having posts in the Soviet would be included.[30]

To be guaranteed of certain privileges it was necessary to be *in* the *Nomenklatura*. No influential position could be attained without recourse to it. A political career could not be established and developed without being a part of it.

The traditional *Nomenklatura* career trajectory began with study in Moscow and then went on to the Soviet, Komsomol, economic or Party apparatus at district level, followed by a recall to Moscow for a one or two year stint in the Central Committee headquarters and then a return to the provinces to a higher level post (often an obkom first secretaryship).[31]

The system nurtured and produced political figures that could progress to the higher echelons of the Communist Party. Paradoxically, it appears that elsewhere in the system the *Nomenklatura* moved away from the influence the Party had over it and formulated specific hegemonies through a nexus of influential cadres who excelled in the manipulation of the system and those directly involved within it. This condition was recognised in the early 1950s.

That is why the inflationary growth of the Soviet Communist Party reveals merely an accentuation of the breach that has been taking place for decades in Soviet society. The *Nomenklatura* ruling class grows more and more isolated, the gulf between it and the Party goes on widening, and the Party increasingly becomes merely a section of the population.[32]

In this sense, the apathy that can be identified with the ideology of the Party can be located within the Soviet establishment itself. Social betterment was not procured through reading Marx and Lenin, but knowing which department or apparatchik could best obtain a good or service, and on what terms, official or unofficial.

The ruling class, the *Nomenklatura*, [was] not interested in economic profitability but only in maintaining its power, its monopoly. For these reasons, what [was] produced [was] not of good quality, it [was] a production that contribute[d] to fortifying and strengthening the position of power.[33]

The corruption prevalent in the ruling apparatus was not a well-kept secret and whilst the worst excesses of it were concealed it was widely recognised that it gained privileges unavailable to citizens outside it. The 'relative independence of the apparatchik from the apparatus through illegally accumulated private wealth'[34] sets it aside from the experiences of the majority in Soviet life.

Social Charades

A brief consideration of the post-Soviet condition illustrates the widespread influence of the *Nomenklatura* in the Central and East European States. Andrei Kolganov and Alla Pokrovskaya at the economic centre at the Moscow State University claim that in the post-Soviet condition that it is the *Nomenklatura* who have reaped the benefits from the collapse of Soviet communism and its institutions.

> The Russians shopping at GUM and audiences at the Bolshoy, the Stanislavsky and Nemirovich-Danchenko Theatre, and the Moscow Conservatory, enjoying the nationalist qualities of pieces by Glinka and Mussorgsky, is part of the top five per cent of Russian society. This class is primarily made up of the Nomenklatura and their families. There is no middle class. The rest are either on or below subsistence level.[35]

Whilst it would not be inaccurate to suggest that in the post-Soviet condition a gradual return to the aristocratic connections and circles of the nineteenth century is occurring, a social class that sees itself above ordinary society is more clearly evident. It appears similar to an earlier impression of Russian life. They are not the cream of aristocracy but the nouveau riche of the communist era:

> who hobnob together in the hidden dacha settlements around Moscow and in other choice colonies around the country have arrogated to themselves a larger system of privileges than being far better clothed, fed, housed and medically cared for than the rest of the population. Their lives simply take place on a different plane from the rest of society.[36]

With the collapse of socialism the gulf between rich and poor has widened and become more obvious. The top five per cent can afford the best commodities and entertainment available whilst the rest struggle to subsist on or below the official 'poverty line'.

> In 1989 the official subsistence income was 140 roubles a month. Between then and 1996, consumer prices rose by 10,000%. On that basis, by 1996 the

subsistence income would have been about 7.4 million roubles a month. As only about 10% had a monthly income above 1 million roubles, that would imply a poverty rate of over 90%.[37]

The extreme differentials between ordinary citizens and former *members* of the *Nomenklatura*, continues, particularly in Russia, to throw light on it previous strength and resilience in the former Soviet system. Whilst it appears not to play a direct role in the political fortunes of Russian politicians, its pervasive history and network should not be ignored in seeking to understand many of the contemporary issues and derogatory events afflicting Russia.

Developed Stagnation

It has been suggested that under the tenure of the corrupt and cynical Brezhnev leadership that the *Nomenklatura* became largely separated from both the ideology of the Party and the needs and aspirations of the multi-national population. It is difficult to place the *Nomenklatura* in a neat taxonomic box. Nonetheless, if it is accepted that a *section* of it separated from the grip of the Party it needs to be measured.

Boris Kagarlitsky, and David Kotz with Fred Weir, have written at length concerning the revolution from above, a revolution they perceive as being orchestrated by a section of the old *Nomenklatura*. Both works are particularly persuasive and provide detailed evidence of the actors themselves. In the latter piece, statistical information is provided to support the proposition that the 'economic, political, and cultural reforms they [Gorbachev] carried out unleashed processes that created a new coalition of groups and classes that favoured replacing socialism with capitalism'.[38] It was not however a revolution prompted by the *Nomenklatura* that ended the authority of the Soviet Union. Nevertheless, it appears that a revolution was prevalent in specific areas of the economy: a shift from national to international wealth creation for a privileged minority. In the political domain it appears that the *Nomenklatura* did not want a radical shift to all out Western democracy, preferring an Asian type model, similar to Singapore, in which State control would continue to dominate the lives of Soviet citizens.

Alternative/counter-culture opposed both the State apparatus dominated by the *Nomenklatura* and the ideology of the Party. Both were perceived to be corrupt, hypocritical and self-fulfilling. The wide opposition to both seemingly undermined the aspirations and plans of the leading members of the Party-State elite.

The bureaucratic nature of the *Nomenklatura* was fundamentally different from the role of bureaucracies in Western European states.

> In European societies the bureaucracy usually executes the will of the ruling class. Naturally, the bureaucrats who administer the state also have their own personal interests. Very often the results of bureaucratic control turn out to be strikingly different from what is expected. But at the same time the apparatus does not advance its own goals and priorities. It merely interprets the will of the rulers after its own fashion as it implements their decisions.
>
> Under the Soviet totalitarian system, by contrast, the apparatus both made the decisions and interpreted them. Without ceasing to be above all the executive apparatus of the regime, the bureaucracy no longer implemented the will of a ruling class. In the strict sense it was no longer a bureaucracy of the old pattern, but a 'statocracy', a class state or class-apparatus without property or stability.[39]

Following the death of Brezhnev, the embedded structural difficulties, paradoxically caused in part by the activities of the *Nomenklatura,* became increasingly apparent. It was widely recognised that change was necessary to add movement to the stagnation that had enveloped Soviet life. The regeneration of the international economic order to a neo-liberal market driven environment led elements of the *Nomenklatura* to recognise the benefits of a move to a quasi market economy.

> Members of the Party-state elite played various roles in the process of abandonment of socialism in favour of building capitalism. Some, as early as 1987, used their connections and access to money and other resources to start private businesses. Others became political leaders of the drive to bring capitalism to the USSR. The switch from the defence of socialism to praise for capitalism appeared to require a drastic change of world-view for the old elite.[40]

When it became obvious that the privileges which had been gleaned from the Soviet system by the ruling hierarchy could not be continued, the *Nomenklatura* ruptured to pursue strategies that would either guard against the loss of its authority and prestige or take advantage of the new conditions. With the cohesion of the Soviet structure abandoned and the wider ideology vulnerable, the culture of communism suffered irreparably; an outcome that could not arguably have been realised without the preceding effort of a coded and vibrant alternative/counter-culture.

Notes

[1] An estimate figure of repatriated nationals and ethnic minorities, in the region of 500,000 to 1,100,000, were murdered in the USSR between 1943-47 alone. *Source: Harff; Conflict Resolution Programme, LA Times; Encyclopaedia Britannica.*

[2] See Robert K. Massie (1967), *Nicholas and Alexandra* for a considered narrative on the strikes and Nicholas' response to them.

[3] Outside the urban centre the Tsar was still venerated as a God.

[4] Bulavka (1998:8), *From the Cultural Revolution of 1917.*

[5] Moynahan (1997:22), *The Russian Century.*

[6] *Op cit* (1998:10), Bulavka.

[7] Gramsci (1998, 1971:20), *Selections from the Prison Notebooks.*

[8] Pasternak's *Doctor Zhivago* provides and excellent record of the tensions between the various groups in favour of the revolution but intent on attaining specific outcomes from it.

[9] Udovicki (1987:249), *The liberal model and the public realm in the u.s.s.r.*

[10] *Op cit* (1998:12), *Bulavka.*

[11] Kagarlitsky (1988:63), *The Thinking Reed.*

[12] Simirenko (1975:35), *A new type of resistance.*

[13] Gibbs (1921:493), *Famine in Russia.*

[14] *Op cit* (1988:13), *From the cultural revolution.*

[15] Koestler (1947, 1940:204), *Darkness at Noon.*

[16] Anon (1933:58).

[17] Russia Today discussion. On-line posting on Russiatoday.com. Posted by Eccly (May 5 1999).

[18] McAllister and White (1995:220), *The Legacy of the Nomenklatura.*

[19] *Ibid* (1995:221).

[20] Russia Today discussion. On-line: Russiatoday.com. Posted by golovkin (May 16 1999).

[21] Tolstoy (1981:45), *Stalin's Secret war.*

[22] *Ibid* (1981:xiii).

[23] Sherman (1990:15,16), *The Second Soviet Revolution.*

[24] Lowy (1991:33), *Twelve theses on the crisis of "really existing socialism".*

[25] *Op cit* (1995:217), *The Legacy of the Nomenklatura.*

[26] Rigby (1988:523), *Staffing USSR incorporated: The origins of the Nomenklatura system.*

[27] Borocz and Rona-Tas (1995:641), *Small leap forward: Emergence of new economic elites.*

[28] Callinicos (1995), *Theories and Narratives.*

[29] Voslensky (1953:69), *Nomenklatura.*

[30] Lane (1997), *Transition under Eltsin.*

[31] Kryshtanovskaya and White (1996:715), *From Soviet Nomenklatura to Russian elite.*

[32] Voslensky (1953:97), *Nomenklatura: Anatomy of the Soviet Ruling Class.*

[33] Djilas (1980).

[34] Heller and Feher (1988:7), *Utopia in Power.*

[35] Andrei Kologonov (1998), Interviewed April 1998.

[36] Smith (1976), *The Russians.*

[37] Standing (1998), *Societal impoverishment.*

[38] Kotz with Weir (1997:5), *Revolution from Above.*

[39] Kagarlitsky (1982:14), *The Disintegration of the Monolith.*

[40] *Op cit* (1997:6), *Revolution From Above.*

4 The System and the Damage Done

The *re-birth* in dissident activity was initiated in response to continued oppression and hardship. The ideas and beliefs that had justified the temporal state were by the 1980s untenable. Vaughan James has suggested that 'an understanding of them [dissidents] can only be deepened by a study of the philosophy from which they dissent, the embodiment of official Soviet culture must be identified to facilitate an analysis of dissent'.[1] The attempt to direct society towards a universal goal in which all ideological deviations were expunged, established a rigorous culture that superficially conveyed an impression of strength, vitality and proletarian purity. In maintaining its hold on all aspects of Soviet life, the Party consolidated its power. The tensions within the system were not however eradicated, but continued in an atomised and coded form.

The Tower of Babel and its Re-occupation by the Atheists

In the immediate aftermath of the October coup, the vanguard of the Bolsheviks was occupied with the conflagration between the Reds and Whites, and *Greens* (the foresters) and the need to secure the grip on Petrograd and then Moscow. The chaos that was typical of this period of Russian history was confounded by the ruthless and contradictory methods established by the Bolsheviks to hold the unity of the revolution and limit the flight from it. Lenin's:

> Preoccupations... were to ensure the most efficient mobilisation of the regime's scarce resources, to instil firm discipline and accountability and to insist upon the authority of the centre. The emphasis was... upon the accountability of the lower Party (and State) organs to the higher ones and this was crucial to Lenin's account of democratic centralism. The self-administration of the Commune model was replaced by a more austere version of the dictatorship of the proletariat which, Lenin acknowledged, had to be exercised by its Party.[2]

The message of freedom that had inspired a revolution would be sacrificed to the mission, which would through pragmatic debate, supersede the demand for cultural autonomy. The social rhythms that had undermined the established institutions throughout the previous century had found expression in a small group of revolutionaries determined to realise their ambitions, many of which were laudable. In the pre-revolutionary environment the cultural distance between the ruling elite and the illiterate was glaringly wide, and an attempt to overcome the injustice by indigenous protest was brutally suppressed by the forces of the Tsar.

Yes. Well. So you see, the whole of the nineteenth century – its revolutions in Paris, its generations of Russian emigrants starting with Herzen, its assassinations of tsars, some only plotted, others carried out, the whole of the workers' movement of the world, the whole of Marxism in the parliaments and universities of Europe, the whole new system of ideas with its novelty, the swiftness of its conclusions, its irony and its pitiless remedies invented in the name of pity – all of this was absorbed into Lenin, to be expressed and personified by him and to fall upon the old world as retribution for its deeds.[3]

Lenin in 1905 had asserted that 'the Party was a voluntary association, which would inevitably break up, first ideologically and then physically, if it did not cleanse itself of people advocating anti-party views'. With the potential increase of literacy amongst the population, it was considered prudent by the revolutionary vanguard to establish mechanisms to control the production, circulation and consumption of the written word and censor anti-Soviet material.

The experience of prolonged struggle against authority had made Lenin keenly aware of the power of underground networks in undermining the ruling elite. He introduced rules that would ironically be used as a framework in subsequent censorship.

What is this principle of Party literature? Is it not simply that, for the socialist proletariat, literature cannot be a means of enriching individuals or groups; it cannot, in fact, be an individual undertaking independent of the common cause of the proletariat. Down with non-partisan writers! Down with literary supermen! Literature must become *part* of the common cause of the proletariat, 'a cog and screw' of one single great Social Democratic mechanism set in motion by the entire political – conscious vanguard of the entire working class. Literature must become a component of organised, planned and integrated social-democratic work.[4]

By the 1920s, with the withdrawal of foreign troops and the failing fortunes of the whites, the need shifted from the demands of war to methods to legitimise the centralisation of Bolshevik control. Direct coercion, which had become widely resented, was relaxed. This was primarily achieved through the campaign to improve literacy throughout the nation. It was expected that the literacy campaign would benefit modernisation, strengthen the proletarian movement and, in the exclusive tuition of the Russian language, establish Russian hegemony.

Social and political education was guided through the State's monopoly of the media and the mechanisms that processed the dissimulation of information. This led to the construction of a reality that seemingly did not correlate consistently with the experience of everyday life; this would become increasingly obvious to both the leaders and led.

Stalin utilised the threat posed by counter-revolutionary activity to eliminate ideas that indirectly or explicitly questioned the methods and ideology of the Soviet power centre. Writers were not allowed to present an opinion that opposed the Party. Without criticism, the power of centre dictates its policy, and debate on it, other than acceptance, is suspended. This position was developed in the summer of 1928 when the Central Committee issued a new resolution on cultural questions:

> In its opening sentences, its most soothing passage, it cited the resolution of 1925, but further on it declared war on any "backsliding from a class position, eclecticism, or benign attitude toward an alien ideology". The resolution declared that literature, theatre, the cinema, painting, music, and radio had to take part "in the struggle... against bourgeois and petit bourgeois ideology, against vodka and philistinism", as well as against "the revival of bourgeois ideology under new labels and the servile imitation of bourgeois culture".[5]

Before his death in 1924, Lenin had the opportunity to reflect on the development of the Bolsheviks. The development of the revolutionary party had not progressed in the manner that he had tentatively foreseen. Everywhere he appeared to recognise the self-interest that typified the worst excesses of the bourgeoisie. In letters and recorded conversations, Lenin raised concerns that the institutions that shaped Soviet life had sabotaged the movement.

> Not until his last writings of late 1922 and 1923, after a second stroke had forced his effective retirement, did Lenin have the leisure to reflect on what had been built in Russia. He was disturbed that the state apparatus had replicated many of the worst abuses of the Tsarist State, that communists were high-

handed, incompetent administrators, and increasingly divorced from the people.[6]

The concerns expressed by Lenin regarding the institutionalisation of a rigid bureaucracy were ignored by the hierarchy within the Party. This is not to suggest however that Lenin rejected Leninism or the idealism that underpinned the revolution, merely that he disagreed with his successor. Following Lenin's death, Stalin embarked on a development programme that systematically removed the potential for cultural inclusion and plurality. The bureaucracy would become all-pervasive; an embedded feature to be experienced daily. All citizens, willing and forced, were subjugated under its development. In a campaign that lasted until 1953, writers, artists, economists, philosophers, musicians, linguists and poets were arrested, murdered and herded into labour camps. Many died anonymously, mainly on the suspicion that they held an alternative view.

The modernisation process was brutal and uncompromising, victimising classes as well as individuals. In celebration of the achievements of communism, Stalin announced the construction of new wonders. Through the exploitation of prison and slave labour, as well as ordinary workers, work began on Stalin's famous 'palaces' and the ambitious Metro system.

> The 'mass spectacles' of the early Soviet years utilised 'topographic reality' and 'real objects and actions' to create a 'utopian and mythological' worldview – for a short time creating a truly popular sense of the appropriation and symbolisation of townscape.[7]

The human cost of the construction of the Soviet spectacle was millions of deaths, incarceration in camps, and a society imbued with fear. The Party had succeeded in its attempt to thoroughly control the various media and its consumption was directed by the sustained application of violence and psychological terror. Despite the attack on opposition in any form, civil society existed in an extremely atomised form. Criticism in literary texts would at this point be expressed in code.

The imposition of a rigid bureaucratic structure alienated large sections of society. Without developing responsibility and accountability, the system failed to address and overcome the exclusion that it had originally sought to eradicate, and created an omnipotent structure that subsumed the operation of everyday life within its rigid confines. The efforts to censor opposition resulted in a totalitarian system and an ingrained personality cult that had little to do with either communism or proletarian emancipation.

Nikoli Tolstoy and Vera S. Dunham have recorded that the construction of the communist utopia would essentially be sacrificed for the luxuries that could, for a connected and privileged few, be accrued from it. The political and industrial hierarchy would separate and construct an exclusive culture that would operate parallel to the widely recognised and official Soviet culture. The social project could not however be abandoned in public, and it continued to be celebrated without the intention of transforming it into a pure form of communism. The state would not whither away, on the contrary it was strengthened to make certain it would not. Stalin orchestrated the quasi ideology that underpinned a façade of social development. Speeches, directives, initiatives, recommendations, programmes, pressures, and policies seemingly did not consistently reflect the interests of the people outside the communist party, and to a degree within it. Despite the difficulties of administrating the vast Soviet region, Stalin's propaganda constructed an identifiable collective will that had its adherents and enemies.

The death of Stalin led to the renewed authority of the CPSU. Despite the thaw period, criticism of the Party was harshly dealt with. The pervasive repression from the late twenties forced many that had supported the revolution to re-assess their ideological position. The increasing circulation of samizdat tracts, which were exchanged and copied extensively, continued the Russian tradition of opposition implicit in literary texts.

In the international arena:

> the constitution itself defined the 'highest aim' of the Soviet State as the construction of a 'classless communist society'. The ideology extended to all spheres of public life; it informed the educational system, defined the view that was taken of organised religion and private property, and ruled out alternative ideas or competing political parties. And the ideology, in turn, seemed to be reinforced by the USSR's social progress, its growing international authority, and the movement towards some form of socialist rule in Asia and Africa.[8]

Following the death of Stalin, the method of coercion was less directly brutal. Subtle techniques of repression, silence and propaganda replaced the mass terror of executions and disappearances. Although some methods, such as the detention of political prisoners in mental institutions, remained barbaric, the widespread terror that had been a feature of Stalin's era receded. This atmosphere prevailed up to the mid-1980s, the point when the political, ideological and economic structures that enveloped the region experienced repeated tensions. The authorities understood the need on the one hand to be vigilant but not to be perceived as philistines. Art could not be allowed to criticise the system nor could it be censored entirely. In this context, the:

> freedom of creation and the problem of art and literature had become central to society, when the biggest revolutionaries turned out to be the non-conformist artists and 'formalist' poets. This wasn't because they wanted it so. It was because the authorities denied all freedom of creation and insisted on ramming Soviet realism down everyone's throats. The resulting situation was paradoxical. In the West, many of the avant-garde were communists while in our country the avant-garde were regarded as outlaws.[9]

The process that led to homogenisation of an official Soviet culture attempted to incorporate or expunge material that was fundamentally alien to it. Local cultures were expected to be subservient to the Soviet culture. Throughout the Soviet Union, the multiculturalism that was a pervasive component of it found difficulty in accepting the version of history propagated by the communists. Whilst by the 1970s, the Soviet Union could be presented with the veneer of cultural cohesion, achieved through extensive cultural genocide and widespread suppression of social experiences, it could not eradicate a nexus of coded cultures. Different cultural sites, which were in varying degrees dormant, re-emerged from exile. The effect of the dominant Soviet culture on millions of lives is indisputable.

> The idea that culture is something to be produced, invented, constructed, or reconstructed underlined so much of the USSR's social vision, and its stunning reach was perhaps nowhere more strikingly seen than in the ways that it transformed the lives of peoples living along its furthest borders.[10]

The unevenness of cultural experience was however a feature of Soviet life. The authorities could not start from a blank canvas. Hierarchies and alliances developed throughout society. Differences of opinion remained. Traditional modes of life, particularly amongst small populations away from the towns, continued, albeit in relative secrecy, to practise traditional aspects of culture subsumed under the dominant mode of social practise.

The example of Soviet man was presented to the outside world. It would be an illusion that would delude sympathisers and protagonists alike. At special ceremonies, particularly if foreign dignitaries were present, comrades were selected to represent the best exponents of Soviet man.

Being strong, good looking, healthy, disciplined and card-carrying members of the Communist Party were the most obvious requirements.

The narrow line maintained by socialist realism, particularly in the various arts, was carefully nurtured to control the social aspirations of the majority of ordinary people. Ideologues cautioned against deviance and where possible demanded that all cultural products comply with a widely and easily recognised form of social *common sense*; a condition that served the interests of the ruling elite.

In the arts, for example, the basic method of Soviet literature and literary criticism demanded:

> of the artist the truthful, historically concrete representation of reality in its revolutionary development. Moreover, the truthfulness and historical concreteness of the artistic representation of reality must be linked with the task of ideological transformation and the education of workers in the spirit of socialism.[11]

With growing literacy throughout the Soviet Union it was demanded that:

> Literature must be popular and accessible to all. Literature must be party minded and conform to the instructions issued by each new set of rulers. Literature must instruct by providing positive characters, creating a cult of heroes – cogs in the mechanism of the state. Finally, literature must depict life in its revolutionary development by portraying what exists in the newspapers and not in life.[12]

The experience of life would be recorded in the currency of propaganda. Human life would be separate from the system that conditioned and directed it. The official pronouncements from the 24th Congress of the CPSU in 1971 maintained the line established by Lenin.

> in line with the Leninist principle of partisanship, we believe that our task is to direct the development of all forms of creative art towards participation in the people's great cause of communist construction...The strength of Party leadership lies in the ability to inspire the artist with enthusiasm for the lofty mission of serving the people and make him a convinced and ardent participant in the remaking of society along communist lines.[13]

The subservience of ideas opposed to the official Soviet culture alienated vast sections of the Soviet population. In all areas of the society unofficial cultural material circulated to undermine the establishment of a pan-cultural identity; a series of actions outside the control of the authorities.

An Homogenous Culture?

It has been made clear that the need to conform to the dominant social practice of Soviet cultural observance was necessary to avoid intimidation and barriers to social progress of all kinds. The realisation of the Soviet man, educated, hard working, displaying good common sense and epitomising the appearance of health, vitality and purity was the product of propaganda and rhetoric, not the benefit of a particular economic system.

A commitment in the service of the Young Pioneers, Komsomol, the army and the Communist Party would superficially construct loyal comrades who would gladly endorse the dictates of the Party. A belief in the fundamental philosophy was not a necessary precondition for development within the Soviet system; the involvement with it was a pragmatic response to a necessary condition, which could enhance social and material development. It was not an ideological commitment to a specific and universal cause (although they were, of course, exceptions).

It was, nonetheless, possible to carefully reject the demands of the system and avoid punishment. The cost of living was virtually nothing and people could get by doing simple work. Generally, people would be relatively left alone to get along with their lives. Those who quietly disagreed with the system but were not prepared to spend time either in prison or a psychiatric hospital distanced themselves from potential difficulties and when necessary played the game to avoid identification.

From the late 1960s, sections of young people became disenchanted with the Soviet regime (other distractions such as Western music and fashion became available). It appears from the interviews that the cultural confusion of the Khrushchev leadership, the activities of dissidents and alternative culture, and increasing contact with the West, contributed to a general lack of trust or interest in the guardianship of the Soviet Union. This corresponded with an awareness of the view that many of the promises made by the architects of the revolution had not been fulfilled; a condition which accentuated the worst abuses and policies of the regime. The cynicism young people displayed disturbed the regime and a fresh wave of intimidation continued up to the mid-1980s. Despite measures to limit direct comparisons with the outside world, the authorities highlighted the worst features of the West nightly on Soviet television.

Young people often denied instinctively everything associated with Soviet culture, or they just ignored it. That was the most common attitude. The interest in the West was incredible, and, I think, it often prevented the young people from participating in domestic culture. On the other hand, that culture was very much pressed upon the Soviet citizens (youth especially in schools, universities etc.), so that denying it was justifiable.[14]

Soviet propaganda followed *Soviet man* everywhere. In the workplace, in the street, in the theatre, school, collage, conservatory, citizens were directed without exception to fulfil the expectation of their roles. From the mechanics of callisthenics to the organisation of production and distribution, each component part was subservient to and responsible for the greater whole. It was therefore necessary that physical and psychological dysfunction be, where possible, identified and made available for correction.

The attraction of Western culture and society could not however be successfully eliminated. On the nightly news broadcasts, state television would focus on the worst aspects of Western society. Unemployment, racial conflict, moral and ethical poverty, and war would be the content of the news that would be presented to a sceptical populace. In the expectation that the comparison to Soviet life would measure unfavourably, these images were played in cinemas throughout the Soviet Union.

In the Eastern bloc, citizens could get access to a range of Western television signals.

Talking about how we were aware of Western culture. My mother spoke German so we all knew German. We used to watch the Western television, although it required great skill of moving around the garden trying to pick up the signal. But that was the way you got away from the rather boring programmes which were broadcast on Czech television. So in the evening we would switch on the German television, and escape from the boring monotony that was all around us. So we had some snippets of the Western life because we lived in the part of the country where we could receive Western television so we could see how people lived. The older generation could remember the good life before the war, then the people remember all the persecutions in the 1950s, apparently in the 1950s it was very bad, but I was very young. Then people completely shut themselves in, not saying a word to anyone. Later every teenager had a programme. We all had to learn Russian. That was very much hated, we had to learn it from quite a young age, 9 or 10 years. It was one of those subjects you had to do.[15]

It was difficult for ordinary people inside the socialist bloc to leave its borders. It helped being a member of the Party but it was not a guarantee that a journey would be deemed acceptable to the authorities. The reasons for travel to the West had to be disclosed and legitimated. Each application was carefully vetted and enquiries could last for months and years before a decision was reached. Because of the high costs associated with foreign travel the applicant would invariably be an important figure and a known communist.

In limiting the contact with foreigners the authorities were able to construct an image of the outside world which was less attractive than the one being experienced in the Soviet Union and its satellites. It was a flawed strategy. In Romania, for example:

> Romanian television, like television in all communist countries, only showed the worst elements of the West. Stories on unemployment, poverty and homelessness, were regular features. No one believed it though. Stories of Westerner's lifestyles were common knowledge. In fact, what ever the authorities said about the West people believed the opposite.[16]

One of the major features in the construction of a common Soviet culture was the use of the Russian language, which 'serve[d] as a vehicular language for all the peoples of the USSR'.[17] Non-Russians resented this imposition and where possible maintained both their traditional language and culture, although this was often in secret and coded in 'ethnic traditions' and the 'revival of artistic traditions'. This function appears to have rendered Soviet culture subservient to both local traditions (although this was primarily coded) and global cultures (which appear to have been widely mimicked). Knowledge of the West as a mythical place of abundance was widespread yet few experienced it directly. Soviet sailors had experiences outside the socialist bloc and traded goods on the black market when home, but the majority of ordinary people were denied or could not afford access.

> I never travelled to the Soviet Union so I didn't have a first hand impression. Russians were not really loved by us, everything Western was wonderful, how decadent or how bad it was didn't matter. So that wasn't a nice relationship, but that's how it was from 1945.[18]

Through education and propaganda, and a repressive police presence, the authorities identified potential social unrest and sought to contain it through either repression or expulsion to less habitable parts of Russia. One of the difficulties for the outsider attempting to understand the formation and activities of opposition (in its various forms) to the Soviet regime is that the conflict that emerged within the system operated partly through the official structure itself. In the youth movements, one could on the one hand be a member of an official group like Komsomol, and informally and unofficially be a committed rock fan with a network of friends and comrades sharing similar interests.

> In the 1970s almost 95 per cent of young people were Komsomol members (I think in the countryside the percentages were somewhat lower, but still more than 2/3 of youth). In fact, Komsomol membership was absolutely necessary for higher education (no chance to enter university without it), and during army service all the young soldiers were forced to join Komsomol. So there was absolutely no opposition between Komsomol members and non-members.[19]

Rather than a body that inspired ideological loyalty, certainly in its late embodiment, the Komsomol appears to have been a requirement to conform to a recognised institution. It did not represent or reflect the wide interests of youth, but established what the youth interest should be. Similarly, the unions represented the interests of the Party and not the desires and aspirations of the workers. The latter could make recommendations through various official channels, such as writing to Central Committee or the Politburo, but these were perceived as being distant institutions which were embedded in social life but cynically absent from the actual and perceived responsibilities to it. In a piece that went against the trend of throwing out such notions of totalitarianism, D.C. Heldman recognised Soviet ideology was fundamentally the material for the conductor of the seemingly perverse orchestra. It had been established, since Lenin, that 'one organisation in the society (the Communist Party, or, more in practice, its upper echelons) had the knowledge, authority, consciousness, or moral right to determine what [was] in the best interests of the whole state'.[20]

It was held that the interests of the workers were best represented by the trusteeship of the Party. Like all institutions in the former Soviet Union, the unions were not autonomous from the Party, and, in effect failed repeatedly to represent the interests of the 'workers'. It was only when the Communist Party began to disintegrate that the unions sought to distance themselves from it.

I was a member of the pioneers and the youth league thing, but I never went near it if I could help it. My parents were members of the trade union but it was only a name, there was nothing for them there. In the factories, I never heard of any strikes.[21]

There is a difficulty in fitting citizens in cohesive class groups. Common characteristics and similar economic and social factors can be identified, but the argument that individuals can be slotted in neat taxonomic groups and alliances is problematic; Soviet rock fans included. It appears that citizens observed the rules of the game. In private, amongst family members and friends, people expressed differing interests and aspirations from the official line. The view that the presence of class distinctions and practice was little else 'than a myth cultivated by Soviet ideologists as a means of legitimising the rule of the communist party and the Soviet State' is credible.[22] The class divisions were not strictly maintained and are not helpful in understanding the complexity of Soviet life. Nonetheless, the us/them distinction between the *Nomenklatura* and everybody outside it was operational (a class distinction) but both the *Nomenklatura* and the people, were composed of various social segments, sharing some similarities in social position, but not encapsulating a consistent and pervasive ideology or cultural heritage.

The various arts invariably become the site of struggle and criticism in hostile and repressive environments. Verse, music, dance, painting and literature were consistently recognised as sources of social guides by the Party.[23] Despite strong direction from the Central Committee, semi-official and unofficial circles continued to undermine the prevailing reality. By the mid-1980s, the cultural poverty associated with Soviet life could not be reconciled with the demands of cultural regeneration blooming throughout society.

Gorbachev, in his address to the 27th Congress, concerned with the stagnation of Soviet society and ideological progress, reflected on the importance of culture in Russian society, suggesting:

a society's moral health and intellectual climate in which people live are in no small measure determined by the state of literature and art.[24]

At an earlier juncture, Lenin had justified the invention in the exchange of free ideas, primarily in regards to Party literature, on the basis that:

Freedom of speech and the press must be complete. But then freedom of association must be complete too. I am bound to accord you, in the name of free speech, the full right to shout, lie and write to your heart's content. But you are bound to grant me, in the name of freedom of association, the right to enter or withdraw from, association with people advocating this or that view.[25]

With the *ownership* of every newspaper, journal, publishing house, radio and television broadcasting in the hands of the Communist Party, all ideas opposing or suggesting constructive criticism of the Soviet State were expunged from the public domain. This appears fundamentally to have contributed to the exhaustion of Soviet ideology. In its place nurtured a crude dogmatism that served the interests of the regime's most powerful and intransigent members.

The Soviet authorities had long attempted, albeit unsuccessfully, to eradicate works that failed to reflect the rigour of social realism. The creative intelligentsia, which was forced underground, found expression in samizdat (self-published works) and magnitizdat (uncensored songs); the activity, and the popularity of it was in stark contrast to the banality of official artistic dictates.[26]

The architects of the Soviet system had become obsessed, not with the ideological development that had initially underpinned it, but its systemic continuation, regardless of its negative and self destructive qualities. Aware of the severe structural difficulties plaguing the system and the embedded corruption at all levels of Soviet life, the reform minded within the Kremlin, sought strategies to rescue the loss of authority and control.

Kagarlitsky has argued that Gorbachev would ultimately allow criticism only to go so far. The intention had been to use the creative intelligentsia who were not prominent or represented in official circles, to aid re-structuring, not to present an alternative and viable political programme. It is clear that he wanted, in response to the enforced stagnation of the Brezhnev era and the phenomenal rise in *suggestions* to the Central Committee, to implement reform and their perceived popularity throughout Soviet society, to re-invigorate and animate society behind a re-articulated Leninist vision. It helped to produce, however, the re-birth of an alternative view, which had been purged but not eradicated from the political agenda.

The artists inspired by their psychological exile in a coded civil space, reformulated their attacks on the system to take account of the new circumstances. The animation of issues previously censored captivated and galvanised a critically starved populace. The topics, eagerly consumed and debated, crystallised antagonisms and disputes long believed forcibly resolved and removed.

Authority, Coercion and Consent

It has been made clear that under Soviet rule, transparency in media information was not forthcoming. It was well known by citizens within the Soviet Union that the two major newspapers *Pravda* (the Truth) and *Izvestia* (the News) were popular mouth-pieces for the Party. It was circulated in Soviet jokes that in *Izevstia*, the News, there [was] no truth and in *Pravda*, the Truth, there [was] no news.[27] In the construction of a communist reality, the Soviet Union created, both internally and externally, the hyper-illusion of order and power.

The Soviet monopoly and manipulation of the media did not simply misrepresent reality – it was to a degree, embedded in the version of the reality it espoused.

> Because the regime [was] captive to its own lies, it must falsify everything. It falsifies the past. It falsifies the present, and it falsifies the future. It falsifies statistics. It pretends not to possess an omnipotent and unprincipled police apparatus. It pretends to respect human rights. It pretends to persecute no one. It pretends to fear nothing. It pretends to pretend nothing ...[28]

Within the Party, Lenin prohibited 'factionalism'.[29] Khrushchev had allowed limited reforms but avoided incursions that undermined the authority of the Party. The mechanical objective of the Brezhnev regime was to deepen the influence of the cadres and eradicate dissent. Gorbachev was to encourage 'openness' in so far as it was directed to the re-vitalisation of the economy, and the re-setting of the compass of the Party and country on Leninist principles. Each failed – some spectacularly.

Flight from the System

The difficulties associated with foreign visits delayed an appreciation of implications of structural changes occurring in the West, which were largely unnoticed by ordinary Russians. Nevertheless, by the early 1980s it became clear that structural, material, and ideological concerns relating to the Soviet system were increasingly being debated in both official and unofficial circles. It was becoming apparent to the CPSU that methods to enlist popular legitimacy would have to be considered to stem the psychological flight from the system.

In the early 1980s, it was a legitimacy attained through the extensive coercion that maintained the power of the CPSU. The stagnation of the Brezhnev era led to opposition, and although it was coded, it was effective in maintaining its presence. Throughout society, remedies were sought to endure the claustrophobia, which was appearing to affect all classes in the classless society.

In the pre-perestroika years, the material divisions that existed in Soviet society were carefully concealed. Special shops containing the latest up-to-date Western goods were disguised in drab respectability and kept distant from the ordinary comrade. It was not liquidity that was important, but the ability to be involved in a network that could provide access to particular goods and services denied to the populace.

Whilst the façade of the Soviet experience concealed the disparities, knowledge of them could not be concealed. The tension between Soviet ideologies and the lived culture of everyday life could not be resolved, nor, at that point, could they be overcome through intimidation or reform. In this light, ordinary people, again suffering the indignity of cultural exclusion, fell back on symbols and icons from the past. Many sought refuge in the consumption of vodka, or released tensions and bile against the regime through coded criticism and less subtle methods of disapproval.

> People grumbled about the regime but only amongst close friends and family. Windows would be closed and people would be very aware who was listening. It increasingly became difficult to survive under communism but there wasn't an alternative. For ordinary people it was difficult to get out. If you did, your remaining family and friends could get into trouble. It was very claustrophobic.[30]

For the younger members living through the Soviet communism, there was some protection. Families could however easily become separated if suspicion fell on a particular member. Nonetheless:

> children were relatively unaffected by the Soviet regime. Parents protected them and kept their young ones out of trouble. You just knew that there were things you couldn't do. You didn't worry that you couldn't do them – it was just how it was.[31]

Official Soviet culture was not rejected outright. Rather than the all-powerful state being seen as a belligerent and interfering parent, its control was deemed by some as protective and caring; a condition the authorities and the councils worked tirelessly at. It was often spoken of in religious terms, in that the environment it constructed was similar to the Garden of Eden. Knowledge beyond its parameters was considered paramount to the fall – a child-like society cordoned off from the adult world. Svyeta, a student in Russia in the early 1970s recalls:

> Our access to information was controlled, but we didn't know any different. We believed what we were told and we were happy. Of course we knew that there was another world out there and we tried to listen to the jammed radio stations to find out more about the forbidden fruit. But it was just curiosity really; we didn't really need it. We were provided for in body and mind, and we didn't even have to make decisions. The adults, that is, the communist party took all our decisions for us.[32]

The system, despite its obvious limitations, had deep roots in the Soviet population and derived legitimacy from its achievements in the betterment of educational, health and welfare. Improvements that the older generation considered with pride. The system therefore could claim legitimacy.

> Some even spoke of a "social contract" existing between the rulers and ruled in which the former fulfilled their part of the bargain by guaranteeing the latter full employment and minimal welfare. But this is not all. The Soviet people, it was argued, were proud of their country's achievements. They were very patriotic too. And they had far more educational opportunities than their parents or grandparents. Moreover, their children crucially had the chance of a better life.[33]

The 'protection' that enveloped the socialist bloc and 'well-being' of society could not however be sustained. The view that 'the Soviet populace ...[was] determined to take seriously the propaganda statements to the effect that it resides in the leading nation of the world, and it expects to see this reflected in household budget' could not be maintained.[34] Increasingly throughout the socialist bloc, citizens seemingly compared the deterioration in the quality of goods and services, and shortages of all kinds with the utopia which was perceived to exist on another planet – *somewhere* in the West.

The centrifugal forces that were prevalent throughout society appear to have gradually undermined the coherence of the totalitarian knowledge and its manifestation in culture.

The clandestine circulation of newsletters, easier access to foreign news, more frequent contact with foreigners-all enabled people to gain a less distorted knowledge of events abroad and also fostered a sense of relative deprivation, and informed comparison that "they" had what "we" lacked.[35]

As more citizens gained access to the BBC World Service, Voice of America and Radio Free Europe the audience for Western popular culture widened and an awareness of events within their own countries deepened.[36] The contents of programmes were copied and circulated in samizdat form. It became more difficult for the authorities to present propaganda that would be believable in any form. Official Soviet culture seemingly fragmented through the nexus of pressures inherent within it. It could only be forcibly held together, through cultural isolation, a strategy that would be particularly dangerous.

Nevertheless, in perpetuating the notion of a big happy family, the authorities succeeded in presenting the impression of unity, an artificial structure that tied ethnic rivalries and cultures to a cohesive and prevalent form of cultural domination.

Glasnost, by accident, undermined the unity of the Soviet Union. This would be realised through the demands made by non-Russians for greater national autonomy. 'Every previous Soviet effort to deal with this question had resulted in subordinating the desires of the nationalities of the USSR, including the Russians, to those of the communist party'.[37] In this context, as events developed, Gorbachev failed, on his own terms, 'to exercise to the full rights of sovereigns' and lost control. Hobbes cites the reluctance to exercise sovereignty as one of the causes of the dissolution of the state, and issues the imperative 'exercise no less power than peace requires'.[38] Gorbachev's shift in policy towards the end of his tenure in office to traditional concerns: order, stability and control, led his associates, both for and against, to castigate his weakness.

The actions of a State may suppress dissent, but dissent is not eradicated from all aspects of a society and nor can it be. A State can virtually lock up or eradicate the entire population and still experience the residue of dissent. The notion that the prisoner, however confined, is still free to think and is therefore 'free' gains, in this context, some credibility. And thus the strength of the state is weakened not by military or economic means, but by the collective act of its peoples to resist oppression.

Where direct political action can be identified, and this is not guaranteed by anything relating to a specific gene for survival (or the history of struggle and survival in Africa for example would be radically different), strategies resulting from dissent seemingly began, however, before being collectively observed. Subtle actions of dissent: trivial in isolation, powerful in unanimity appear to accumulate exponentially. Each, in reaching a point where the absence of freedom becomes unbearable, succumbs, in varying degrees to a form of primitive politics; an option may be indifference or capitulation to the dominant mode. Motivated by cultural circumstance and experience, where resistance is present, each acts as a Machiavellian, using the elements in the social world for his/her own ends. It is within this chaotic and uncoordinated nexus of social activity that the leaderless expression of dissent materialises. Ultimately, it proves too difficult for authorities of any ideological persuasion to either prevent or contain. Here lies the motivation for Hobbes' Leviathan to intervene and restrain the self-interest in voluntary human acts: it is the foundation of control. That the Leviathan can be swept aside by its inner 'bodies' highlights the tensions prevalent in the assessment of human nature, its management and its degree of *freedom*. Correspondingly, if 'every man is presumed to do all things in order to his own benefit',[39] the Leviathan must continually be seen to be of benefit, both to the architects and the citizens who live within it. Despite its all perceived pervasive power over intellectual and physical capital, the Soviet condition appeared to fail both its people and its architects.

The nirvana or nightmare of Soviet culture could not be sustained. In place of the early idealism and utopianism embedded in a radical science developed a form of communist culture foundered on fear and greed: the antithesis of communism. In the light that the Soviet regime ruled by coercion, it should not be unexpected that social forces however atomised and heterogeneous should seek to expose and ridicule it. The methods that it adopted and the successes it recorded will predominantly fill the concerns of the remaining pages.

Notes

[1] See Vaughan James (1973), *Soviet Socialist Realism.*
[2] Bottomore (1983, [1997]:310), *Marxist Thought.*
[3] Pasternak (1958 [1971]: 505), *Doctor Zhivago.*
[4] Lenin (1905), *Party organisation and party literature.*
[5] Cited in Heller and Nekrich (1982:268), *Utopia in Power.*
[6] *Op cit* (1997:310), *Marxist thought.*
[7] Milner-Gulland (1997:226), *The Russians.*
[8] White (1994:8), *The decline and fall of the USSR.*
[9] Bulovsky (1978:117), *To Build a Castle.*

[10] Grant (1995:xi), *In the House of Soviet Culture.*

[11] Reavey (1968: xiv), *The New Russian Poets.*

[12] Plyushch (1977:52), *History's Carnival.*

[13] 24th Congress of the CPSU, Moscow (105, 107).

[14] Sergey Pantsirev (1999), On-line e-mail 11 December 1999. Moscow citizen, former Komsomol member. Keen Soviet and Westen Rock music fan. IT specialist, webmaster of Seva Novgorodsev's official website.

[15] Anna Nirmalendran (1997), Interviewed December 1997.

[16] Aszabo (1998), Interviewed February 1998. Former Citizen of Bucharest, Romania.

[17] *Op Cit*, Milner-Gullard.

[18] *Op Cit*, Nirmalendran.

[19] *Op Cit*, Pantsirev.

[20] Heldman (1977:196), *Soviet Labour Relations.*

[21] *Op Cit*, Nirmalendran.

[22] Teague (1992:115), *Manual Workers and the Workforce.*

[23] This point is made clear by Milner-Gullard (1990:167) who suggests that 'literature has always been open to cross-fertilisation and co-operation with the other arts: the remarkable development of Russian Opera for the early nineteenth century, to take one example, is neither 'literature led' nor 'music led' but a real partnership of music, text and spectacle. In the context of indigenous unofficial Soviet rock music, there is a clear juxtaposition between 'literature', dissident poetry and the 'music'.

[24] Gorbachev (1986), Report made to the Central Committee of the Communist Party.

[25] Lenin, Party Organisation and Literature.

[26] For a comprehensive assessment of a collection of self-published works see *Samizdat: Voices of the Soviet Opposition*, edited by George Sanders.

[27] Maclean (1992), *Stalin's Nose.*

[28] Havel (1985), *The Power of the Powerless.*

[29] Barghoon (1973:27), *Fractional, sectorial, and subversive opposition in Soviet politics.*

[30] Joanne Eccles (1998), Interviewed February.

[31] Ibid, Eccles.

[32] Roxburgh (1997), Roxburgh's Russia, Radio 4 broadcast, August.

[33] Anon.

[34] *Op cit, Utopia in Power.*

[35] Coser (1999), *The intellectuals and Soviet reform.*

[36] Radio Free Europe and Radio Free Liberty (RFE/RL) are private, international radio services funded by the U.S. Government. The station broadcasts to Central and Eastern Europe and the former Soviet Union. In contrast to Voice of America, the U.S. Government broadcaster whose mission focuses on American society and U.S. policies, RFE/RL concentrates on developments within its audience countries.

[37] Wimbush (1989: viii), Glasnost and Empire. See B.Grant, *In the House of Soviet Culture: A century of perestroikias*, for an excellent insight into the experiences of national minorities in the former Soviet Union.

[38] Sorrel (1990), *Hobbes's Persuasive Civil Service.*

[39] Hobbes (1651[1985]:293), *Leviathan.*

5 Alternative/Counter-Culture: Coded Change

The Soviet system, its fear, its guarantees, its expectations, its requirements and *laws*, were valued higher by its architects than the life that functioned along with it. The *will* of the state, driven by authority, became a mechanism of systematic control, serving specific interests and denigrating others. The vast numbers incarcerated in Soviet institutions indicate the threat of ideas to the regime.[1] Crucially, alternative/counter-culture operated to present an alternative view, an anathema to the Soviet regime. The reactivation of counter-culture in the 1960s, a force relatively impervious to systematic social control, recorded and communicated the inconsistencies, the flaws, and the contrariety, embedded in the Soviet system through various methods of criticism: art, music and literature being popular outlets. Whilst all expressions and ideas are to some degree creative, literature, music and art are examined to exhume the construction of an alternative view and its correlation to, and influence on, a lived reality.

In the totalitarian environment of the former Soviet Union, alternative/counter-culture functioned in direct opposition to an official culture, established and manipulated by the regime. Hannah Arendt wrote 'terror becomes total when it becomes independent of all opposition, it rules supreme when nobody any longer stands in its way'.[2] The body of dissident acts in the former Soviet union includes a range of activities that were not homogenous (in fact, many would be appalled that a comparison between differing styles and interests could be satisfactorily linked). In recognising the difficulties associated with the label of alternative/counter-culture it should not be forgotten that there were expressions that deviated from Soviet ideology which were not necessarily alternative culture (e.g. traditional common sense). Given the differing agendas and concerns, alternative/counter-culture, and *common-sense* formulations, exhibited however a solitary activity in the Soviet context: the shared deviance from Soviet ideology and culture.

Counter-culture: the Rattle in the Iron Cage

Counter-culture is a problematic concept. There is a danger that it encapsulates and speaks for social phenomena that is strictly not associated with it. In the West, counter-culture generally refers to the ideology of the sixties that challenged the social conventions and institutions of the establishment.   In the former Soviet Union, it shared the idealism of Western counter-culture, and to a degree its methods, but was more embedded in a form of alternative culture that held a range of firm philosophical positions, specific to its past experiences.

As Ramet suggests, *Counter-culture*:

> may be defined broadly or narrowly. Broadly defined, any culture that challenges the Party's official culture, which is premised on the concept of a single legitimate general interest, can be seen as counterculture. More narrowly defined, counterculture could be a set of ideas, orientations, tastes, and assumptions that differ systematically from those of the dominant culture, recognising that *dominant* culture and *official* culture are not the same.[3]

The definition above is useful in making clear the existence of phenomena deemed alien to a commonly accepted *normalised* culture. The method through which the inherent deviance of counterculture operates can however contradict its appearance in the environment in which it takes place. It may encapsulate coded expressions that render it circumspect, a category in need of further elucidation and not superficial clarification.

Sabrina Ramet, for example, suggests, in writing on rock music and counterculture in communist occupied Eastern Europe, that 'the spirit of the age is perhaps best captured in the famous "Get Out of Control", performed by Televizor[m]'.[4] The song may have captured the defiance of rock, but for many unofficial Soviet rock fans, it was deemed too explicit, too crude and did not contain the subtle expressions of dissent that developed a sophisticated alternative view through the method of coded criticism. It appears more accurate to claim that the 'spirit of the age' in unofficial rock music is related to its specific poetic content, and circulation of coded criticism, through repetitious reference to style and the banality of beauty in everyday life.

The signification of alternative culture as a political label that defines a space of ethical organisation, should not be separated from the ideas that influenced the composition of it. An influence that can be traced back to the early nineteenth century and the specific struggles that have dominated

Russian history. The work of Pushkin (1799-1837), Gogol (1809-52), Turgenev (1818-83), Lermontov (1814-41), Dostoyevsky (1821-81), Tolstoy (1828-1910), Pasternak (1890-1960) Solzhenitsyn (1918-), Pastenak (1890-1960), Bulgakov (1891-1940) and Vladimir Majakovski (1893-1930), the leading Russian poet and one of the founders of the *Russian Futurism* movement, illustrate the on-going concern with oppression, injustice and intolerance.[5]

In the Soviet condition the presence of a counter-culture established a separate site of refuge, guidance and organisation. It presupposed the term the Hungarian socialist, Elemer Hankiss, used to describe the 'second society' that existed along with the bureaucracy of the Party and the state. These were identified in the form of:

> The combination of the small-scale private enterprises, black market enterprises, samizdat publishing, informal welfare networks, political and intellectual clubs.[6]

In essence, it is argued, that in questioning the authority of the regime, alternative culture acted as an *idea*. A form of 'double-think' founded on experience and philosophical insight. Active in various sites, it operated to put pressure on established structures and the ideological justification of them. The conflict between the artists and the Soviet State, Russian despot or Tsarist monarchy provided a source of material that, for the beleaguered Russian author, regardless of the genre, was ingrained in the hardships of everyday existence and re-occurring conflict with authority.

For example, Poprishchin, hero of Gogol's *The Overcoat*, is, in Ronald Wilks' words, 'engaged in a hopeless struggle with the rigid, highly impersonal state bureaucratic machine of Nicholas 1's oppressive regime'.[7] Turgenev's *Sketches from a Hunter's Album*, denounced as subversive by the offices of the Tsar in 1852, embodies and reveals the existential potentialities of the peasantry in their day to day encounter with the possibilities of freedom and the realities of survival.

Oleg Kostoglotov, the central character of Solzhenityn's *Cancer Ward*, reveals through his progressive illness and subsequent recuperation and 'rescue' the deepness of coded criticism and its unregulated motion, measure for measure, in meeting the injustices and the symptoms of paranoia that derive from the oppression of human spirit.

From this tradition the Russian bards, the rock poets and the creative intelligentsia revisited established struggles and utilised the method in a contemporary setting to make clear the realities of Soviet life.

The voices of those who have suffered blend with the voices of those who still have hope. Therein lies the essential drama and rekindling of power of the new Russian poetry as it struggles to rise to new human rights above the welter of conflict and falsehood, and above the "daily grind" against which Mayakovsky's "boat of love" had crashed, and renew itself in the purer "running stream" of lyrical energy.[8]

Solzhenitsyn's other great masterpiece, *The Gulag Archipelago*, illustrates how widespread opinion arrived at the conclusion that socialism was lost, and perhaps irrevocably sacrificed, in the gulag.   The rehabilitation of communism following the death of Stalin failed to meet the expectations of a curious society, distanced by the activities and crimes associated with the Party.   Whilst a brief relaxation of censorship under Khrushchev allowed coded activity to tentatively surface, it did not allow the free exchange of ideas in the public domain.   The activities of the Church continued to be suppressed with venom and in the numerous prisons throughout the Soviet Union, political prisoners remained incarcerated.

In October 1964, Khrushchev had been removed for 'reasons of health'. He, like Gorbachev later, had been guilty of overestimating his individual power to influence the course of events.   Despite the beginnings of Soviet Conformism by the mid-1960s, it could be observed that:

> there [was] growing alarm that the younger generation has outgrown the stale clichés of the old type propaganda.   And there [was] a great potential audience for the new poetry, which offer[ed] freshness of language and a novelty of image that had long been lost...but even more than that, poetry today ha[d] spilled over from the more restrictive habitat into the streets, the public squares, the concert halls, and even the stadiums.[9]

The purges against artists and writers that resulted in intimidation and arrest rather than execution accelerated after the Soviet intervention in Czechoslovakia, and curtailed the activities of alternative/counter-culture and forced it underground.   The creative atmosphere was suppressed and forced to stagnate, along with other aspects of Soviet life.

> The history of Soviet literature in the Brezhnev era – and literature can serve here as the model for Soviet culture in general – was marked by a constantly recurring phenomenon.   A talented writer would appear, his first works to be published would be published, but as soon as he began to present a true picture of reality his work would no longer be printed.   Then he would begin to write

for "his desk drawer" in the hope of being published later or outside the USSR, or he would censor himself and become a genuine Soviet writer.[10]

It would in the West be claimed by the early 1980s, be widely claimed that dissidence in the Soviet Union had been eradicated, it appears that the presence and activity of coded criticism within the Soviet system was prevalent throughout this period. In light of Soviet evidence and experience, the claim that dissent was not important to the Soviet change process appears extremely misleading. It will be made clear that the coded nature of Soviet rock lyrics was, in the absence of celebrity dissidents, a crucial element in maintaining the profile of social dissidence.

Art and Censorship

It has previously been made explicit that the explosion of writing critical of authorities that appeared, particularly in Moscow during the 1980s, was part of a deep and subversive literature that had historical ties with earlier expressions of dissent. With the appointment of Mikhail Gorbachev as General Secretary, censorship was relaxed and with it, a wealth of previously guarded work entered the public domain. 'The effects of glasnost [took] on their most visible and dramatic form in the cultural life of the country'.[11] Tengiz Abuladze's well known 1984 film, *Repentance*, exposed Stalinism to Glasnost, and caused a sensation, to the annoyance of Ligachev and other traditionalists, on its eventual public release. The reformers viewed a relaxation in censorship as a prerequisite to prolong the whole Soviet system, which had been eroded during the Brezhnev era. The traditionalists, recognising the need to allow certain amendments, drew a line at rebutting Soviet history and attempted to limit all criticism directed at the Party.

It is no secret that Gorbachev had initially encouraged the intelligentsia to express their opinions through the unhindered publication of articles and open debate. This led to the proliferation of discussion and expectation appeared prevalent at all levels of society. Despite its cautious introduction, it gathered momentum and incorporated difficult issues relating to the autonomy of the individual, national self-determination and republican agendas, human rights and religious matters. New ideas found furtive ground in the old grievances and long denied cultural aspirations. In mobilising words as weapons, in various forms, in opposition to the Soviet regime, alternative/counter-culture challenged directly the authority of the

CPSU, and accelerated the discourse for political reform in a range of previously closed 'official' spaces.

The apparent softening of official censorship in Gorbachev's early reforms was not accompanied by a relaxation in KGB's monitoring of the situation. In a previously top secret report to the Committee of State Security of the USSR, March 21 1988, Chebrikov informed the Central Committee of the increase in anti-Soviet material. In response:

> the KGB [was] implementing measures to prevent and suppress in a timely fashion negative incidents connected with the distribution of anonymous materials of hostile content and to increase the effectiveness of the effort to identify the authors and distributors of these materials.[12]

By 1989 the 'official' encouragement to the intelligentsia and the media had waned. Gorbachev had belatedly recognised that the reform process was spiralling out of control. The intention was not to terminally undermine Soviet communism but to rescue it from its economic and social decline. The rhetoric of democratisation had been a convenient tool to direct change in a direction favourable to the Soviet establishment. The benefits from the reform process had become difficult to discern. It seemed likely to the traditionalists in the Party that without the re-establishment of firm control in all aspects of Soviet life, the impetus from anti-Soviet elements would destabilise the Party's remaining interests and cumulate in social chaos. Censorship and familiar methods of social control were re-introduced to limit the shift toward the capitulation of Soviet power. Gorbachev was not an unwilling member of the countervailing trend to reintroduce discipline and social control.

> The press was no longer talking about the prowess and the Soviet worker – the reports from Vorkutta were saturated with hatred for the strikers, who were depicted as being solely responsible for all of the country's ills. The time when the regime safeguarded glasnost had clearly receded into the past. The authorities strove to remove Vladislav Starkov – editor in chief of *Argumenty i Fakty*, one of the most radical and indisputably the most serious newspaper in the country ...the person trying to obtain the dismissal was the 'architect of perestroika' himself, 'the outstanding leader of the Soviet people', the initiator of the new thinking, the father of glasnost and democracy, and the star of Western television – Mikhail Gorbachev.[13]

The forces that urged the leadership to abandon reform seemingly sprung from the social activity that had de-stabilised and terminated earlier reforms. The desire and willingness of counter-culture to go further than the reformers intended was fundamental to the change in direction. The residue of alternative culture (the fundamental ideas debating social organisation), presupposing observable appearance, had through various forms widely circulated and collected discontent, and had infiltrated processors that had direct influence on the consolidation and loss of Soviet power. Without the reintroduction of severe repressive measures, the pressure to accelerate political reform could not be controlled.

The Sound of Opposition

Along with literature, music had been particularly influential in reflecting the desire for change in society, capturing, amplifying, guiding and being guided by the mood or spirit of the *times*: its hopes and concerns. In music, dissent was not confined to folk and rock with its subversive and satirical lyrics. Instrumental music could be viewed as decadent and dangerous if it did not confirm to rigid musical structures that could be utilised in the communication and construction of the Soviet idea. Dmitri Shostakovich's Symphony No 4 (written in 1936 but premiered in 1961) and No 5 were considered too dangerous to perform during Stalin's reign due to its hidden agenda and coded criticism.[14] Material on the work of Shostakovich, Prokofiev, Vainberg and Kanchek under Soviet rule is instructive in that it reveals the effects of censorship and the rationale behind the numerous pressures to maintain and support the all-embracing Soviet reality.[15] The constructed reality, however, continued to be critiqued in a range of musical styles, encapsulating comedy, farce and political satire.

Bolat Okudzjava, poet and songwriter, active during the Brezhnev era, reveals how the authorities disliked the arts when they critiqued the system

> Soviet songs were supposed to be uplifting, and along came this guy with a strange name and a strange moustache, playing the guitar badly and singing sad songs, anti-war songs, songs that didn't inspire people to greater things – Ah, they didn't like that.[16]

The display of opposition did not pass without a response. Musicians, as well as artists and writers were investigated. Saxophones were particularly susceptible to being confiscated by the authorities. They were perceived has being decadent instruments, which were used, in avant-garde jazz to incite rebellion. Performances were cancelled and difficulties were introduced to frustrate efforts to arrange concerts and organise recordings.

In an effect to halt the publication of unofficial tracts, the authorities raided the homes and premises of suspected publishers. In this way:

> some of the underground magazines were seized by the authorities and their editors arrested. Poems by Okudzhava, Akhmadulina, Brodsky, Kharabarov, and Slutsky have been first presented in this form.[17]

During 1965-1972, the rock scene exploded throughout Moscow. 'New beat clubs appeared in Moscow almost every month', recalls Soviet rock critic Artmy Troitsky, 'but were constantly closed down again by frightened officials'.[18] In the late 1960s, despite the conservative atmosphere, the authorities felt cause for alarm: 'the city was shaking with a rock music epidemic. Hundreds of garage bands, thousands of guitars, hundreds of thousands of fervent fans', suddenly, like in the West, found a powerful weapon with which to rebel: rock 'n' roll.[19]

Music had long been used in the Soviet Union, both as a form of coded criticism and transmogrified concealment (the presentation of ideas in a grotesque or bizarre forms). The struggle of poetry, faith and the fundamental beliefs of long established cultures had been subsumed under the all-embracing Soviet culture. Ironically, the enthusiasm for a wider – counterproductive Western secular force – had not been eliminated. For many years it had operated in relative secrecy in defiance of the omnipotent Soviet culture.

> In contrast to the material culture with its prevailing unification tendencies, the spiritual culture of the Soviet peoples largely retained its ethnic distinctions. This is part due to the further flourishing of the ethnic arts and crafts and the revival of artistic traditions.[20]

This was particularly the case with Islam in areas such as Uzbekistan where Muslim Uzbeks were persecuted. In rural Russia, the Chastushki songs made allusion to the cultural genocide. Shamanic songs, composed after 1917, maintained cultural links and commitments through music. These crucial activities rejected the atheism of the Soviet regime, typified on a Soviet propaganda poster in the form of an astronaut returning from a space mission to pronounce with scientific certainly that 'God is Dead', and numbing rhetoric that daily rattled out of the village loudspeakers. Although the Russian Orthodox Church rejected the use of instrumental music, liturgical music arranged around vocal harmonies and chants, it sustained too, an ethereal version of alternative-culture. Interestingly, the church was against the rebellious nature of rock music, believing it against the values of religious faith.

The intertextual activity of the Russian literate expression imbued the various arts with a spiritual content that celebrated the role of creative and intuitive perspectives that were at odds with the Soviet system. In this context, to convey the *message* (conceptualised around an alternative view – encapsulating a range of ideas – and confidence with it) and circulate it within a censured environment 'it is clear at a glance that the new poets use[d] a variety of forms. It is certainly not any particular poetic form that unite[d] or distinguishe[d] them from their immediate predecessors. They [were] freer to experiment and use various combinations'.[21]

Russian artists have repeatedly revealed influences in their work from the West, but traits alien to it are also present. Anatoly Anotolyevich Strigalyov, writing in the introductory notes to the exhibition catalogue *Art and the Revolutionary Period 1910-1932*, reveals a similar trait in the work of artists of an earlier generation:

> The Russian artists had very quickly absorbed, processed and utilised the experiences of contemporary Western European art in autonomous, original works...they amalgamated the new achievements in the fine arts with the national traditions and with the autonomous programme of the new Russian art. This is why the efforts of the Russian avant-garde of the 1910s were partly similar to, and partly consciously opposed to Western artistic objectives.[22]

The Soviet authorities, however, acted swiftly to purge works that celebrated random and chaotic influences. Artists such as Kasimir Malevich and Alexander Rodchenko experienced difficulties with the authorities. Movements such as Dada, Surrealism and Cubism were immediately seized upon as being subversive and decadent. Work that contained no aesthetic principle and was considered to be against the progress of Soviet realism and a criminal slight on the development of the new Soviet man. The various arts were forced underground, and new ordered and chaotic networks evolved.

It was only in the energy, innovation, and stylistic diversity of the artists of the 1960s that the Russian avant-garde of the 1910s and '20s found a worthy successor.[23] In April 1998, The Second Avant-Garde exhibition held at the Dom Nashchokina Gallery, displayed graphic works and small sculptures produced by artists during the period of Khrushchev's 'thaw'. The exhibition included pieces by Eduard Shteinberg, Ernst Neizevestny, and Ilya Kababov. What was amazing about the exhibition was the originality, freedom and power of the works on show – a vitality that would not be out of place in the sixties London art scene.[24]

The technique adopted by the satirists within Russian new music was influenced by the experimentation of the avant-garde and the surrealists. A starting point, if one can be provided, encapsulates the perspective of declared artist and sound-poet Kurt Schwitters, 'the medium is as unimportant as myself. What is essential is only the idea'.[25]

The idea that the omnipotent reality was an imposition by a trickster, a maverick of dubious intent was gaining currency. Various methods were adopted to make clear the deception. Music was one such form.

> New music has emerged out of a protest, however, a protest of a special kind. It is neither political nor social. It is spiritual. It is protest against hypocrisy and consumerism. No wonder new music found such favourable soil in the Soviet Union, although it came from the West with some delay.[26]

'Music and youth culture', suggests Victor Sumsky, leading researcher at the Institute of World Economy and International Relations at the Russian Academy of Sciences 'played an important part in adding to the formulation of an active counter-culture. It [Western music] gave optimism and widened the desire for our freedom. In the 1960s, I and many of my friends learnt English from records and tapes of the Beatles. Popular music was incredibly important to many people'.[27] Whilst some may have learned English from Western rock lyrics it appears generally that it was the sound of Western rock that was important. The popularity of American and English groups, particularly the Beatles, the Rolling Stones, Bob Dylan, Pete Seeger, and amongst hard rock circles, Led Zeppelin and Frank Zappa, was in the former Soviet Union uneven, but significant. Zappa would later become involved in Czech politics, an intervention that irritated republicans in the United States. The lyrics however were at the time not widely understood or considered politically valuable, unlike unofficial Soviet rock lyrics, which circulated criticism of the Soviet regime.

The extensive efforts undertaken by the Soviet authorities to monitor and 'police' the rebellious content of 'serious' rock, particularly Soviet rock lyrics that rallied against the establishment and promoted cultural experiences, illustrates the seriousness with which the authorities treated this form of cultural terrorism.

> The most important part in Western rock is the sound and feel of the music. The lyrics are just an embellishment. In Russian rock it is the opposite. The

lyrics are of primary importance, much more important than the music and the sound. The music is just an embellishment. The lyrics should tell you something that the censorship would not be able to understand or suspect of being dangerous. The connotations are extremely subtle, which brings rock lyrics to the levels of high-class poetry.[28]

The potential for learning a foreign language such as English was extremely limited for ordinary Russians. Only special representatives of the Soviet hierarchy would be allowed to travel abroad and meet with Westerners. Foreign visitors to the Soviet Union would be monitored and contact with indigenous Russians would, unless in exceptional circumstances, not be encouraged. Other methods associated with learning a language, books, private and public tuition was forbidden. In not an isolated example of irony, it would appear that political prisoners studied English through access to English speakers and painstaking study in prison, aided with the concealment of books and papers. The use of English between political prisoners allowed them to overcome the censorship imposed by the authorities and enforced by the guards.[29]

The recourse to radio could provide access to knowledge that was denied or censured. The authorities attempted to interfere with the radio signals – Radio Liberty and Deutsche Welle were jammed regularly while the BBC World Service and Voice of America were targeted less. For both technical and creative reasons, the authorities found it difficult to prevent people attempting to tune into foreign radio broadcasts. The widespread use of mercury based aerials is perhaps an exaggeration, most seemingly attached a simple piece of wire to a regular aerial on a VEF receiver and manipulated the tuning control by hand. Outside Moscow, interference with Radio signals would be less noticeable. The material that was broadcast from the West was regularly copied and circulated throughout an accessible social network.

A particularly influential figure who contributed significantly to social attitudes and change in the former Soviet Union was the broadcaster Seva Novgorodsev. Transmitted from the BBC's Bush House in London on the world service wavelength, the broadcasts contained popular music and chat. From the 1970s onwards, the show drew vast audiences throughout the former Soviet Union. His unique radio voice, its intonation and character, was a revelation in comparison with the usual wooden style of Soviet broadcasters.

Seva's influence to Soviet counter-culture, it was VERY significant during the pre-perestroika times. In fact, his broadcasts were the only widely available source of information about the Western music scene. That's why these broadcasts were recorded, typed out and distributed among music fans in some kind of samizdat. Most of Seva's broadcasts weren't anti-Soviet at all – they were rather informative about latest releases, top charts, or focused on band's/artists' history. However, Seva did never miss a chance to mock-up the Soviet system, often in somewhat by-the-way style. His jokes were even more famous than he himself – often people recited them without mentioning their origin. It would not be overestimating to say that Seva was known to virtually everyone – even for those who never heard his broadcasts.[30]

Seva was undoubtedly influential in popularising subtle forms of dissent, the degree to which he directly inspired counter-culture to nurture an alternative view is however impossible to measure accurately. His technique – laid back but extremely clever and humorous is, akin to many influential figures that reach a trans-national audience, largely dependent on life experiences and a particular talent to communicate them. In this context:

> Seva's jokes are extremely difficult to translate and even more difficult to make clear. The reason is that the BBC authorities asked Seva to be "politically correct" and not to make "wild jokes" about the communists. So Seva started to make jokes that were obscure to his supervisors from the BBC but nevertheless quite clear to his audience in Russia. (How we loved him for that!)[31]

An over enthusiastic observer could perhaps claim that Seva was as influential on the Soviet change process as – in a diametrically opposing way – Gorbachev and the on-going rhetoric of the Soviet machine. The idea that a disc jockey, broadcasting from a conservative institution outside the Soviet Union, was as important as the General Secretary in contributing to a redirection in Soviet history, seems ludicrous. Nonetheless, is this a crucial example of globalization in its most *destructive* or *constructive* creative form? Seva's role in undermining the authority of the system may be an exaggeration but it clearly raises some interesting questions.

There is ample evidence; the post received by Seva from the beginning of 1970s includes thousands of letters from listeners in the former Soviet Union, which has been carefully recorded by the broadcaster. The mail suggests that the role adopted by Seva was extremely important in undermining the Soviet reality imposed on all aspects of society. It is seemingly the subtleties of the humour that caused such extensive cultural conflagration. For example:

> I was completely sold to his programs the whole '80s. Not that there was some significant or outstanding music information, you know, who wanted it, could get access from various sources. The matter was in the way Seva delivered the information, spicing with authentic Soviet jokes and observations. I liked his jokes and comments though forgot almost all of them. But some still remain in memory. For example, commentating 1984 Iron Maiden album "Powerslave" he said... "Powerslave" – "Rab sily" (in Russian), but not "Rab sila" (in Russian for working force, typical term referring to employees), they sound almost the same. May seem corny now, but those times I think he found a brilliant way of carrying slight "Anti-Soviet", as it was officially called, context.[32]

The power of humour and irony, the weapon of the unbeliever, is an on-going activity that is present in both Russian literature and society. Under Soviet control, the prevailing atmosphere encouraged a black humour that circulated throughout society in a coded form and released tension from the stifling social conditions. In this context it may not necessarily have been deemed consciously subservient, but it highlighted deficiencies within the system and as a direct consequence undermined the authority of those responsible for the institutionalisation of them.

> Laughter can be threatening, a form of 'anti-behaviour', associated with, for example, carnivalistic excesses and topsy-turverydom, with the 'unmasking' absurdities of holy fools, with Ivan the Terrible's corrosive and theatrical sarcasm. This dangerous aspect of laughter is never far away in Gogol, Dostoyevsky or their successors in the twentieth century such as Beliy (in his novel Petersburg), and once again was analysed by Bakhtin, who saw it as deriving from the ancient genre of 'Menippean Satire' – through its early folklore roots.[33]

The seriousness that was perceived as an enduring part of the Soviet system was founded and maintained by fear. Whilst it could not be cajoled or loosened it could be effectively ridiculed: a strategy that appears to have exacted compensation by returning the fear produced by the Soviet beast to its originator. Laughter is a well-known tonic to ease physical pain, less appreciated is its ability to relieve psychological pain. In this way:

> the role of laughter, essentially, is to help us overcome fear, death and everything deadening and dying. It has been said that Rabelais's laughter broke

the ground for the French revolution.   The Russian Revolution was accompanied by buffoonery and satire. Similarly, the jokes and laughter of the samizdat satirists are cleansing society of its prejudices. Galich's songs put an end to the dead ideology of the Soviet rulers. They make room for a new seriousness, a new struggle among living ideologies.[34]

This leads to the question regarding the consequence of its presence and circulation in the Soviet system, and its influence on the decision-making process at the highest political level. Fred Halliday raised a crucial question when he considered the motivations behind the change in Soviet policy:

> that the leadership of the most powerful state in the system decided to introduce a radically new set of policies, within the USSR and within the system as a whole: it was not that the ruled could not go on being ruled in the old way. The question is what it was that led these rulers, who cannot be accused of having in the past lacked a desire to retain power or of being initially covert supporters of the West, to introduce the change they did.[35]

Humour, rock music and satire? Were these culturally based expressions of social dissent considered important in an analysis of East-West relations or were more serious, scientific, *real* political issues valued above what are often perceived to be trivial expressions? A review of the literature implies that coded activity arising from humour and rock music within the Soviet Union was particularly neglected by the analysts of International Relations, regardless of the preferred paradigm. Humour is however important to political and social change.

Whilst it has been argued that Western rock was not consumed by the Soviet people for its direct lyrical revolutionary message, a consideration of the effects of the global counter-culture movement from the 1960s needs to be considered to measure its cultural and economic influence in the Soviet Context.   Despite the perceived anti-consumerism of Soviet counter-culture, items such as Jeans and records were a crucial component of the emerging youth culture from the 1960s onwards.

In the Soviet Union, the material of Western cultural commodities were obtained either through *blat* networks or the black market. Many who were able to obtain records or fashionable cultural accessories from the West were able to either gain influence in particular circles or make desirable exchanges by taping them on to blank tapes or counterfeiting them to supply the active but illegal marketplace. This significantly destabilised the operation of the command economy, an introduction that paradoxically widened the experience of consumerism.

The nexus of trans-national links that undermined the political and cultural separation between the Soviet Union and the West were innumerable. It could be, for example, activated by official East-West visits. Russian diplomats, industrial representatives, and *celebrities* received gifts and material inducements from the West, which were seemingly traded within the Soviet Union.[36] Contacts were also made between businesses, ethnic groups and relations abroad. There were also émigrés, sailors, modern communication such as radio (the BBC World Service, Radio Free Europe and Voice of America) straggling the East-West duality. In the former Soviet Union, a multi-national workforce and a virtual global representation of prison detainees, added to an experience of a non-communist world and its possibilities.

In 1874, Russia was a signatory to the international postal union. The Soviet postal service subsequently accepted and followed strictly the internationally recognised rule-book.[37] This resulted in international letters and parcels being delivered to the addressee (although items were regularly checked by customs and the KGB, the contents were not generally lost or damaged).

Whilst it is incomprehensible to believe that Gorbachev and the politburo would have been unaware of the persuasiveness and resilience of alternative culture, it was grossly underestimated by the leadership. Although the reforms had been initiated to overcome the tensions prevalent within the Soviet system and allay the protests of its harshest critics (increasingly Soviet youth), by the 1980s 'he [Gorbachev] was surprised by the power of society, and didn't except it to go as far as it did'.[38]

The measures that were instigated by the Soviet authorities in direct reaction to criticism, which rallied against it, weakened not the opponents of the communist regime but the cohesion of the Soviet system.

Notes

[1] It is impossible to arrive at an accurate figure concerning the number of political prisoners with dates in Soviet prisons and mental institutions. New evidence is regularly coming to light. For an up-to-date number, it is advised that contact be made with: The Andrei Sakharov Museum and Public Centre for Peace, Progress, and Human Rights 57 Zemliano Val, building 6, 107120 Moscow, Russia Federation. Telephone and fax: 7 (095) 917-2653.

[2] Arent (1986:464), *The origins of totalitarianism.*

[3] Ramet (1995:236), *Social currents in Eastern Europe.* Alexander Kan suggests the Televizorm were thought of as second rate by alternative culture in the former Soviet Union because of their obvious opposition to the system.

[4] *Ibid* (1995:261), *Social currents in Eastern Europe.*

[5] Disappointed in love, alienated from Soviet reality, and denied a visa to travel abroad, Majakovski committed suicide in Moscow.

[6] Kalder, Holden, Falks *et al* (1989:8), *The New Détente.*

[7] Gogol (1972), *Diary of a Madman and Other Stories.*

[8] Reavey (1968:xxiii), *The New Russian Poets 1953-68.*

[9] *Ibid* (1968:xviii).

[10] Heller and Nekrich (1986:680), *Utopia in Power.*

[11] Ali (1988), *Revolution from above.*

[12] Statistical Report. Special Folder. Committee of State Security of the USSR March 21, 1988 No. 458-Ch Moscow – to Central Committee of the CPSU titled 'Results of the work of the KGB in investigating authors of anonymous materials of a hostile nature'.

[13] Kagarlitsky (1990:197/8), *Farewell Perestroika.*

[14] The totalitarianism that was imposed throughout the Soviet Union from the 1930s onwards eradicated opposition in any form. It appears from the field research that both alternative culture and civil society were present from an early stage, but atomised.

[15] See Ian MacDonald's resource site:
http://www.webcom.com/beatlebk/musov/contents.html

[16] Roxburgh's Russia (1997), BBC Radio 4. August.

[17] Reavey (1968:xix), *The new Russian poets.*

[18] Troitsky (1987:22), *Back in the USSR.*

[19] Ryback (1990:108), *Rock around the Bloc.*

[20] Bromley (1988:449), *Ethnographic studies of contemporary Soviet life.*

[21] *Op cit* (1968), *The New Russian Poets.*

[22] Catalogue (1988:14), *Art and Revolution, Russian-Soviet Art 1910-1932.*

[23] Wood (1998:9), *Artistic Results of Political Thaw* (The Moscow Times. Tuesday April 7).

[24] See David Mellor (1993), *The Sixties Art scene in London* (book published by the Barbican Art Gallery on the occasion of the exhibition 11 March – 13 June 1993).

[25] Baldwin (1988:126), *Ethnographic studies of contemporary Soviet life.*

[26] Leo Feigin (1992), *Russian New Music.* Associate films for Channel 4.

[27] Victor Sumsky, leading Researcher at the Russian Academy of Science, interviewed in Moscow (April 1998).

[28] Leo Feigin (1999) on-line e-mail:leorec@atlas.co.uk (26 March 1999).

[29] See in particular Vladimir Bulkovsky's *To build a castle.*

[30] Sergey Pantsirev (1999) online e-mail: webmaster.seva.ru. (15 February 1999).

[31] *Ibid*, Pantsirev.

[32] Climos (1999), Russia Today discussion. On-line message posted (February 22 1999).

[33] Milner-Gulland (1997:168), *The Russians.*

[34] Plyushch (1979:301), *History's Carnival.*

[35] Halliday (1994:206), *Rethinking International Relations.*

[36] Extract from a letter received on 8 March 1999 from the Foreign and Commonwealth Office concerning an enquiry to the Russian section on this matter reads as follows: 'Our information on this matter is, like your own, anecdotal, although there is little reason to doubt its accuracy. We agree with your understanding that Soviet officials bought Western goods such as books and clothes when visiting the UK. Pop records were particular popular. It is worth remembering, however, that Soviet officials did not usually have much spending money, and this would inevitably have restricted their purchases'.

[37] Verified by the Russian section of the Royal Mail's customer services in London.

[38] Joanna Eccles (1998).

6 The Meaning of Dissent: From Grumble to Revolution

The presence of dissent is a feature of any political, economic and social system. Its appearance may be suppressed, ignored or inadvertently nurtured through the application of rules, convention and culture. Dissent can be recognised in a physical act or mental activity, unconsciously and deliberately, within various time-space environments. It is an on-going activity within all social relations, which undermines the quest for finalities. The Bolshevik revolutionary vanguard, which wrestled control from the disorganised in-fighting of the provisional government led by Alexander Kerensky, cumulated in a struggle to impose domination. This led to the 'mass social cultural movement [being] gradually relocated into formal, excessively organised institutes, and certainly by the Brezhnev era culture had become nothing more than a ritualised adjunct to ideology'.[1] The intention to remove all competition to Soviet authority resulted in a mechanism incapable of widespread coercive social inclusion.

Dissent and Dissidents

From the first moment, the Bolshevik grip was a form of government as ruthless as that of any Tsar, a dictatorship ostensibly of the proletariat but actually of a few men who controlled the Communist Party. Freedom of speech and opinion, other than the Bolshevik line, was permitted in the press. All religions were suppressed and the power of the Russian Orthodox Church destroyed. All classes of persons, from peasants to factory workers to artists and intellectuals, had their lives ordered by government fiat.[2]

The Soviet system was not intended to reflect the interests of a broad church. It demanded total acquiesce to its authority. In the process of systematically enforcing its will and solidifying control:

It substitute[d] for the boundaries and channels of communication between individual men a band of iron which held them so tightly together that it [was] as though their plurality had disappeared into one man of gigantic dimensions.[3]

It was expected that control would be total. The coercion administered by the Party and the promise of a realisable utopia that would benefit the majority rather than the few provided the legitimacy of the regime. The Party would dictate direction and society would without question be expected to follow. It was widely believed that change motivated by the collective will of the people was impossible (they were without political representation and their cultural interests were diverse and often in conflict. The unifying theme would be the opposition to Soviet communism and its prolonged rule). Nevertheless, by the 1980s, it was, within the system, difficult to avoid the initial signs of change. It was felt that 'only the Sovietologists and émigrés commenting on the progress of events in the USSR in the pages of the popular Western publications, could have any doubt about it'.[4]

Dissent from the Soviet communist project had not at any time been eradicated. The various ideas and faiths in opposition to the regime, continued on a parallel line from the Soviet system. Throughout the book it has been argued that the primary source of change in the former Soviet Union was initiated by the wide activity of dissent.

It was raised at the outset that in the former Soviet Union, the black marketer, the political prisoner, the non-compliant comrade, the rock musician, the comedian, the poet, could through various modes share the generality of deviance. 'In its most general sense the term *dissent* conveys disagreement about something. This is clarified beyond mere nay saying through the contrary belief or opinion expressed in the form of an alternative or, at any rate, a different position of the matter'.[5] The activity of dissent in the Soviet totalitarian environment was radically different from the discontent found in the everyday situations in supposedly Western democratic societies. A moan, a grumble, was tantamount to a rejection of the ideas that organised and managed Soviet society. Dissent in the Soviet Union was an act that challenged directly the strength and authority of the Party.

Protest thus is conceptualised here as a set of strategies of interest articulation for those who perceive themselves as relatively "powerless" in resources and influence and access to decision-makers. To exert effective impact on the decision-makers the protesters perceive that they must build political resources through some unusual, dramatic and often non-conventional means of communication.[6]

In the social commentary on everyday Soviet life, doubt in the system was largely expressed through coded criticism. A sigh, a gesture of annoyance or a slip in composure could be interpreted as a criticism of the system. Non-Russians would be particularly vulnerable to intimidation from the authorities and would be reported to the authorities if they defied, however innocuously, the authorities.

I never met anybody who was openly a dissident, maybe because my parents were from a different class and didn't meet that circle of people. We had friends in the factories that were constantly complaining and they had no chance of promotion. They would be constantly harassed. Some didn't go to May Day parades but we did. We did go. I did go because at that time it was the easier option. I am probably not...or I feel in some ways I am...typical dissident. I think the dissident movement was very small, mainly artists or that group. You hardly heard a dissident openly speak; you had many many people who moaned. I certainly never met anyone who had signed up or were a part of Charter 77. I would say the majority of people lived as well as they could. Everybody dreamed of saving up enough money to buy a car. Perhaps get to university or college. As long as the children got some training and got a good job – again it was not so much what you know but who you knew. You had to constantly give things to get things back. Nothing was done without the little exchange of something. There was a lot of people complaining, like you know, there was this classical thing that the character that led the Soviet Union was really stupid man maybe who didn't know anything. We had to spend hours standing in some square listening to some idiot talking about how grateful we should be to Russia, and it would be maybe cold and windy, and listening to these pointless monologues going on for hours. You had to be there or there could be trouble. On May Day, everybody was clapping and waving and kissing members of the Communist Party or the government, but they were hated. It wasn't real. No one believed it. But you went, because if you didn't go, and if you weren't a member of the Communist Party or a family member had been born in Germany, you would be investigated and trouble would follow.[7]

In identifying the motivation for dissident acts Rudolph Tökès identified the flexibility between the various categories and highlighted the role of existential acts present in the method of opposition. Tökès' main focus was however on the shared and constituency-specific grievances with which the dissidents have sought to promote change by making demands on the political leadership to alleviate or eliminate unacceptable conditions. In the absence of a viable political program and cohesive ideology stemming from an officially recognised opposition, the immediate concerns of the various actors opposing the regime were methods through which an alternative view and its circulation could be formulated and exchanged. In accessing the dynamic of reform and dissent under Khrushchev, it becomes clear that 'Tökës summary offers the best analytical description available'. Nonetheless, there is a caution against it 'becoming a universally inclusive category'.[8] To avoid the neatness of invisibility, it is important to remember that:

> the sites and strategies of subversive opposition are extraordinarily varied. Sites range from farm fields through factory workbenches on up to the most sensitive nerve centres of the political, administrative, and military structures. Strategies include almost any that human ingenuity – restrained, however, by fear of reprisal and by the effects of the official system of surveillance – can devise.[9]

The dissidents in the Eastern Bloc and the Soviet Union had, for example, varying objectives and, in some cases, conflicting aims. In Romania:

> the dissident movement was not organised. There was a very loose network of dissidents compared with other East European states. It was, in fact, too dangerous to rebel. If you wanted trouble you would be removed, and in all probability you wouldn't be seen again. It was a very effective deterrent.[10]

Whilst dissent in Romania continued to be repressed by Stalinist methods, sensitive material was present and circulated throughout society. Without doubt, 'people exchanged illegal texts but generally kept political writings and ideas to themselves – it was too dangerous to get caught'.[11] It appears, however, that there was little communication between Romanian dissidents and other dissident groups throughout the eastern bloc. Cultural exchanges of any kind were restricted and monitored closely, making it difficult to form alliances and share interests over a wide region.

Romania opposed the United States and to a lesser extent the Soviet Union. It had no Russian troops on its soil and attempted to follow a mercantilist policy that acquiesced to its belligerent neighbour on certain points whilst maintaining the will of its former leader Gheorghiu-Dej and his protégé, Nicolae Ceaucescu.

Ceaucescu was a ruthless and cunning dictator. He was paranoid with power and the possibility of losing it. On public visits to factories workers would leave their jobs and go outside to wave. People knew the consequences of not registering their support. Ceaucescu may have believed that he was popular – no one would dare tell him otherwise. If an official informed him of a particular problem he would be held responsible, so no one said anything on matters of concern.[12]

Romania, despite its nationalist aims, was communist, and as such it was part of the ideology dominating the region 'one [however] realistically conceived in term's of Romania's geographic location, achievements, traditions, and the paramount interests of the Romanian Communist Party'.[13]

The opposition movement in Hungary was different from that in Poland. Romanian opposition had different concerns to those in Czechoslovakia. Rudolph Tökès, Ludmilla Alexeyeva and Sabrina Ramet raise the subtleties between various dissident activities in operation throughout different parts of the former Soviet Union and Eastern Bloc and make clear the different strategies that were initiated and articulated from the residue of historical struggle and complaint.

The concerns and goals of dissident groups in the Soviet Union had orientations that were specific to its political, cultural and social conditions and experiences. Despite the differences, *dissidents* were related by the unanimity of constructing and communicating an opposing position to the Soviet condition. Some alliances were made, but they were far from an all-embracing opposition movement, and co-operation proved to be tenuous and often contentious.[14] The opposition to Soviet life has been widely communicated through the various arts.

It is an old tradition in Russia that the spirit of the people is expressed not by political figures but by writers.[15]

In the absence of political plurality the dissimulation of the truth and its content was debated through the method of coded criticism, an activity embedded in literature. A similar technique had been used by secret agents in the Second World War: coded messages in poetry to communicate foreign operations. The *truth* served the interests of the Soviet elite. It was not a question of it being right or wrong but which policy would sustain power and authority in the hands of the Soviet regime. The dispersion and consumption of tracts through Samizdat sources acted as a countervailing force to the weight of official publications that proliferated in regards to all political, economic and social matters. The content of the prolific copies of Samizdat overwhelmingly reflected on the:

> struggle of "liberal" Soviet writers for freedom of expression, like that of Soviet artists, is potentially of exceptional import. Not only is there a tradition in Russia, as in many other countries which until recently were economically undeveloped, of looking to writers and artists as custodians of the community conscience; but literary and artistic professionals, far more than other intellectuals, possess the capability of projecting their influence to relatively wide circles of public opinion. Moreover, the weapon of creative imagination that they wield had a singularly powerful impact on the shaping and inculcation of social values.[16]

Despite the momentous power of the Soviet regime, its weakness lay in its inability to remove the negative aspect of deviance from within Soviet society. It was recognised that opposition could not be presented in the form of traditional political organisations. Ironically, the authorities had made it difficult to identify 'the opposition' – each recantation was a defiant act.

> We had grasped the great truth that it was not rifles, not tanks or atom bombs that created power, nor upon them that power rested. Power depended upon public obedience, upon a willingness to submit. Therefore each individual who refused to submit to force reduced that force by one 250-millionth of its sum. We had been schooled by our participation in the civil rights movement, we had received an excellent education in the camps, and we knew of the implacable force of one man's refusal to submit. The authorities knew it too. They had long since abandoned the idea of basing their calculations on communist dogma. They no longer demanded of the people a belief in the radiant future – all they needed was submission. And when they tried to starve us into it in the camps, or threw us into the punishment cells to rot, they were demanding not a belief in compromise, but simply submission, or at least willingness to compromise.[17]

The realisation that the system was vulnerable was realised not only by the political dissidents. Despite repeated purges, arrests, and forced exile, the presence of opinions, derogatory of the Soviet regime, could not be removed, although attempts were made with an appalling human cost. The perpetrators of the non-compliant view would be:

> simply a physicist, a sociologist, a worker, a poet, [musicians], individuals who are merely doing what they feel they must, and consequently, who find

themselves in open conflict with the regime ... dissidents can be found on every street corner.[18]

Whilst the activities of alternative/counter-culture were typically coded, frustrations, hatred and religious beliefs would lead to open recalcitrance with the regime. On a political and cultural stand:

> non-compliant individuals assume that the Party has no right to govern and consequently go about their lives as though the Party did not exist, irrespective of the danger this may present to their personal safety.[19]

This led to repeated intimidation through physical and psychological violence on people who refused to accept or coalesce with the reality imposed on them by the ruling elite. By the early eighties it was generally assumed that 'all the dissidents' small organisations and printing operations ha[d] ceased to exist, and it [was] now difficult to speak of dissidents as a political movement or a key factor in domestic or foreign policy'.[20] This view ignores the evidence that unofficial Soviet rock musicians were widely ridiculing the Soviet system and making clear the perversity associated with the imposition of Soviet culture on people largely alienated from its stage-managed development.

The Use of Humour

The coded nature of high poetry as subtle resistance in Soviet rock music reiterated to a generation the failings of the authoritarian system. Its literary duplication in the forms of samizdat and magnitizdat seemingly galvanised interest in opposing the regime without alienating general accessibility. The message contained within the prose appeared to compliment the wide disillusionment with the Soviet regime. An emotional and spiritual condition reciprocated in kind through social participation, thereby weakening the system both numerically and psychologically.

> I am old enough to remember the reaction of the authorities on rock music back in the sixties. Reaction was very oppressive to say the least and described in detail in Vassilii Aksyonov's "The Burn" ("Ozhog") it was the same reaction to jazz in the thirties: "Jazz is the music of the fat ones", – "Today he is playing jazz and tomorrow he'll sell out the motherland" – most famous Soviet posters of the period. Authors of the text Maxim Gorki and Sergi Mikhalkov the most decorated Soviet writers.[21]

Whilst the authorities removed known dissidents and attempted to restrict the activities deviant of Soviet culture, the jokes that attacked the system continued to be widely circulated and could not be terminated. The circulation and digression of humour worked to undermine the regime; the jokes became part of everyday life.

> The only time my parents would complain about the regime would be at home with close family friends who could be trusted. In fact, that was mostly done when people expressed their anger or frustration at the system, not so much by marching on the roads shouting "down with the communists", because they knew that would result in prison. But by having close friends at home and having glasses of vodka and picking up all these wonderful political jokes, which is something you do not have in Great Britain, that was the way you could ridicule the system.[22]

There is a clear relationship between the humour against the Soviet system and the need to maintain a spiritual faith in an alternative view. The criticism of repression found the literature of Dostoyevsky ('supporters of socialism usually declare *The Possessed* to be a parody, a slander on socialism')[23] Pasternak's *Doctor Zhivago* and numerous references to folk culture, reveal the counter-charge against the indoctrination of order through the circulation of sceptical criticism embedded in humour. Mikhail Bakhtin has written at length concerning the power of laughter as a liberating force. In *Rabelais and His World*, Bakhtin reveals how the role of laughter in opposition to the officially constructed truth is, at its most simplistic, a test of it.

Many of the political anecdotes below have been documented and provide an example of the humour that would be common to people in the former Soviet Union. In listing a brief selection, the impression of the incompetence of Soviet reality is incisively revealed.

> A speaker tells his listeners, "The communist ideal is already on the horizon".
> The audience wonders quietly, "What IS a horizon?"
> Answer: an imaginary line where the sky comes together with the earth; it moves off when you try to get closer.

In viewing society through the imposition of iron laws drew the response:

> Is communism a science?
> No. If it were, they would've tried it on dogs first.

There were numerous jokes relating to the stupidity and actions of Brezhnev:

Brezhnev rebukes his speechwriter:
I asked you for a 15-minute speech, but you made it one hour.
No, sir, it was written exactly for 15 minutes – you just read all four copies.

Brezhnev complains to Gromiko that he can't get used to summer and wintertime changes.
It's simple, replies Gromiko. Just move the hands on the clock one-hour ahead in spring, and then move them one-hour back in autumn.
Well, says Brezhnev that sounds really simple. Nevertheless, when I sent a telegram of my condolences to Egypt regarding Anwer Sadat's assassination last summer, it arrived one hour before his death.

Gorbachev came in for no less subtle bile, and numerous examples relate to his incompetence and inaction in making clear decisions. His failure to address domestic concerns and the failure to improve the quality of Soviet produce were topics that received scurrilous attention.

Gorbachev sent some sausage overseas for analysis. Soon he received an answer.
Mister Gorbachev, no helminth (any parasitic worm) were detected in your excrement.[24]

Less obvious methods were used to illustrate the lunacy of the Soviet system. Havel, for example, drew on and utilised the prevalence and circulation of the double entendre to undermine Soviet communism. A greengrocer displaying a party poster with the words 'Workers of the World Unite' in the window of his store gives out a signal other than its textual representation. Through a process similar to that which Skinner refers to as illocutionary redescription, where, by way of recovering the agent's illocutionary act, the underlying reality of the action is made clear. Read in the context of the actual social conditions that prevailed directly from Soviet control, the call for the 'workers of the world to unite' in support of a continuation in the *imagined* Soviet situation was absurd.

Jan Sverak's 1996 film *Kolya*, included a similar device to that applied by Havel. Louka (played by Zdenek Sverak) displays the Soviet flag next to the Czech flag in his apartment window not out of support for the former but out of benign acceptance of the coercion placed by the latter. Both Havel's greengrocer and Sverak's Louka fundamentally do not pledge allegiance or alliance by their actions to the beliefs of the Soviet ideology. They are functional acts, robotic necessities conducted on the one hand to avoid trouble from the Party. The banality of the act consequently reaffirms the monotony and tedium that is responsible for its origination.   The necessity was in Havel's words to play the game. The desire of the deviant was to alienate, and be alienated from, the system.

Reason and Reaction

The struggle to reassert the direct power of the CPSU, and the ructions caused in 1956 by Khrushchev's secret speech, led to a fresh burst of optimism and material activity, which enveloped Soviet society.   Whilst the effort to dominate and control the popular mind continued with a shift from death squads to psychological terror, the provision for the physical body in the Soviet world improved. The degree to which an opposing opinion could be expressed in public was however slight and controls were immediately introduced when the authority of the regime was challenged in any serious manner. It was evident however, that young people were seeking:

> wider knowledge of contemporary art, music and literature, and the right to think and write and talk as they please.   At times [as demonstrations within Moscow University in support of the Hungarian revolt in 1956 reveal] they have even openly questioned the Party's propaganda efforts.[25]

From the late 1950s, a general improvement in Soviet life occurred. The long problem of scarce or cramped accommodation was partly relieved with development and completion of residential buildings around the major Soviet cities.   Families who had long shared sparse rooms and living quarters with other families were gradually able to achieve a modicum of privacy. Relative subsistence had been achieved and improvements were taking place in health, education and work.

Despite the apparent betterment in Soviet life, conflict over ideas and social organisation continued at the highest level. Khrushchev had succeeded in disturbing the sensibilities of the Stalinist fraction and through ill-advised programs and outbursts which alienated his support within the Kremlin for the necessary political, economic and social reforms. With Khrushchev's removal, the brief and limited thaw was ended.   Despite the swing back to a conservative approach and the acceleration of successive campaigns and arrests: the evolving alternative view could not be eradicated.

Since the 1950s, the improved accessibility to tools of communication within the Soviet Union allowed material to be produced and circulated without the imposition of a range of laborious difficulties to limit such expressions.

> The underground used leaflets to communicate and demonstrate. Through this method, the Poles were aware of the Hungarian uprising in 1956. It was used to organise increasingly large protests. The first in my memory would be the 1958 student/worker protest in Gdansk. [26]

In the 1920s, the Bolsheviks, had to their credit, addressed the problem of widespread illiteracy. This had partly allowed the wide consumption of official publications. In opposition to the material supplied by the regime, self-published tracts and the duplication of novels proliferated; the demand for which appears to have been insatiable.

Forty years later the wider access to television, newspapers, cinema and radio allowed the Soviet system to co-ordinate and circulate its rhetoric and propaganda. Despite the monopoly of the Party over the various media, the advent of new forms of communication provided a forum for the introduction of subtle and oft unconscious acts of defiance and ridicule.

The authorities allowed only material that would be beneficial to the Soviet system, deviation from the grand design was interpreted as a direct attack. The official line was the only point of view that could be held without it being censored and removed. The Party considered criticism of it an affront, 'a repudiation of the proletarian struggle and a violation of Marxist-Leninism, and thus a threat to its authority'.[27] This resulted in an extremely tedious and wooden media, a feature that appeared to further the desire to ridicule the control of the system and search for modified forms of fulfilment. The rhetoric and the:

> strong ascetic undercurrent in Soviet ideology had an additional function of further disarming concerns for individual sovereignty. In the light of the promise of collective well being, basic individual freedoms (such as freedom of thought, assembly, speech, press, religion, etc.) were easily interpreted as obstacles to progress and as morally unacceptable.[28]

Whilst official institutions proliferated to guide and deliver the *true* intentions of the revolution, it appeared that experience with it in everyday life did not correlate with the propaganda and the pronouncements of the 'good Soviet life'. Force was a tool in constant use to overcome difficulties in the project that could not be disguised. The collective fear that had enveloped Soviet life did not evaporate with the death of its worst exponent of terror. Many of the controls instigated by Stalin remained in place, and in some sectors they were developed to meet the demands of the new conditions.

> During the reign of terror, people typically suffered from two kinds of phobias: some, unable to shake off a sense of imminent danger hanging over them, suspected everyone, even their husbands, of being informers; others feared that they themselves might be taken for provocateurs, and surrendered to a feeling of uncommitted guilt lurking to be pinned on them at any moment.[29]

The methods of social control applied by the Soviet regime following the end of Stalin's reign shifted from the application of direct terror to the extensive contact with a pervasive bureaucratic structure. In the knowledge that repetitive enquiries could be initiated at any time, people retreated further from direct exposure to the system. The vast human resources directed at extensive surveillance of the population resulted in inconsistencies and incompetence that led to the investigation of trivial matters, which created additional administration and physical effort to process and monitor.

> Assessing the populace, checking up on it, is a principal and never-ending social activity in communist countries. If a painter is to have an exhibition, an ordinary citizen to receive a visa to a country with a sea coast, a soccer player to join the national team, then a vast array of recommendations and reports must be gathered (from the concierge, colleagues, the police, the local party organisation, the pertinent trade union) and added up, weighed, and summarised by special officials. These reports have nothing to do with artistic talent, kicking ability, or maladies that respond well to sea air; they deal with one thing only: the "citizen's personal profile" (in other words, what the citizen says, what he thinks, how he behaves, how he acquits himself at meetings and May Day parades). Because everything (day-to-day existence, promotion at work, vacations) depends on the outcome of the assessment process, everyone (whether he wants to play soccer for the national team, have an exhibition, or spend holidays at the seaside) must behave in such a way as to deserve a favourable assessment.[30]

The intensity of the control appears to have nurtured a feeling that was common in the former Soviet Union: the futility of complaint against the violations of rules, injustice and misconduct. Against the bureaucratic monolith 'protest had no effect ...it was impossible to prosecute the guilty party, or to identify the decision-maker'.[31] Without recourse to the right to publicly discuss injustices and recognition of the lack of responsibility at all levels of the Soviet hierarchy, individuals seemingly moved away from the psychological hold over them and performed their duties without either belief or camaraderie in and with the system.

Foreign visitors to the Eastern Bloc and the former Soviet Union were monitored during their stay in the country. In restaurants, attempts were made to record conversations between diners, particularly if the Party included a foreign visitor and a Soviet citizen. Hotel rooms of foreign visitors would be regularly searched. Although items would not generally be removed, incriminating material (books, papers etc.) would be recorded and action (deportation, expulsion, arrest) would be initiated if concerns (however unwarranted or innocent) were reported and documented. This appears to have been largely decided on the zeal or stupidity of the investigating officer, a Kafkaesque world of gigantic proportions.

The post-totalitarian nature of the Soviet system revealed its failure to transform itself from the damage that had been inflicted by Stalin. It could not seemingly separate the falsity of its condition from either its aspirations or rhetoric.

> Government by bureaucracy was called popular government; the working class was enslaved in the name of the working class; the complete degradation of the individual was presented as his or her ultimate liberation; depriving people of information was called making it available; the use of power to manipulate was called the public control of power; and the arbitrary abuse of power was called observing the legal code; the repression of culture was called its development; the expansion of imperial influence was presented as support for the oppressed; the lack of free expression became the highest form of freedom; farcical elections became the highest form of democracy; banning independent thought became the most scientific of world views; military occupation became fraternal assistance.[32]

The resulting claustrophobia administered by the system on the Soviet people appears to have contributed, out of desperation, to a range of personal strategies activated to manage the experience of relations with it. The regime had:

> its officials and members of the intelligence service everywhere. Surveillance using hidden cameras, tape recorders and bugging devices were used with

regularity and varying degrees of competency. Informants observed everyone, and everyone was suspected. Everyone was paranoid. It resembled one great lunatic asylum.[33]

To the totalitarian regime and its post-totalitarian embodiment deviation from Soviet realism was considered by the authorities to be irrational – a condition that required correction and re-education. In its worst manifestations, it was a condition deemed worthy of necessitating incarceration and clinical surveillance. The logic that prevailed rhetorically was that the system was perfect. Therefore, deviance from it would be recognised by the regime as a form of madness that required correction, in the interest of the individual who suffered from the delusion.

This procedure applied to individuals:

who peacefully engage in political dissent, those who attempt to exercise minority, ethnic, or national rights, to emigrate, or to practice their religion, as well as those activities that are merely bothersome to the Soviet authorities.[34]

The intimidation of scientists, documented in Zhores and Roy Medvedev's, *A Question of Madness*, illustrates the lengths the authorities were prepared to go to repress and eliminate dissent. Other less well-known cases of intimidation and incarceration took place. Some were recorded, as the documented evidence catalogued by the Sakahrov Museum and Archives reveal.

The reverse side of the iron wall consists of metal bars – the eternal symbol of imprisonment. This side of the second nave is devoted to the memory of victims of political repression. Recesses and file cabinet drawers embedded within the barred wall contain previously classified photographs and "execution lists" of people buried in common graves in the greater Moscow area. The opposite wall displays materials documenting resistance to the regime. The human and non-violent character of the resistance is underlined by the wooden construction of this wall, which resembles bookshelves in a library or archive.[35]

The technical intelligentsia received a modicum of protection, particularly if they were internationally recognised figures. With the development of an active international news media, the Central Committee was increasingly cautious not to create a situation whereby the arrest or intimidation of a publicly known figure could lead to action or criticism against them. In this context:

It was all right for Zhores Medvedev- he was well enough known in the scientific world. But what could be done for the workman Borisov, the bricklayer, Gershun, the students Novodvorskaya and Iofe, or the stage designer Victor Kuznetsov? For them there was no prospect of academicians raising hell with the Central Committee or the world community of scientists threatening a scientific boycott. According to our information, there were little known individuals being held in psychiatric prisons for political reasons. Who would take up the struggle on their behalf?[36]

The ability of political prisoners to frustrate the penal administration by utilising their knowledge of Soviet law was initiated by requesting the hearing of their right to petition any state or public institution and any public official with a compliant. It appears that the sheer vigorous activity of this function overwhelmed departments and officials with complaints, and caused chaos and bureaucratic conflict. This appears to have led to substantial disruption within the Soviet administration, a development that would have consequences on the formulation of policy and strategy at the highest level.

Bureaucrats are bureaucrats, always at loggerheads with one another, and often enough your complaints become weapons in internecine wars between bureaucrat and bureaucrat, department and department. This goes on for months and months, until, at last, the most powerful factor of all in Soviet life enters the fray – statistics.[37]

The number of complaints that the authorities received were recorded and examined. Investigators from elsewhere in the bureaucratic hierarchy checked a committee, department, and institution receiving a large number of complaints. This resulted in the involvement of bureaucrats and departments from *outside* the original site of complaint. To avoid interference it was common that a department or influential official would not act on the identification of a specific problem or issue. It would simply not be recorded and the matter would largely disappear. The embedded corruption, incompetence, and pervasive deception continued within the functioning of Soviet administrative structure. With official compliance, the atmosphere nurtured the condition of neglect, which did not improve the system but disabled it.

The transfer of power to a new leader in the Kremlin resulted in the arrival of thousands of letters (and this was amplified by millions in Gorbachev's case) being sent to the Politburo or the Central Committee. The messages had to be read and responded to. They contained:

not just congratulations but suggestions, projects, requests, complaints, demands for justice, appeals on behalf of those serving prison sentences (more than 2 million people), from prisoners themselves or from dissidents of all kinds (almost every known Soviet dissident began his career by writing to the Central Committee or Politburo).[38]

The ability to criticise without relative retribution or retaliation for anti – Soviet behaviour was provided by Article 49 of the constitution, which specified:

> Every citizen... has the right to submit proposals to state bodies and public organisations for improving their activity, and to criticise shortcomings in their work. Officials are obliged, within established time limits, to examine citizens' proposals and requests, to reply to them and take the appropriate action. Prosecution for criticism is prohibited.[39]

The legitimate process of submitting complaints through official channels appears to have substantially contributed to the gross inefficiency of the Soviet bureaucratic system. This situation became increasingly worse and burdensome with Gorbachev's encouragement to citizens to utilise the organs of the Party to make recommendations and identify failings in the Soviet system.

With the re-occurring abuses and acts of treachery promulgated by the Soviet regime, the opposition had developed exponentially, in various coded forms, to undermine the illusion of a collective culture and the ideology that sanctioned it. The explosion of unofficial Soviet rock continued a poetic struggle of deviance that had been endemic in Russian life for several generations. Its articulation and circulation would seemingly shatter the Soviet experience and the effort to prolong it.

Notes

[1] Bulavka (1998:13), *From the cultural revolution of 1917.*
[2] Leonard (1956:85), *The History of Russian Music.*
[3] Arendt (1986:466), *The Origins of Totalitarianism.*
[4] Kagarlitsky (1990: ivv), *The dialectics of change.*
[5] Tökès (1975:8), *Dissent in the USSR.*
[6] Diddulph (1975, 1976:96), *Dissent in the USSR.*
[7] Anna Nirmalendran (1997) Interviewed (8 December 1997).
[8] Cutler (1980:16), *Soviet dissent under Khrushchev.*
[9] Barghoorn (1973:81), *Regimes and Opposition.*
[10] Antony Aszabo (1998) Interviewed (4 February 1998).

[11] *Ibid*, Aszabo.

[12] *Ibid*, Aszabo.

[13] See Fischer-Galati (1967), *Rumania*.

[14] The material collated at the Museum of Peace, Progress and Human Rights in Moscow provides an invaluable insight into the opposition movement active in the former Soviet union.

[16] *Op cit* (1973:62), *Regimes and opposition*. The interviewees commenting on the ideas and material contained in this investigation support the view that creativity expressed in various cultural forms presented a threat to the authority of the Soviet system.

[17] Bukovsky (1978:32), *To build a castle*. The strategy of 'living within the truth' takes on a direct political standpoint when viewed in the context described by Bukovsky. Havel (1986:42) describes it 'a bacteriological weapon, so to speak, utilised when conditions are ripe by a single civilian to disarm an entire division. This power does not participate in any direct struggle for power; rather it makes its influence felt in the obscure arena of being itself'.

[18] Havel (1986:58), *The Power of the Powerless*.

[19] Simirenko (1975:36), *A new type of resistance*. Actions of this type appear in the main to have been provoked on religious grounds. The intimidation during the Khrushchev era on individuals and groups openly practising and celebrating the demands of their faith was particularly harsh and often resulted in violence.

[20] Medvedev (1983:226), *Brezhnev: a bureaucrat's file*.

[21] Koroviev: Ein discussion board (10 October 2000).

[22] *Op cit*. Nirmalendran.

[23] Shafarevich (1976:54), *Socialism in our past and future*.

[24] For an excellent and detailed list of jokes from the Soviet era see: http:// russia.uthscsa.edu/Humor/politic:html.

[25] Thayer (1960:108), *Russia*.

[26] Joanna Eccles (1998), Interviewed (8 February 1998).

[27] Revelations from the Russian Achieves: http://1web.loc.gov/exhibits/achieves/atte.html.

[28] Udovicki (1987:257), *The liberal model and the public realm in the u.s.s.r.*

[29] Mandelstam (1976: 34, 88, 95).

[30] Kundera (1984:96), *The Unbearable Lightness of Being*.

[31] Bonnell (1989:313), *Moscow: A view from below*.

[32] Vaclav Havel *et al* (1986:30, 31), *Power of the Powerless*.

[33] *Op cit*, Aszabo.

[34] Gershman (1984:58), *Psychiatric abuse in the Soviet Union*.

[35] Museum Catalogue, *Peace, Progress, and Human Rights*, The Andrei Sakharov Museum and Public Centre, Moscow. The Sakharov Archieves, apt.62, Zemlyanoi val Street 48b, Moscow 103064, Russia. Phone and fax: (095) 916-24-80. The archives provides documents for display in exhibitions, provides access to scholars, and answers requests, concerning Andrei Sakharov's life and activities.

[36] *Op cit*. (1978: 286).

[37] *Ibid* (1978:35).

[38] Medvedev (1986:209), *Gorbachev*.

[39] Construction of the Union of Soviet Socialist Republics. Moscow. Novosti Press Agency, (1980:46): *op cit* from in Medvedev 1986.

7   Emancipation and Coded (Dis)chord

In an attempt to avoid the censorship administered by the Soviet regime, musicians and lyricists utilised musical and associated cultural forms imported from the West to influence and augment strategies of native struggle. The facility of musicians both directly and unconsciously to present an alternative view, placed a question mark against the authority of the Soviet experience. Performance of unofficial Soviet rock was not however explicitly political, but was seemingly charged with a social significance, which the authorities could not ignore.

The material that follows focuses on music as the most 'popular' art form and its relevance to the presence of counterculture in the former Soviet Union. The spontaneous revolution in popular music including avant-garde, jazz, progressive rock and folk rock is recovered to highlight an 'electric' version of globalization. In seeming to undermine the conservative culture, the performance and circulation of unofficial rock music, through the distribution of recorded material and the duplication of lyrics in samizdat tracts, expanded and drew converts from a curious generation. The wider global counterculture movement was not separate in substance from the aspirations of youth culture within the Soviet Union. It flowered from the same sea as it were. It is recognised however that many in the Soviet Union, as in the West, were unaffected by the social movements and *atmosphere* that arrived, evolved and evaporated in the 1960s. Nonetheless, it appears that the consciousness of a global counterculture, however tenuous the label may be, was identifiable in both the West and the Soviet Union.

Routine and Spontaneity

Music is renowned for both celebrating established systems (the authorities in the Soviet Union commissioned numerous works in recognition of the achievements of the proletariat) and applying pressure to popularise revolt from them.

The subversive nature of music has long been recognised by rulers, religions and moralists. Plato condemned the use of specific intervals; William Byrd risked his life by composing music in secret for the Roman Catholic Church; Verdi had to tailor his libretto to avoid political censorship. What is the particular threat music poses? Probably that its meaning is ambiguous and that its power gives dignity to people in awful predicaments. Whatever the cause, it is in our own 'beautiful pitiful century', as Osip Mandlelstam called it, that the censoring of music and musicians, from Shostakovich to Marilyn Manson, has particularly flourished.[1]

It has been established that in the aftermath of the revolution and the Bolshevik coup d'etat, that it was expected the arts would reflect the achievements of the proletariat. It required specific icons, testaments and cultural products to celebrate its achievement.

> The music conservatories went on as before, but with a new class of proletarian students who, it was expected, would create the new music and culture of the proletarian society...A typical manifestation of the times was the formation in 1922 of the famous Moscow Persimfans Orchestra, which operated without a conductor.[2]

In the drive to construct a homogeneously integrated Soviet culture the creativity that had been evident in the previous decade was expunged from the public domain by the 1930s. The view espoused by C.L.R. James had seemingly been discarded by the Party-State elite, its potential sapped by the Soviet institution, its residue forced underground.

> His studies of the Haitian Revolution, the Paris Commune, the Russian Revolution, and of the infinitely plural and diverse struggles for democracy waged around the world, convinced James that the self-activity of ordinary citizen and workers held the key to social change.[3]

The loss of social inclusion, other than that which the rhetoric of the Party alluded to, had been hastened with Gorky's doctrine of 'Socialist realism', which had been expounded on at the First Convention of the Soviet Literary Union in 1934. It was prudent for composers of all styles to reflect on their previous works and correct errors which failed to celebrate the development of Soviet communism and revel in its glory. Failure in these matters would result in immediate action by the authorities to censor material with which it disagreed and arrest the perpetrator. A little after a decade later from the first Literary Union conference, the Soviet grip on the creative arts would tighten.

On February 10th the Central Committee of the Communist Party published its Decree on Music, one of the most extraordinary documents in the history of Russian music. The Decree bluntly warned the composers of the Soviet Union to "liquidate the faults", and to "become more conscious of their duties to the Soviet people".[4]

Despite censorship, intimidation and intrusive surveillance, the coded criticism inherent in a number of musical works could not be extinguished. It appeared in a variety of compositions, Shostakovich, Prokofiev and Miaskovsky being particular culprits, who went against the directives concerning correct Soviet harmonies and conventions. In public they vowed to 'correct their errors', in private they continued with them.

1960s: Revolution in the Head Revisited

The sound of rock 'n' roll, typical of the music revolution in the West, reached a wide audience during the later part of the 1950s. Its association with rebelliousness in criticising the bourgeois establishment, both intrigued and disturbed the Soviet hierarchy (a feature that led to an uneven policy in regards to its import). To aid precession the term rock 'n' roll will include its later connections with electric folk, hard rock and progressive rock and will be used interchangeably (as it was in practise). Whilst the Soviet authorities feared the decadent attitude instilled in young people as a result of association with rock music, it was recognised that in certain performers an anti-capitalist message did not sit comfortably with the bourgeois sensibilities.

Robin Denselow, in the book, *When the Music's Over* has recounted in detail the atmosphere of paranoia that prevailed in the West, concerning the link between popular music and communism. The conservative majority in the United States saw rock 'n' roll imbued with a communist message: sweeping the nation and corrupting American youth. Woody Guthrie and Pete Seeger were recognised and labelled as 'red' exponents who incited workers to rebel and challenge authority. Rock 'n' roll's working class credentials were seemingly considered important in allowing the first performances in the former Soviet Union. In the early 1960s, Pete Seeger made appearances in Moscow. Elsewhere behind the iron curtain others such as The Rolling Stones were allowed to perform in Warsaw to a selected Komsomol audience.

The spontaneity of rock, its improvisation, its rebelliousness, its concern with physical and psychological repression, proved a viable vehicle to raise an awareness of the paradoxes of everyday life. Through the celebration of an opposing view, it seemingly encouraged critical thinking and practise: one not necessarily intellectually developed but suspicious of all forms of authority.

In the late '60s – foreign-made records were listened to in many houses (even from our iron curtain a lot of people travelled abroad, for business or, let's say, sailors). Tape recorders helped in the spreading of music, though the quality was terrible! In the '70s Russian rock became more and more popular. It was sometimes protest, but not always. It was lifestyle, as Aquarium leader, Grebenshikov, said. He himself tried writing, drawing, was part of the so-called "Mit'ki" group which hardly fit any definition. "Generation of street sweepers and storage guards", from some other song. In the '80s, the amount and variety of groups became enormous, so each one could choose what to listen to according to individual preferences. You could tell "Alisa" fans coming out from a concert in a big hall from "Aquarium" ones. Age and manners different. I also have to mention author's song. It was no less a popular trend, especially amongst students. Originated in the '60s, it was a mixture of poetry, music, simple guitar accompaniment and close connection to the audience. On that site you can read a little about some people and listen to songs. Music was very important part of life, it filled souls, united people, gave chance to many to be not just a passive listener, but try oneself to express and so on. There was resistance of course (groups were not allowed to perform in good halls etc), but it was part of the fun! If it would be easy and without troubles, it would not be the phenomenon we know.[5]

Throughout the world in the twentieth century, music that had been dominated and regulated by the commission and patronage of the powerful became democratised, albeit unevenly.

It is in this context that we must understand the reception of syncopated dance music in the early 1900s, of rock 'n' roll in the 1950s, and of punk in the late 1970s, as not only new but *unnatural.* These are movements involving elements of social crisis, or at least social unrest, when the strength of accepted articulated patterns decline.[6]

The content of rock music as anti-establishment, its association with attacking traditional social values, its derogatory social implications undermining authority, control and order led the Soviet authorities to limit access to it. In a move to lessen its attraction, the Soviet Ministry of Culture endorsed official Soviet rock, music that to a degree utilised the

Western sound but contained lyrics, which celebrated and reflected the achievements of the Soviet system.

> In 1966, the Ministry of Culture approved the formation of the first state-supported beat-music ensembles. Musicians willing to cut their hair, moderate their decibel levels, and purge their repertories of offensive Western songs, could enjoy the benefits of State sponsorship – national concert tours, appearances on the radio and television, recording opportunities on the Melodiya label.[7]

There does not appear to have been strict instructions against rock musicians from the West visiting the former Soviet Union. In every case, an official within the administration had to make a decision on the suitability of the visit. This would be arrived at through a consideration of a particular artist and the political, economic and social circumstances, both domestic and international, surrounding the visit. Pete Seeger, The Rolling Stones, Elton John, Queen and Uriah Heep had at different times visited various parts of the socialist bloc, the management of each act meeting different bureaucratic conditions related to domestic considerations and international affairs.

From the 1930s up to Stalin's death in 1953 information about the West had been controlled and distorted. During the Khrushchev era 1953-1964, a period that was at first called 'glorious' was later censured as a period of 'voluntarism' and 'subjectivism'.[8] Nonetheless, Khrushchev's limited reforms facilitated the import of cultural forms relatively absent from Soviet life and this included the repertoire of rock 'n' roll.

Kan recalls how the 'cultural visits by Westerners to Moscow in 1957 and in particular the spectacle of Western rock 'n' roll was explosive' to Russians denied access to popular Western cultural forms.[9] It galvanised interest in young people to experiment with sound, dress and style. The later US Exhibition in Sokolniki Park in Moscow in 1959 (in which Western consumer goods were on show) affected Soviet society, but in a different way from the previous cultural invasion. Although the authorities generally selected visitors to the exhibition, the official press reported it and selections were passed to circulate throughout the Soviet Union. A visitor to the exhibition remarked:

> The communist party lost their hold over so many people by raising the iron curtain even for a month. It was as if we were discovering a new planet, stepping into the future. We were stunned, we couldn't believe people really lived like that.[10]

In Moscow and Leningrad the earliest signs of an observable emerging counterculture, interested in Western music and style, was the *stilyagi* (style hounds). They were similar to:

America's former zoot-suiters and the 'teddy boys' of Britain, the stilyagi... [was] to wear odd clothes: tight trousers, strange hats and gaudy neckties.[11]

The stilyagi had their own style (stil') which was an interpretation of American rock 'n' roll styles incorporated along with their own idiosyncratic jargon. They were ridiculed by the authorities, and laughed at by less enlightened proletariats. The police regularly made indiscriminate arrests and forced the stiligi to take haircuts and change into sensible clothes, with immediate effect.

Rock 'n' roll was labelled degenerate by the establishment on both sides of the Atlantic. Marcuse observed how it challenged communism: 'miniskirts against the apparatchiks, rock 'n' roll against Soviet realism'. In the West, the conservatives and religious attempted to defend institutions, which had been rocked by an outburst of pluralism.

At this point, they were only archetypal dropouts. I mean, they weren't art students but they should have been, they had all the symptoms, that aggression, that scruffiness and calculated cool, that post-beat bohemianism. And in these very early sixties, before the age of T-shirts and baseball boots, the heavy art school cults were Ray Charles and Chuck Berry, and Bo Diddley, Muddy Waters, Charlie Mingus and Monk, Allen Ginsberg and Jack Kerouac, Robert Johnson. If you were pretentious about it, you might stretch to a paperback translation of Rimbaud or Dostoevsky, strictly for display. But the Stones weren't pretentious – they were mean and nasty, full-blooded, very tasty, and they beat out the toughest, crudest, most offensive noise any English band had ever made.[12]

The atmosphere of 'freedom' was not confined to the west. In the Moscow area, spontaneity and experimentation exposed counterculture. The 1960s revolution in music reflected and inspired the wide rejection of the principles and demands associated with the established authorities. It momentarily appeared that the global appetite to reject the flawed 'adult world' would result in chaos. To the delight of the propagandists within the Soviet Union, who actively reported on the social turbulence occurring in the West in the various Soviet media, rock 'n' roll could briefly be reported as a reaction to bourgeois decadence and capitalist values.

In the West, the marches, riots and sit-ins disturbed middle class sensibilities and popularised theories of communist inspired activity. The issues that inflamed public opinion ranged from America's involvement in Vietnam, racial discrimination, sexual inequality, religious piety and hypocrisy. Ken Kesey and his posse of Merry Pranksters (reviewed famously by Tom Wolfe in *The Electric Kool-Aid acid Test*), a chaotic group that included Neal Cassady, the beat icon on whom Jack Kerouac had based his Dean Moriarty character in *On The Road*, rejected the dullness of industrial society. Alan Ginsberg, Timothy Leary, Jimi Hendrix, Bob Dylan, James Dean, The Beatles, The Rolling Stones, Marilyn Monroe and the Grateful Dead, and Dennis Hopper's cult road movie *Easy Rider*, became the icons of a generation, which had followers in both the East and West.

The propaganda and paranoia that circulated throughout the West mirrored fears relating to the arms race and potential conflict between the superpowers. It suddenly became important to question and satirise the absurdity of the 'cold' relations that threatened to toast humanity. The protagonists were clearly identified in the Kremlin and on Capital Hill. An active media drew on the tension and raised attention to the potential of a nuclear calamity and its consequences.

The film *Dr Strangelove* (a classic from the 1960s, starring Peter Sellers) in which the living world is destroyed by a nuclear exchange galvanised the anti-war movement. In the movie, the scenario of a crazed American general convinced that the Russians had contaminated the American people's bodily fluids, shocked the world. In Rocky and Bullwinkle's *Goof Gas Attack*, an epidemic of intense stupidity swept through the country. The cause of the Goof Gas: Boris Badenov's new secret weapon. On American television, the heroic squirrel and mouse, Rocky and Bullwinkle, popular cartoon characters, saved America repeatedly from the sinister duo, Boris and Natasha. Nevil Shute's apocalyptic 1957 novel *On the Beach* reached a wide audience with its transfer to film. Starring Gregory Peck and Ava Gardner, it raised the popular consciousness regarding the threat and aftermath of nuclear annihilation. Hellers' *Catch-22*, in aftermath of Vietnam, was again widely thumbed by concerned readers, well aware that stupidity is not the possession of a single generation or context.

In America, France, England, and Germany, and elsewhere in the east, 1968 was a year of revolution and change. For many, America's hopeless and ruthless war in Vietnam was the catalyst: the Tet offensive, draft resistors, violent protests in the streets (the infamous revolt in Grovesnor Square, London) and in the universities, questioned the legitimacy of

Governments to wage war. The demonstrations throughout France challenged the fundamental values and fabric of modern societies. In Czechoslovakia, Dubceck and the participators of the Prague Spring attempted to reform socialism and democratise it with a human face.

The explosions of social revolutions from Prague to Paris to USA were essentially directed at democracy, a democracy not framed on Hobbesian or Lockean notions of liberal-democracy, overseen by the all-powerful monarch or by a strong parliament of the people for the people. This was a direct democracy – a post democratic state – one that Petr Ulr believed would lead to 'a society wide system of self management'.[13]

> The effort to unite intellectuals and workers faired better in Eastern Europe, especially in Alexander's Dubcek's Czechoslovakia during the "Prague Spring". There Paul Berman recalls in "A Tale of Two Utopias", they won broad support when they championed the young, humanistic Marx against the old, iron-laws of history Marx, Hegel against Engels, Lenin against Stalin, left-wing humanism against "scientific" leftism, artists and intellectuals against office-clerks and censors, the avant-garde against the Party-mandated arts.[14]

Music accompanied the social turmoil. The sounds of crowds and police vans during the 1968 Paris riots were captured along with the iconic sounds of the electric guitar on Francios Bayale's *Solitude* of 1970. John Lennon's *Revolution 1* from The Beatles' *White Album*, screamed literally with the anger of protest and frustration.

Ian Mcdonald, in his book *Revolution in the Head* has argued that 'much of what happened in the sixties had been spiritual in impulse, the free festivals being expressions of shared feeling intrinsic to the times in which they took place'.[15] Moreover, huge sections of [global] society were effectively part of a concurrent local and global revolution.

> The Revolution of 1968 challenged liberal verities, in all their manifestations. It challenged above all the belief that the state was a rational arbiter of conscious collective will. The revolutionaries of 1968 challenged not only those in power in the state structures themselves but all those in power in the "ideological apparatus" of the state.[16]

The Western variant of counterculture capitulated through its own devices and the measures introduced by the establishment. By the end of the decade, hopes of political reforms faded. The *establishment* throughout Western society defeated the revolution of 1968 and the spirit of social, economic and political reform. On 4 May 1970, with the shooting dead of four American students by the National Guard at Kent University, Ohio for disagreeing with the Government, the American public turned against the idealism of a generation, allowing a conservative backlash to gather momentum.[17] The dream of peace and love disintegrated into violence. At the Altamont rock festival, the Hell's Angels, employed by the Rolling Stones management to maintain *security* caused a conflagration and a death. At the Isle of Wight festival, the encroachment of a business ethic in the organisation of the event was widely criticised. The idealism of peace and love faded in prominence to the increasingly virile demands of an ascendant consumer society.

> The hippie movement was shot down by many factors, but drugs – naively taking drugs – was a big factor. The hippie movement seemed like a worldwide movement, in concept, but still the establishment was bigger.[18]

The entertainment industry that had exploded along with the prosperity of 1960s consolidated its gains, and increasingly acted as a gatekeeper. The political content and experimentalism eschewed by many artists in the 1960s was increasingly expunged and replaced by the American stadium sound of the 1970s. In numerous areas artists suffered decreasing opportunities to develop and perform their work in large public settings. By the late 1960s, in the Western world:

> the new social patterns, technologies and musical styles had been substantially assimilated into a reorganised music-industrial system: a technological oligopoly of vast entertainment corporations, supplied to some extent by 'independent' producers; serviced by mass audience radio and TV channels (with some 'minority' TV shows and channels), by a symbiotically pliant music press and by related leisure-products businesses; and directing itself at a series of separate audiences whose distinctiveness is less subcultural than a creature of market researchers' consumer profits.[19]

East/West Social Turbulence

The content of rock music in the West throughout the 1970s abandoned its association with rebellion and struggles and capitulated to the medium of entertainment, dominated by celebrity. In the late 1970s Punk would be a reaction to the increasingly sterile FM world, but it did not become available in Eastern Europe and the Soviet Union until much later.

The abundance of cultural products in Western markets allowed easy access for foreign investors to obtain cheap and unfashionable stock. A lot of this material appears to have entered Eastern Europe and the former Soviet Union. Western cultural commodities: jeans, tee shirts, records and tapes increasingly penetrated the Soviet region and were obtained through friends (this was the most favoured route) or recourse to the black market. In the light of radically accelerating demand, particularly in relation to music by The Beatles and the Rolling Stones, the black market became increasingly sophisticated, and expansive, attracting businessmen, apparatchiks and organised criminal gangs. Whilst attempts were made by the Soviet hierarchy to limit the spread of unofficial commodities, the attraction of deviant forms typical of unofficial culture could not be halted.

The authorities in the various parts of the Soviet Union, and the Soviet influenced East European states, reacted to the cultural invasion and introduced measures to limit it. It was taken to be an extremely serious matter. In Eastern Europe, indigenous rock music had its own problems. The response of the East German authorities towards GDR rock musicians, highlights the seriousness with which the authorities monitored the methods through which the *products* of counterculture were articulated and circulated.

> Where else in the world would politicians at the highest level (politicians within the Politburo) watch the lyrics of every rock song with great care, while presiding over a political system which afforded rock musicians sufficient institutional power to instigate the systems demise? The attempt to institutionalize rock culture as a state enterprise, to turn it in to an organ of state-run political education, played a central role in the processes of disintegration which led to the country's dissolution.[20]

In the former Soviet Union, Western Rock music appears to have generally been associated with noise. An acceptable noise for many that added to the mythical impression of the West as a *place* of freedom, experimentation and affluence. Western rock music did not directly attack the Soviet system. Its political content against a range of issues was either absent or not widely understood. It essentially added to the general sound of the bands, but contributed almost nothing politically.

> No lines from Western rock were used to set any criticism against the Soviet system. The main reason is that Russians, in common, know English very little, and the typical rock fan doesn't understand the lyrics in English at all! The curious thing is this fact never reduced the popularity of Western music in Russia, but the vast majority of its listeners remain ignorant about their meanings (I know a lot of funny examples of misunderstanding). That's

because the significant difference between the two languages, and because of the extremely bad system of education in the Soviet Union (and, sadly, in Russia so far).[21]

Correspondingly, unofficial Soviet rock was primarily subversive in attacking the Soviet establishment, its institutions and ideology.

> Rock poets were literally at the forefront, a strong voice. In a way they were indeed overcoming censorship as their songs were distributed outside any official routes. But at the same time they rarely went into an outright political comment or defiance – not only because it was fraught with more severe repercussions, but also because it was much "cooler" to be able to express the same sentiment in a more sophisticated "Aesopian" language of poetical metaphors – pretty much in the refined Russian tradition. There was for instance this band Televizor whose lyrics were very straightforward in their defiance (Get Out of the Control! – a telling title). They were respected for their courage, but artistically thought of as second rate, precisely for this reason – their straightforwardness.[22]

The quote above suggests the opposite to Ramet's observation mentioned earlier that Televizor were one of the key groups generating change. The groups importance should not be underestimated, but they were not part of the subtle movement generating change.

Musical influences from the West had long been influential in the former Soviet Union. Jazz was deemed elitist. Whilst it attracted the attention of the authorities, its musicians, despite intimidation were relatively unharmed in conflict with the authorities.

The avant-garde was considered dangerous and particularly subversive but it too attracted an elitist audience, drawn mainly from the creative intelligentsia and the wider intelligentsia, who appreciated the abstract ridicule of social conventions, through a composite of abstract forms. The musician Sergey Kuryokhin was the leading exponent of this genre during the Soviet era. It was particularly difficult to produce and professionally record original work in the Soviet Union. Nonetheless, Kuryokhin's concerts are legendary in musical circles, and the recordings that were made, capture the vibrancy and creativity of this unusual artist.

A note to Kuryokhin's music reads:

> My only wish for everyone who reads this booklet and or listens to the music is to remember that all the recording and events presented here happened not in the cosy concert halls in front of nicely dressed and perfumed audiences. They

happened not in the spacious recording studios with perfect acoustics. These events happened in the very midst of the most cruel totalitarian regime. It was dangerous to play this music, and it was dangerous to be seen at Kuryokhin's concerts, for a certain part of the audience was KGB employees or informers.[23]

Similar intimidation was accorded earlier to the Russian bards such as Bulat Okudzhava and Alexander Galich. They performed in small environments, usually a kitchen, and contributed to the *atmosphere* of dissent.

An effective form of social resistance was the work of the so-called "bards", who performed their own works. By the late 1950s, the songs of Bulat Okudzhava were well known, and in the 1960s, songs by Alexander Galich, Vladimir Vysotski, and Yuli Kim became equally popular. The bards' work revived the Russian tradition of singing to guitar music and incorporated the style of "Blatnaya", or criminal song, born (like the blues) in oppression – in prisons and labour camps. The songs of the Russian bards expressed the liberal values of the post-Stalin generation. The authors of these songs did not have access to the mass media. Their audiences usually gathered at illegal home concerts. In the mid-1960s, inexpensive tape recorders expanded the reach of these singers, and the authorities could no longer control this process.[24]

Throughout the Soviet Union it was common that a circle of close friends would regularly meet. Music would be a constant guest, stimulating the mood from the apparent confines of Soviet cultural convention. It was a social necessity that:

everyone gathered around the table and imbibed tea and more than tea. Affairs were begun: families formed and were broken up. Together everyone sang, danced and listened to music. Tape recorders had gone on sale, and they were not prohibitly expensive. They facilitated the distribution of songs by Bulat Okudzhava, Vladimir Vysotsky, and a little later Aleksandr Galich that took the country by storm.[25]

The culture that appears to have developed from these social gatherings prefigured the emergence of unofficial rock, which was to incorporate similar methods to savour and communicate ideas and social comment. It drew on the unwritten popular culture of the peasant, based on folk-tales and religious legend, and provided an alternative to authority and culture of the ruling elite. It is important to understand the root of the oppression, which was repeatedly referred to in the lines of the *dissident* lyric.

Many circles had their own bard who performed these songs, as well as his own and the camp songs that spread over the entire country after the mass return of prisoners from the camps. These songs were a form of contemporary folklore, like the anecdotes, inspired by every important event. Exchanging anecdotes is a favourite pastime for Soviets from all walks of life because they allow one to formulate and express political judgements and observations on life.[26]

Music that did not conform to the official view spread throughout the country like a virus.

In Siberia, the most popular groups were "Mashina vremeni" and "Aquarium". The most popular album was David Tuhkmanov's "Along the waves of my memory". The most popular performers were Berger and Gradsky. It was not dangerous to listen to music but Gradsky was banned in our City after his first concert where he sang "A monologue of a loaf of bread for 20 copecks" ("Monolog 20kopeechnogo batona").[27]

Unofficial Soviet rock music operated as a creative and tactical bomb that imploded throughout society. In addressing the concerns of the audience, the rock lyrics and celebrated an alternative view. It was adopted, modified, circulated by the groups, the intelligentsia and rock fans in the audience in both magnitizdat and samizdat forms..

Between the aims of the post-totalitarian system and the aims of life there is a yawning abyss: while life, in its essence, moves towards plurality, diversity, independent self-constitution and self-organisation, in short, towards the fulfilment of its own freedom, the post-totalitarian system demands conformity, uniformity, and discipline...[28]

Despite efforts to stem the flow of Western influences, technically competent citizens modified their radio sets to receive the foreign radio stations. Seva Novgorodsev's weekly rock programme drew a loyal audience on BBC wavelength. Radio Free Europe/Radio Liberty (*peasants' radio*) made inroads into the restricted cultural wasteland. The propaganda associated radio broadcasts was a key component in American foreign policy, which sought to undermine Soviet authority through the import of Western culture.

The introduction and availability of magnetic tape and the machines to record and play them on, rapidly increased the copying and illegal circulation of popular music.

Before 1986 Aquarium had no "records" as such. Their recorded "albums" were "released" on reel tapes with photographic design plastered on the cardboard box. About 30 original copies were produced. Later on recordings would travel all over the country just dubbed from one machine to another. "Magizdat" a version of "samizdat" (from magnitofon – tape-recorder). Authorities certainly intervened. Originally all rock 'n' roll was subversive. Then at a later stage they made a ludicrous and clumsy attempt to ban a long list of performers and records under ludicrous pretexts. Aquarium was there as well as most other interesting groups. I remember Pink Floyd's Final Cut was there because of the "Brezhnev took Afghanistan" line.[29]

Whilst it appeared that Soviet society stagnated culturally, it was official Soviet culture that experienced severe tension. Alternative/counter-culture by the early 1980s was registering a cultural renaissance, and through coded criticism, channelled its creative energy to lambasting the lethargic Soviet system.

From the late 70s – early '80s those rock groups that were not overtly political got the opportunity to play quite freely, including sports complexes and concert halls. At the same time, the more "underground/alternative" bands were reduced to playing in front of small audiences in run down clubs, schools etc (which was actually part of the attraction).[30]

Nonetheless, it only became publicly recognisable 'towards the end of the Brezhnev era when voluntary associations begin to reappear. The late seventies and early eighties witnessed the formation of unofficial clubs among young sports fans, rock music enthusiasts, and others'.[31]

A new generation of filmmakers recognised the importance of the underground and active youth culture. Films such as *The Burglar* (Vzlomshchik, 1987), *Is it Easy to be Young?* (Legko li byt' molodym? 1987) and *The Courier* (Kur'er, 1987) addressed themes such as the alienation felt by disaffected youth. The extreme strategies 'hard rock, punk attire, drugs, me-generation syndrome [and] mystical flights into the world of Hare Krishna' began a cultural flight from the dictates and indoctrination of official culture.[32]

It is difficult to locate youth culture in the former Soviet Union in a neat category. Youth culture was institutionalised by Komsomol. This may not have meant very much to most of its members but the involvement in the official culture, however tentatively is recognised. Informal groups certainly operated within it and formulated relationships that were either unofficial or semi-official. Kan suggests that during the 1970s and 1980s the age group making and listening to rock music were generally in the twenties and thirties. Younger people were certainly aware of it, but it must be recognised that the age difference of even a few months, produced strikingly different views of both the Soviet Union and the world.

The separation of official and unofficial codes of conduct is problematical in the sense that institutionalised and official youth movements such as Komsomol contained informal networks that circulated and listened to rock music.

> In being a Komsomol member meant in 1970s-1980s that you had to pay a minimal membership fee, participate in semi-annual general meetings – and, in most cases, that was all. Even so-called activists hadn't a lot of Komsomol work. So there is no contradiction and no need to emphasise it. When I was a student in the early 1980s, our institute had its own "Dom Kul'tury" (House of Culture), controlled by Komsomol and Komsomol ruled Students' Union. Nevertheless, there were some almost underground rock concerts, including Mashina Vremeni and even punks like Grazhdanskaya Oborona. It was impossible to organise these concerts bypassing Komsomol leadership of the institute. And I'm sure they knew everything – but either they were secret admirers of the bands, or, more likely, they just didn't care. Komsomol of the rock generation was an old rusty corrupted machine, hardly able to do anything, so Western influences targeted equally both Komsomol members and a small number of non-members. Taking this into account you realise that most informal young people were formal Komsomol members (of course, there were some people refusing to join Komsomol for one reason or other, religion was the most common, but their number was small).[33]

The emphasis on lyrical style parodying the banality of the system and its ideological legitimisation continued a form of dissent that had its emotional residue in the poetic works of the Russian creative intelligentsia.

> You can trace with many of the better Russian rock lyricists, through the previous generation of dissenting singer-songwriters (Vysotski, Galich, Okudzhava) to Kharms, Akhmatova, Mandelstam, Yesenin, Mayakovsky, all the way to Pushkin, Lermontov or Dostoevsky, Saltykov-Shchedrin or whatever.[34]

In the early 1980s, when it was widely assumed that dissident activity in the former Soviet Union had been largely silenced or eradicated, unofficial Soviet rock bands, performing in relative secrecy from the authorities, paradoxically on occasion in Komsomol buildings, ridiculed the system and encouraged dissent from it. The existence of this social action exposes a failure in Soviet studies to recognise and identify indigenous forms of social dissent and the method of their coded expression.

The response of the authorities to criticism would be predictably hostile but it appears that in relation to Soviet unofficial rock the authorities were uncertain of its revolutionary potential. In its dealings with unofficial Soviet rock, the regime miscalculated its popularity amongst Soviet 'youth'.

It clearly failed to censure, for example, brilliant bard singer Alexander Bashlachev's song called "Black Holes":

We were building a temple but we've built a WC:
An error in the project, but we were so sure…

and later in the same song:
They're good guys on the wrong way,
No reason to go if you're just thinking of falling down.
I'm certain I will never be able to find
What I'm looking for, what is so easy to steal.

Since my early years I couldn't toe the line,
When I look at the flag, the sun makes me blind,
I'm reaching for open hands [to shake]
Meeting their fists over and over again…

The band Kino, extremely popular in the last pre-perestroika years, and their hit "Local Train":

The local train is taking me there, where I don't want to go.
It's cold but it's somehow warm.
The fresh air is filled with cigarette smoke.
Why do I keep quiet?
Why don't I shout, keeping quiet?
The local train is taking me there, where I don't want to go.

Another song, "For Me and You", also by Kino:

The stones are looking like soap here
And gold resembles copper
And I didn't like everything that was here,
And I don't like what is here either.

Sometimes allusions to coded criticism were by their nature less straightforward. For example in his early song, "A piece of life", Boris Grebenschikov ("Aquarium") sings:

> I came to the concert
> Not to get bored
> Let play who must play
> And knock who must knock

The Russian word 'stuchat' has different meanings: 1) to knock, like knock at a door, 2) to beat, like drums, 3) to squeal, to inform. Rock concerts were prohibited, and often concerts were stopped by the police, informed by neighbours or agents. So the actual meaning of the text was: 'let's have fun, even if someone will tell the police'.[35]

The importance of unofficial Soviet rock was recognised by the emerging left. Rock affected the social atmosphere and generated interest in a range of cultural forms.

> 'Change!' our hearts demand.
> 'Change!' our eyes demand.
> 'Change!' We want change!

So sing the 'Kino' group, and such songs are encouraged under the conditions of Gorbachev's perestroika. But the crux of the matter is that many young rock groups, including some in the provinces, had begun to sing about freedom and renewal even before Gorbachev had come to power. Their initiative was not a response to any appeal from above. Independently of the leadership, a new cultural milieu began to be formed already in the first part of the eighties. A group of young admirers of Marx gathered around a rock ensemble – that would have been hard to imagine ten years ago. This actual case illustrates very well the processors that have taken place. As in the West in the sixties, interest has increased sharply in both Marxism and utopian socialism. Some are interested in Kropotkin others in Narodnik ideas about a free commune, others still in the theory of alienation.[36]

The point raised by Kagarlitsky concerning the connection between rock music and Marxism is not however shared by prominent figures in former unofficial Soviet rock circles.

Only in Boris Kagarlitsky's mind as far as I'm concerned. If there was a certain interest – which frankly speaking I do not recall – it had nothing to do with the rock movement. Most of the rock musicians/audiences were not concerned with political/philosophical ideologies at all. You could trace some influences of left radicalism (Markuse, Reich) or occult mysticism (Kastaneda), anarchism. Hippy idealism was still quite strong in the early 80s. But most of it would be acquired sort of second hand through Western rock music anyway.[37]

The appearance of punk rock in the Soviet Union and Eastern Europe, made explicit the depth of opposition to the communist regime and life within the socialist bloc, particularly amongst young people. It did not, however, introduce a unique alternative view, but added to the circulation of protest embedded in everyday life. The first original punk banks appeared in the late 1980s, and viciously attacked the system that had curtailed their freedoms.

The punk lifestyle was very important and influencing. First of all, punks were more into politics than anyone else. Also, it was the way of saying "no" to the establishment. The music itself was far less known. So, punk (and, later heavy metal rock) was very popular. Everyone has heard about the Sex Pistols (at least, the name of the band, that was a big deal itself, because the word "sex" was not of everyday use: that was the age of purism). The only other punk band to be relatively famous in Russia was The Stooges. Other acts like The Ramones, The Clash, MC5 and the New York Dolls were known only by dedicated music fans.

There were a lot of so-called "punks" in the last Communism years, but they were carbon copies from the Sex Pistols, so it was not impressive. On the verge of perestroika several pure Russian punk bands had appeared. The first Russian punks were, I think, Petersburg band "Televizor, with their aggressive social protest. Later the famous Grazhdanskaya Oborona appeared with their rude language and dark pessimistic lyrics. The band has survived until now, and all of their songs are still banned from the radio, and I have never heard of their concerts advertised anywhere. The band's leader, Egor Letov, thinks that protest itself is more important than the target of criticism. Ironically enough, now Grazhdanskaya Oborona hold with those who favour communism...Also I have to mention the Siberian band The Red Octobers who started together with Grazhdanskaya Oborona, but their female singer/songwriter soon became a solo artist. Her lyrics had something from Russian Folk Songs with noticeable influence from blues and punk. Her melodies are simple enough and all the punks think she was punk too. Maybe, but I think she was more than punk, trying to reach new levels of poetry until she committed suicide in 1991. Here is an example of Yanka's lyrics (but any translation loses all her alliterations, all allusions to Russian folk songs, tales of nursery rhymes that are often in her songs):

The false crucifix has been burned on the bridge

It was made of paper, it was yesterday
The leaves are falling like empty bag
And there's a blizzard blowing from different places
The great holiday of barefooted ideas
Sowing bread, yielding rush
The price of sugar in your tea is your life
Then you'll get salt in a foreign land
And long howling is our jolly barking
And grass is burning on the background
My face is nothing more than a pay-list
A signal of alarm: good night
A stubborn guard is looking forward
Not remembering his mean wife
And the primeval forest is ringing his eyes
Look out of your window: you'll see the bridge
Close your eyes: you'll see the cross
Unmask yourself: you will taste the smoke
Remember: it's only cardboard scenery burning...[38]

The lyrics of many of the Soviet rock bands were not explicitly directed at communists and politics. The role was ambiguous: the struggle of youth reawakening spiritual experiences (a re-occurring Russian tradition), the realisation of inner and outer freedoms, and the need to express choice, re-vitalised feelings perceived eradicated in socialist order.

It has been argued that in the absence of a recognised political opposition, counterculture was fundamental in maintaining and developing an alternative view in the former Soviet Union, a view that expressed a belief in a rejection of the monolithic order and imposition of Soviet culture. The pervasive nature of unofficial Soviet rock and its appearance throughout the Soviet Union points to a social momentum that impaired the acceptance and legitimacy of Soviet culture to young people. It can be inferred from the above that unofficial Soviet rock contributed extensively to an alternative view, a condition that undermined and weakened the remnants of a tarnished Soviet ideology.

In the context of the Soviet change process, it is claimed the occurrence of change was not in response to the bureaucratic relations between states. The emphasis appears to be resolutely placed on the cultural tensions occurring within Soviet State, coupled with the global and local social influences, which historically contribute to the shape and development of them. It is to the local and global social factors that the investigation now turns.

Notes

[1] Editorial (1998:5), *Index on Censorship.*

[2] Leonard (1956:286), *The History of Russian Music.*

[3] Lipsitz (1994:137), *Dangerous Crossroads.*

[4] *Op cit* (1956:292,293).

[5] TG Ein discussion board (11 October 2000), www.russiatoday.com.

[6] Middleton (1990:9), *Studying Popular Music.*

[7] Rycheck (1990:106), *Rock around the Bloc.*

[8] Burlatsky (1991), *From the other shore.*

[9] Alexander Kan (1999).

[10] Alexi Kozlov, interviewed for the BBC's *The Peoples' Century.*

[11] Thayer (1960:108), *Russia.*

[12] Coln (1989), *Ball the Wall.*

[13] See Petr Uhl 'The alternative community as revolutionary avant-garde' in Havel's, *Power of the Powerless.*

[14] Anon (1996), *In the Mirror of the 1960s* (The Economist. October 19th. 3-4.)

[15] Macdonald (1995:4), *Revolution in the head.*

[16] Wallerstein (1991), *Geopolitics and Geoculture.*

[17] The National Guard read the riot act before shooting dead the four students. Report included in BBC 2 television documentary, *Decisive Moments*, broadcast on 1 November 1997.

[18] Yoko Ono (1996:12), *The Guardian Newspaper.*

[19] *Op cit* (1990:15), *Studying popular music.*

[20] Wicke (1993:25), *The Cabaret is Dead':Rock culture as state enterprise – the political organisation of Rock in East Germany.*

[21] Sergey Pantsirev (1999) 'Led Zeppilin' Online e-mail: webmaster@seva.ru. (18 April 1999).

[22] Alexander Kan (1999), 'Research' On line e-mail: alex@amkan.demon.co.uk.

[23] Alexander Kan (1997), *Divine Madness.*

[24] Gnedovski (1996), Catalogue notes: *The Andrei Sakharov Museum and Public Center.*

[25] Alexeyeva (1987:269,270), *Soviet Dissent.*

[26] *Ibid* (1987:270), *Soviet Dissent.*

[27] Anon, Protest music in Siberia on-line e-mail (11 October 2000) www.russiatoday.com.

[28] Havel (1986), *The Power of the Powerless.*

[29] *Op cit* (1999), Alex Kan.

[30] Potapych (9 October 2000), www.russiatoday.com.

[31] Bonnell (1989:317), *Moscow: A view from below.*

[32] Lawton (1989:44), *Toward a new openess.*

[33] *Op cit* (1999), Pantsirev.

[34] *Op cit* (1999), Alex Kan.

[35] I am indebted to Sergey Pantsirev for spending the time searching through his tapes in Moscow for examples of coded criticism. There are literally thousands of examples that should occupy numerous researchers for years to come.

[36] Kagarlitsky (1988:332), *The Thinking Reed.*

[37] *Op cit* (1999) Alex Kan.

[38] Translated by Pantsirev (1999).

8   The Intelligentsia

Throughout Russian history, the intelligentsia have been a point of reference, schismatically arranged: the messenger in the tradition of the Greek drama, 'a witness and living testimony to events rather than as an anonymous reporter' who commands respect through his or her efforts to represent the world in its clearest form.[1] In essence, the specific function of the Russian intellectual was to present an accurate depiction of everyday life (although allusions were occasionally made to grand programs, which may be similarly flawed). Its role within the general complex of Soviet social relations, however, was to make clear the nature of the dominant system, its political economy and ideological justification, regardless of the recriminations, its flaws and hypocrisy.

The use of categories to distinguish the Russian intelligentsia between those who used their minds in an altruistic manner to contribute to a form of human well being and responsible citizenship, and those who applied their knowledge purely to gain personally from it is fraught with difficulties. The wider philosophical concerns of the intelligentsia in Russia are a complex topic imbued with history and struggle. Whilst not removed from the concerns of this book, it is a separate journey to be embarked upon.   Despite this, an effort will be made to identify the role of intelligentsia in underpinning the strategies of alternative/counter-culture.

The Russian Condition

The intelligentsia was not autonomous from the lived experience of everyday life – it was fundamentally a part of it. The hunger, isolation and harsh treatment of political prisoners exposed irrelevancies that did not oppose the system. 'The readiness of a thinker to sacrifice his life and freedom for the sake of his convictions gave a deeper meaning to the very profession of the philosopher' – it invariably became an act of political opposition. The dissident Bukovsky is one example of this unusual character. His extensive experience as a political prisoner in Soviet prisons draws attention to the sacrifices made by thousands of the political prisoners who made the personal choice to 'live within the truth'. This was a strategy that has little to do with either wishful thinking or romanticism, however hard the conservative critic imagines it.

Within the Soviet system two broad and general categories of the intellectual activity can be made clear, this is not however intended to be a rigorous separation but an illustration of a social divide familiar in practise. The analysis presented does not include the wide subtleties of Russian thought, which is not inclined to neat location within an unscrambled taxonomy.

During the Soviet era the necessity for pragmatism in the formation and articulation of ideas and beliefs was overwhelming. Two strands of thought, which encapsulate divergence and conflict, separate the communication of ideas throughout Russia.

> Political thought since the mid 19th century and up to now continues to develop among the main division line – Westerners and anti-Westerners. Therefore each philosopher or thinker in the history of Russian political thought would be picked up by one of the camps and used in their argumentation.[2]

In encapsulating a dogmatic and extreme science, the Soviet system arrived at a version of reason that would result in a society that would espouse social justice and communist well being. Its supporters held that collective benefits would be attained through the strict adherent to scientific laws discernible in the natural and social world. To dissent from the rigour of science would be to tempt loose thinking, unsystematic capitulation, and a mystical flight in search of covetous but insubstantial thought. The Soviet ideologues believed that:

> loyalty to the teachings of dialectical and historical materialism was the prerequisite of civil loyalty and professional success. Neither worker nor peasant, scientist nor politician, writer nor artist, could succeed in their respective fields without a specific philosophical preparation, at least an understanding of the ABCs of "dialectical forms of matter's movement".[3]

The cogs in the machine were expected to expel personal idiosyncrasies and commit mind and body to the realisation of the communist project. It would be viewed by the Soviet authorities as the only viable route to rid society of its ethereal demons, bourgeois parasites, and historical chains that shackled the proletariat to the ruling class. Its articulators thought it scientific and therefore inoculated against the vagaries of chance and the handicap of emotion.

In the attempt to neutralise culture and class divisions both materially and psychologically, the Soviet vanguard embarked on a project to construct a homogenous culture, which could be manipulated and directed towards specific goals.   Where necessary, pervasive coercion would be applied to remove counter-revolutionary forces that opposed Soviet culture. The early and extensive introduction and availability of education to the masses resulted in a *social lift*, which may primarily be related to the general improvement of literacy.

This improvement appears to have won converts to the communist project that would otherwise have been disabled by illiteracy and poverty. The improvement of education throughout society *civilised* areas that had been ruled by superstition and ignorance.   In urban centres, the effort in the early stages to construct a Soviet culture resulted in an atmosphere of social betterment.

> I always laughed at the Russian longing to be perceived as members of an "intelligentsia class", as opposed to workers, farmers or "meshcanes". While "intelligent" means "intellectual" to whom 1 would assign artists, writers etc., absolutely everyone in my days claimed they were intelligentsia – military, construction workers, nurses, and few street-sweepers.[4]

Regardless of material redistribution, the cultural differences and social experiences that continued to divide social relations could not easily be expunged from the collective consciousness, Rather than identities being reconstructed from a clean sheet as it were, the residue of experience could not be eradicated.   Nonetheless, roles were adopted and adhered to a rigid script to meet the pragmatic necessities of the turbulent and often cruel social conditions.

> By the way Platonov worked as a street-sweeper for a while according to legend. And in Russia "intelligentsia" does not necessarily mean occupation, it is rather a state of mind, remember Polesov – "slesar" – intelligent"? All this division by classes is very conditional.[5]

The intellectual, in the specific Soviet context, is not exclusively the scholar, the academician, the technician and the rhetorical ideologue.   It is the constructive social *critic* who, recognising his or her position in the social structure: be it a labourer, professor, or the unofficial Soviet rock musician, communicates, often through *coded criticisms*, the abuse of powers initiated by the organising authority.   It is a moral reference point;

guidance from passivity. The act of defiance is initiated through personal choice; it leads without explicitly being led.

Whilst it is widely recognised that 'students, academics, and professionals [were] in the vanguard of the struggle for freedom in the satellites',[6] the coded activities prevalent through the wider Soviet population necessitated the need for intellectual cunning and disguised acts of cultural terrorism. In response to the system's systematic punishment of the perceived political and cultural impropriety, the method through which ideas were communicated became increasingly sophisticated. The high poetry found in unofficial Soviet rock lyrics being one obvious example. In response to the widening activity of non-compliance the regime intensified its methods of censorship and punishment:

> Books and magazines viewed as no longer politically correct were removed from libraries. Scientists, artists, poets, and others, including others who did not think themselves as dissidents but whose work appeared critical of Soviet life, were systematically persecuted and even prosecuted. Often they were declared enemies of the state and imprisoned, or they would be diagnosed insane and committed to punitive mental hospitals.[7]

The regime failed in its efforts to halt the widespread disillusionment found at all levels of Soviet life. The repulsion towards censorship itself, which had reintroduced a form of cultural apartheid, undermined the intent of the revolution to sweep such impositions and power differentials aside.

The Intelligentsia and the Intelligent

The perception of a figure belonging to the *intelligentsia* during the Soviet era is generally referred to as someone who was clever or highly educated, or had a specific view of the world. With varying degrees of clarity, tolerance and sophistication, the objective would be to reflect on the nation's struggles and experiences.

In response to the prevailing atmosphere of the *acting* communist culture, the *intelligent* would however be recognised through the studious accumulation and communication of practical knowledge that would assist in the transition from a socialist to pure communist society. The desire to engage in controversial issues or comment on them would be avoided unless it was politically astute to do so.

It has been set out that indoctrination in the young pioneers would be undertaken to ground the impressionistic minds towards correct thinking and attitude. In the Komsomol youth movement, the character would be nurtured and strengthened through a range of physical activities and political education.

Access to the Party was necessary in the search and procurement of a place at a good university. An acceptable student would be expected to be at all times diligent, courteous, loyal, compliant, and dignified. The attainment of a certificate would signify two fundamental attributes. The student understood and unquestionably accepted the philosophy of the Party. He or she recognised that the accumulation of knowledge for uses other than in its practical and positive use in the service of the Soviet system was irrelevant and meddling with it could be an admission of counter-revolutionary activity.

The committees, official leisure and work groups, were part of the policy to bureaucratise the social activities of everyday life. A strong mind that raised questions regarding the nature of the pervasive social organisation could be identified and singled out for attention. Where one stood on issue of the free association or denial of ideas could lead to promotion or paralysis.

There was a world of difference between a comrade labelled or using the title of an *intelligent* and the *intellectualle*. The distinction is one of attitude, of world outlook and of morals. The work of Lev Shestov, Vasily Rozanov and Nikolia Berdiaev influenced the cream of the intelligentsia in these matters. 'These books were mainly studied in the capitals and influenced quite a few in these circles'.[8] The intelligentsia are generally caring people, people who abhor violence, people who respect the truth, who want knowledge but only so that it can be imparted to others. In this context, the *intellectualle* consistently doubts his or her ability. He or she can laugh at the efforts produced.[9] The *intellectualle* therefore has the ability to be both indispensable and redundant, prioritising creativity over strategy and policy.

Conversely, the *intelligent* seeks to profit from the experience of an elevated position and manipulates the responsibility bestowed on it in the service of the system to reap opportunities and siphon off value in whatever form it is presented. The world-view of the *intelligent* generally reflected a serious persona, secretive and compliant with authority, and allegedly embroiled in a plethora of narcissistic political projects and programs, which seek in part to modify the method of the control without changing the nature of it.

In the West, the names of Alexander Solzhenitsyn and Andrei Sakharov represented a form of intellectual criticism that opposed the vulgarism of the Soviet State. Solozhenitsyn's famous novels with the implicit call for the Christian regeneration of the Soviet State attracted wide interest in the Soviet Union and the United States. Sakharov's work on the thermonuclear bomb in 1948 preceded his public association with the human rights movement and correspondingly contributed to safeguarding the academician from extensive psychological and physical punishment.

Following the publication of a number of essays, of which *Progress, Coexistence and Intellectual Freedom*, written in June 1968, was a part, the authorities directed official recrimination against the academician, encouraging a display of bile from the Soviet people. To intimidate Sakharov, the KGB in the 1970s widened the pressure to his colleagues and friends. 'In the early 1980s, after Soviet troops had entered Afghanistan and on the eve of the Moscow Olympics, the repression against dissidents intensified. In January, the authorities decided to get rid of Sakarov as well'.[10] Sakharov was exiled to Nizhniy Novgorod and remained there until being released from exile in December 1986. In a media staged act, the release of Sakharov was intended to enhance the international reputation of the reformats within the Kremlin, and avoid the potential conflagration both within the Soviet Union and world outside were the sick physicist to die in Gorky.

Sakharov, Solzhenitsyn and perhaps Medvedev brothers, Zhores and Roy, were internationally known figures representing different points of view but sharing an opposition to the intransigence of the Soviet regime. Voluminous material has been collated concerning their actions. It should not be forgotten however that a multitude of political prisoners and intimidated citizens, whose names either appeared in the print of the authority's penal records or the memories of friends and comrades, were equally vehement and active against the regime.

Human Rights, Human Wrongs

The cultural repression that accompanied the Tsarist regime had been expected to dissipate with the end of Romonov rule. The identification, surveillance and repression of behaviour not in line with the ruling autocracy had been brutally dealt with. Lenin had had experience of its methods. Despite the emancipation of the serfs by Alexander II in 1861, the peasants were tied to the land and remained financially servile, tied to the service of the landlord. In the city factories, the bourgeoisie fed well on the brawn of working class.

In the aftermath of the revolution, the cultural segregation was not successfully overcome. The Party vanguard of the professional revolutionaries, who according to Lenin were required only in the struggle to end Tsarist rule, continued after the massacre of the Romonov family at Ekaterinburg by the Cheka execution squad, to solidify and extend its power. The special police received a new title but continued in secrecy to purge all residue of opposition. At the end of the civil war the proletariat owned everything and nothing. Freedom of movement within the Soviet Union and between States in the international arena was strictly curtailed to limit movement both in and out of the region.

The terror of Stalin's reign silenced the concern with fundamental human rights but it did not eradicate them.

> The Communist interpretation of human rights is based on economic materialism and the treatment of individuals as mere units of mass production. In return for work and bread, coupled with economic and social benefits such as "full employment" and public services for health and education, the Soviet Russian government demand[ed] from all members of its society a total and unquestioning obedience. It [was] justified on the grounds that the Communist Party was the creator and guardian of the beneficent new order, and that its permanent and infallible monopoly of power serves the highest common interest. There [was] no need, nor room for bourgeois notions of personal liberty, which have now become obsolete and irrelevant.[11]

The abuses that stemmed from the Party's monopoly of power were orchestrated through its use of force. The subsequent personalisation of the most negative aspects of control by Stalin resulted in what is repeatedly referred to as a claustrophobic asylum, which denigrated personal decency and sociability. The move away from rigid totalitarianism to a deeply controlled social society that regulated personal activity led to demands for greater autonomy and personal choice.

> Despite the Thaw, no human rights movement developed in the USSR until 1965. Any protests by individuals or small groups were quickly repressed by the authorities...The catalyst for the creation of the Soviet human rights movement was the trial of Sinyavsky and Daniel (1965). On December 5. 1965 Constitution Day, the demonstrators unfurled banners reading "Respect the Soviet Constitution!" and "We Demand Glasnost [Openness] in the trial of Sinyavsky and Daniel!". They were immediately arrested. This was the first public human rights demonstration in the Soviet Union.[12]

The demonstration in Pushkin Square correlated with the circulation of dissident activity through song and poetry. It had been further politicised with the contributions made by the creative intelligentsia and political prisoners translating experience of intimidation and abuse through music and prose.

The attack on Joseph Brodsky is one example amongst many. Brodsky was convicted as a "social parasite" in 1964. The testimony from his trial, leaked to the western media, propelled him from a little known twenty-three-year-old poet to an individual's rights against the state. An extract reads:

Judge: Who recognised you as a poet? Who enrolled you in the ranks of poets?

Brodsky: No one. And who enrolled me in the ranks of humanity?

Judge: Did you study this?

Brodsky: This?

Judge: To become a poet. You did not finish school where they prepare, where they teach?

Brodsky: I didn't think you could get this from school.

Judge: How then?

Brodsky: I think that it...comes from God.

Following his trial, Brodsky's poems began appearing in the West. Within the next few years, translations of Brodsky's poems appeared in English, German, French, Hebrew, Polish and Czech. Foreign visitors beat a path to Brodsky's door. The KGB took notice. In the May of 1972 during a visit from Carl Proffer, University of Michigan, Professor and small publishing house, a message came for Brodsky to report to the Ministry of Visas and Immigration. An ultimatum was presented leaving Brodsky no choice. He had to leave the country of his birth and language. Proffer helped to arrange a position at the University of Michigan; Brodsky accepted. The Soviet authorities assumed that once Broadsky left the country he would become only one more émigré among many; his importance would accordingly diminish. This could not have been further from the truth. In fact, rare for a poet, Brodsky gained celebrity status with his dry humour, his openness for the media, and his prolific writings.[13]

The fear of immediate retribution from the authorities had relaxed slightly and throughout Moscow, and in particular near Pushkin Square and the Arbat, poets gave impromptu readings that conveyed the intensity of a radicalised alternative view. The Conservative faction within the Kremlin reasserted its authority with a direct attack on all political opposition and repealed the optimism that had accompanied the cultural thaw.

The arrests and trial of dissidents between 1966-68 led to the creation of an organised human rights circle. It quickly widened and produced activists that would challenge the system.

> The "selection process" was not primarily based on sympathy towards liberal ideals (such sympathies were, at least in Moscow, too widespread), but on the readiness to openly stand up for such ideas in the face of attempts from above to restore Stalinism. The first round of the selection process consisted in letter writing campaigns. Under Soviet conditions such participation was a serious test of one's civic-mindedness.[14]

The Soviet invasion of Czechoslovakia clearly signalled the end of the thaw period and a return to neo-Stalinist rule, which shifted the method of terror from direct physical eradication to psychological torture and extensive incarceration. The struggle for human rights continued but on an atomised scale, with political activists such as Vladimir Bukovsky, exposing the continued abuses of the regime.

The physicist Yuri Orlov, Corresponding Member of the Armenian Academy of Sciences, created the Moscow Helsinki Group in May 1976.[15]

> The MHG's activities served as an impetus for the creation of a broad Helsinki movement. The MHG collected, checked, and dissimulated information about Soviet violations of the humanitarian articles of the Concluding Act of the Conference on Security and Co-operation in Europe, signed in the summer of 1975 by 35 states, included the Soviet Union [who cynically used the conference to improve their access to economic credits and technology transfer without intending to grant human rights] and the United States. The information they gathered was then included in documents addressed to the government of the USSR and other participant states, as well as the international community.[16]

Part of the Russian intelligentsia: technical, creative and moral had been fundamental in the foundation of the human rights movement in the former Soviet Union and despite the repeated intimidation vented by the Soviet authorities it continued to work towards the identification and recording of the human rights abuses. The accusation that in the post-Soviet condition the intellectuals are simply attempting to make a name for themselves as key players in the Soviet change process fundamentally misunderstands their specific function, concerns and method. They were crucial to the change process not autonomous from it.

The Role of Education

In the Soviet Union, the opportunities, particularly in the natural sciences, were available to the most well connected students. The education syllabus served the perceived requirements of the State. Behaviour that did not conform to the rigor of a one-dimensional culture was isolated and *corrected.* No line of study could be undertaken without Marxist-Leninist indoctrination, which was compulsorily taught in educational institutions and the workplace. Philosophy was fundamentally a part of social life, not an abstract occupation seeking to make sense of it.

Political education was not intended to inform. It was structured to facilitate instruction and expunge 'loose thinking', which could be fused with deviant ideas and contaminate either Soviet ideology or its material. On these grounds:

> philosophy was the most dangerous occupation in Russia, and the majority of first-rate thinkers, such as Berdyaev, Shestov, Florensky, Bakhtin, Losev, were persecuted, exterminated, or silenced (exile, death sentence, prison camp, ban on publications etc.) This persecution testified, as never before in history, to the vitality and validity of philosophical thought for the cause of spiritual liberation.[17]

Despite the extensive concerns of the authorities towards intellectual activity of all kinds, the education in non-political activities was of a consistently high standard, and institutions initially had resources to produce strong graduates.

> Generally, education was very good. At the Gymnasium there would be some political teaching but no one believed it. It was obviously too dangerous to object and I am not aware of anyone who actually did, certainly not in public. The authorities censored Polish history and traditions. Whatever lines the authorities expressed people believed the opposite. It was all constructed around pretence, they knew it and we knew it. My saddest reflection on the period is the waste of talent that suffered at the hands of the communists.[18]

Likewise, in Romania:

> Education in Romania was very good. People had a lot of choice about what education they wanted to pursue. Political education was particularly bad. Students had to go and listen to a talk by a Party member. Students pretended that they believed what they were being told. It was obvious they didn't, most of them used the time to go to sleep. The students were aware that many of the teachers didn't believe it either, and went through the motions so as to keep out of trouble. If, however, anyone rebelled they were quickly removed from the sessions and dealt with. No one failed political lessons. If any had, the teachers would get into trouble and they could lose their jobs. In was thought that good communists should believe in communism and as such should be able to communicate it. No one believed it, but you had to pretend to believe it.[19]

It has been made clear that deviance from the Party line was not tolerated. An innocuous comment made and overhead and taken out of context could result in a prison term for its originator. Milan Kundera, in the novel, *The Joke*, conveys the risks associated with deviance from social realism, however banal. When the central character of the story writes a joke on the back of a postcard it leads to an investigation by the authorities and a prolonged and painfully absurd intimidation of the perpetrator.

On the rare occasion that disagreements were raised in public in objection to an official policy or the regime was critiqued in any way, it was deemed part of a wider conspiracy to subvert the entire Soviet system.

> According to party dogma, a man is incapable of arriving at certain thoughts on his own, just like that. There has to be someone's 'influence', either that of bourgeois propaganda (discover how it got through!) or some anti-Soviet individual (uncover him and bring him in for observation!). In the last resort, the investigation is obliged to confirm that not enough educational work has been done with citizen N. This is very bad, and means that one of his party colleagues at work or in the faculty will be reprimanded. But they prefer not to take the matter that far and urge him: 'Come on now think. Who was it that influenced you? Who?'[20]

If a satisfactory admission could not be obtained, and even if it was, the accused, whether guilty or not, if holding a position of authority such as a doctor, surgeon, teacher and so on, could be relieved of his or her duties and forced to engage in menial work. Members of the technical intelligentsia were repeatedly harassed. To limit communications between colleagues and departments technical staff were organised in small groups and monitored by a supervisor known to the authorities. If suspicions were raised against a member of staff the authorities would investigate and the enquiry could last until evidence was collated, which could drag out for years, or, in some dubious manner, the concern was removed, without the suspicion being annulled. This seemingly widespread paranoia deepened the absurdities found in the system, and severely stifled an atmosphere that had been conducive to technical innovation and creativity flowering elsewhere in the world.

Whilst the effect of censorship inspired the opposition to sharpen its creative talents the outlet for its public performance beyond self-published material and 'artistic shows' was limited. It appears that many working in the various arts would have attained international status had it not been for the limitations placed on the exhibition and performance of their work. Csaba Kozak, director of the Mucsarnok gallery in Budapest, puts the work of the late artist Geza Samu in this category, an artist of stunning originality, which, during his lifetime, transgressed boundaries if not borders.

Access to the outside world was extremely difficult. The repercussions following an attempt to leave the Soviet Union without official acknowledgement were serious. If a relative or a close friend of a citizen remaining in former Soviet Union had left the Soviet sphere of influence without permission and the necessary papers, family members or associates remaining in the communist world would be intimidated. If young members were related to the exile and had remained behind they would invariably be denied places in the University system, and would lose security in regards to health and welfare. The careers of those with close connections to exiles could also be halted or terminated. The authorities would claim that because one member of a family had left the Soviet Union or Eastern bloc, the association with the West had infected him or her with bourgeois ideology and tastes. Therefore associates would be vulnerable to subservient ideas and likely to commit similar acts of treachery, an identifiable danger requiring official intervention and surveillance.

Despite efforts to limit contact with the west, 'foreign' cultural forms impacted on Soviet society and complimented the change process.

> ...it now emerges that Soviet paranoia took a fascinating turn in the 1960s. According to Dr Yury Pelyoshonok, a Canadian doctor of Soviet Studies who grew up in the Soviet Union, the soviet authorities thought that the Beatles were a secret weapon of the cold war because "the kids lost their interest in all Soviet unshakeable dogmas and ideals and stopped thinking of English-speaking persons as the enemy".[21]

It has been inferred that literature provided a device through which the cultural intelligentsia could reject and subtly convey the inherent contradictions of the Soviet regime. One of the most popular works that inspired critical reflection on the system through the satire of its flaws was Mikhail Bulgakov's, *The Master and Margarita*, written in 1938 though not published until 1966/67 in the literary magazine *Moskva*. Bulgakov's novel occupies a unique niche in Soviet Culture. In the book, the devil and his bizarre assistants visit Moscow and cause mayhem, largely at the expense of the incompetence and hypocrisy endemic in the Soviet system. The book exists prominently in three cultural domains. It was 'part of the official literary process, hence it was subject to literary criticism, and attempts were belatedly made to institutionalise Bulgakov as a Soviet classic; it struck a powerful chord with the intelligentsia subculture; and it was eventually taken up by popular culture'.[22]   A subject of the Russian literary commission, Bulgakov's masterpiece weaves together a range of satirical stories that reveals the incompetence, corruption and stupidity associated with censorship and ideological indoctrination inherent in Soviet totalitarianism. 'Bulgakov's target in these virulent satirical passages is easy to define, as is the reason for the writer's final and mystico-philosophical auto-apotheosis'.[23] It is, however, its reading of coded criticism and of conscience, in the presence of re-occurring cowardice, to overcome the hypocrisy and face the uncertainty of fear, which is the most destructive element to the longevity of totalitarian regimes and despotic tyrants from whatever source they emerge.

The Master and Margarita, along with other works from the wide artistic field, notably Solzhenitsyn, Pasternak, Sinyavski, Galich, Korzhavin, were responsible in keeping alive incarcerated cultural flames that had been utilised in the construction and presence of an alternative view. The efforts of the above, along with unofficial Soviet rock musicians, and the long chronology of dissident Russian poets, arguably inspired much of the creativity that intuitively opposed the regime and its effort to reform.

It must be remembered that the particular cultural forms overlap. There is no neat cultural representation that adheres to the ABC of culture. For example:

In talking about Golovin's songs one has to mention his "The Live of Remarkable People" cycle. A special brand of "black humour is employed as the ideology of the "ZhZL" (Golovin borrowed the name of a book series – the Russian acronym for the series is "ZhZL" – published by the Molodaya

Gvardiya publishers). Aesthetically and ideologically the cycle is akin to the irony-orientated New Wave, to the ironic ideology of contemporary rock.[24]

Romantic Politics?

The argument made by Paul Hirst that 'the Soviet Union collapsed for reasons that had little to do with opposition in Eastern Europe or with the growing dissidence in the Soviet Union'[25] radically understates the role of alternative culture and the nature of philosophy in a specific Russian context. Hirst argues that 'Soviet power ... ebbed for straightforwardly economic and political reasons in both the USSR and Eastern Europe'[26] and that 'the West "won" the cold war, but only because the Soviet leadership possessed the rationality to give way'.[27] This view fundamentally misunderstands the nature of the Soviet change process.

It is stipulated in this investigation that the social pressures which emanated from alternative/counter-culture, sprang, in part unconsciously, from the prolonged contract and experience with the lies that prevailed throughout the Soviet Union and the intuitive need to reject them. In this context, Havel's existential strategy of living within the truth is not simply a condition 'that repeats a classical theme of Enlightenment thought – the opposition of absolute power and truth located in the free conscience of the citizen, a personal refusal based on living in the truth'.[28] It is, on the contrary, aligned with the counter-Enlightenment liberalism of Isaiah Berlin – the recognition, and rejection, of the Enlightenment aspiration to organise society rationally in accordance with a universal conception of truth, a process that 'seriously threatens the liberal commitment to the freedom of individuals to pursue their own ends and values'.[29]

In the Soviet State:

> philosophy, more than anywhere else in history became a supreme legal and political institution, acquiring the power of a superpersonal, universal reason, which in unrestricted dominion was equivalent to madness – since, being a State philosophy, it ruthlessly victimised individual thinkers.[30]

In response to the claustrophobia and pervasive repression of the Soviet State, the personal choice and contingency of living within the truth was not an illusion inspired by the intoxication of romanticism – 'an imaginary alternative',[31] but a practical and extremely alluring act of opposition.

One method through which opposition intuitively arrived was circulated through the popular unofficial rock music network. In Czechoslovakia:

the security police took drastic measure to repress this new form of musical dissent. The worst use of force took place in March 1977 near Ceske Budejovice, when troops and police with dogs invaded a concert in which the Plastic People group was taking part. About 200 people were arrested and several of them were given prison sentences, but the musical 'maquis' continued its work. In March 1976 the police made over a hundred raids and numerous arrests of political performers and their supporters. Some of them were sent to prison for up to eighteen months on charges of 'disturbing the peace'.[32]

Havel appears to be one of few philosophers to care about such matters. 'Havel envisions that deliberative democracy brings the experience of dissent against totality into professional politics'.[33] With the appearance of Charter 77, and the spiritual and intellectual climate surrounding its appearance 'created by the trial of some young rock musicians associated with a rock group called "The Plastic People of the Universe"', an important band influenced by Western acts such as Lou Reed and the Velvet Underground, an atmosphere took hold that celebrated the coolness of non-conformist activities amongst young people. Suddenly, the public receptivity for an open debate concerning freedom and its abuse was advanced on a range of fronts. The Charter of the Czechoslovak civil rights movement, led to an animated response from the creative intelligentsia that materialised in both essays and performance. It would be suppressed but the ideas that were associated with it would gradually materialise throughout society and maintain the momentum that had accumulated in the aspiration for human liberty.

The spiritual content of Soviet rock cannot be understood without reference to schizoid culture – it forms a crucial link with criticism of the prevailing Soviet system – a social development that occurred in the 1960s.

From its very outset, schizoid was an attempt to break the bounds of common sense. In a narrow sense, schizoidism is an anti-thesis to the conventional. In the avant-garde, the quest for the unconventional is an absolute pre-condition. Paradox, misplaced proportions and outrage are program methods of artistic liberalism. Obviously, the avant-gardist sees himself as a David confronting the Goliath of the routine. Common-sense is to him the hallmark of conservatism, dogmatism and stagnation. To a schizoid, the conventional mind is a product of censorship. But the schizoid imparts a clear-cut metaphysical accent to the notion of censorship. Censorship walls the individual from reality by fostering a conventional mind – a fortress with walls and towers of salutary lies, protective hypnosis, all manor of mental clichés, run-of-the-mill wisdoms, spiritual idols and mental taboos without which a normal person would be unable to exist.[34]

In other areas of political thought, influences from the West continued to impregnate the region. Philosophical ideas from France in particular were available in the former Soviet Union through a nexus of subtle unofficial networks.

As far as I can see, Russian philosophy was less popular in Russia than the Western one – books by Nietzsche, Schopenhauer, or, say, French existentialists were far more known and demanded. But, of course, Russian philosophers were influential too: Shestov and Berdyaev more than Rozanov and Tolstoy, I suppose. The important thing is that Russian philosophy is inseparable of Orthodox Christianity – or denying orthodox Christianity, which is the same. But in the beginning of the reforms, the Russian Orthodox Church wasn't so popular, so I think people were missing an important part of Russian philosophers' ideas. It's funny, but now we have quite an opposite situation: the church is fashionable – namely fashionable – but nobody seems to be interested in philosophy any more...I think the main influence of Russian philosophers on alternative culture was providing an alternative viewpoint. We had to learn that there is always more than one viewpoint. It was unusual at first. But the ideas themselves weren't very influential, I think.[35]

The construction of an alternative viewpoint and the popularisation of it, beyond a narrow intellectual circle, was arguably facilitated by the efforts of unofficial Soviet rock musicians and the audiences who intuitively experienced the inherent flaw in Soviet ideology: its failure to represent the spiritual needs of the citizen. Whilst unofficial Soviet rock may be less recognisably intellectual than the 'products' of the intelligentsia, at least superficially, it served a similar end, to reflect life as it is and not as it ought to be.

Notes

[1] Keane (1996), foot-note in *"The Message"*, Volcano Theatre Group.
[2] Alexander Kan (1999), 'Philosophical Residue' (29 May 1999).
[3] Mikhail Epstein (1995), *http://www.an overview of Russian Philosophy.*
[4] P. Vanych, (1999) Russian Today Discussion. On-line (May 4 1999).
[5] Eccly (1999), Russia Today Discussion. On-line (May 4 1999).
[6] Coser (1990:183), *The intellectuals and Soviet reform.*
[7] Revelations from the Russian Archive, http://lweb.loc.goc/exhibits/achieves/atte.html.
[8] *Op cit* (1999), Kan.

[9] A.Roxburgh (1997), *Roxburgh's Russia.* BBC Radio (4 August 1997).

[10] The Andrei Sakarov Museum and Public Centre, Moscow. Catalogue notes.

[11] Beamish and Hadley (1979:15), *The Kremlin's Dilemma: The Struggle for Human Rights in Eastern Europe.*

[12] Sakarov. Catalogue notes.

[13] Discussion board (11 October 2000) www.russiatoday.com Press release Hoover Institution Exhibit.

[14] Alexeyeva (1987 [1985]:282), *Soviet Dissent.*

[15] The original members of the Moscow Helsinki Group were Liudmila Alekseiva, Mikhail Bernstam, Elena Bonner, Alexander Ginzburg, Piotr Grigorenko, Alexander Korchak, Vitali Rubin, Anatoli Sharansky, Malva Landa and Anatoli Marchenko.

[16] Sakarov. Catalogue Notes. Also Thomas Oleszczuk (1985: 132,333) makes an important in 'An Analysis of Bias in Samizdat Sources' that 'repression does not reduce the volume of *samizdat* reporting. Either the lost activists are replaced by new ones, or higher levels of activity on the part of other dissidents compensate for the absence'.

[17] *Op cit,* Epstein.

[18] Joanna Eccles (1998), Interviewed (8 February 1998).

[19] A Aszabo (1998) Interviewed (4 April 1998).

[20] Bukovsky (1978:226), *To build a castle.*

[21] 'For Lenin, read Lennon: How the Beatles transformed the cold war', The Guardian Newspaper (November 18 2000).

[22] Lovell (1998:29), *Bulgakov as Soviet culture.*

[23] Stenzl (1991:10), *York Holler's 'The Master and Margarita': A German opera.*

[24] Igor Zaitsev ed (1990:25), *Soviet rock: 25 years in the underground and 5 years of freedom.*

[25] Hirst (1991218), *The State, civil society and the collapse of the Soviet Union.*

[26] *Ibid* (1991:221).

[27] *Ibid* (1991: 228).

[28] *Ibid* (1991: 222).

[29] Garrard (1997:281), *The counter-enlightenment liberalism of Isaiah Berlin.*

[30] *Op.cit,* Epstein.

[31] *Op cit* (1991:225).

[32] *Op cit* (1979:81), *The Kremlin's Dilemma.*

[33] Matustik (1993:x), *Postnational Identity.* The implosion of the former Soviet Union has been followed with a myriad of musical styles in Russia. Hilary Pilkington's extensive research has made clear the development and role of popular music in the post-Soviet environment.

[34] *Op cit* (1990:15), *Soviet rock.*

[35] Pantsirev (28 May 1999).

9   A Weak Utopia

The connections between the Soviet political economy, the presence of counterculture, and the tensions within the Soviet system, which contributed to the prevalent social ambivalence towards all institutions associated with Soviet communism, require elaboration. The material outlined in the proceeding chapters has demonstrated the social flight from the rigid socialist bloc. Clearly, the collapse of communism in Eastern Europe 'damaged the modernist belief that social change could be rationally planned and managed'.[1] It is claimed in this book that social change occurred within the former Soviet Union and led to an institutional collapse.

The theory that the disintegration of Soviet life occurred through pressures originating and manifesting within it is not compliant with the Western stories that celebrate ends of ideological projects. The need to identify the nexus of relations typical of the political, economic and social dynamics is necessary to successfully map and relate the underlying forces, primarily originating in alternative culture through coded criticism, to the Soviet change process. It is therefore crucial to assess the conditions and atmosphere in which change took place.

At an earlier juncture, it was introduced that Soviet rock music was pivotal in explicitly facilitating the shift in the prevalence of pre-political opposition (operational in everyday life) to a force capable of causing political reform. This was not achieved through the organisation of political parties recognisable in Western democracies, but through alliances that developed spontaneously from a range of counter-cultural sites that had continually been present in various forms within the system.

Reform, what Reform?

Despite Russia's on-going national economic problems, Moscow is a dynamic city in the post-Soviet environment. Surprisingly, perhaps, to the 'outsider's gaze' it shares a similar atmosphere to New York or London. Like cosmopolitan cites in Western states, it has its contradictions and puzzles, many of which are fundamentally different from the cities in the

United States and Britain. Nonetheless, the excitement of a dynamic urban space is there.

> Just take any neighbourhood in Moscow, look at it one month and then return the next. You'll be amazed how different it looks. Take-over, swaps, change of business use takes place everyday; every hour...it's very energetic.[2]

Whilst the above could be offered as evidence of market reform, which it obviously is of sorts, the fact remains that it is a minuscule of activity that has little effect on the economy as a whole. It is not a power that can provide immediate support to the pressures directed at large industry. Large Throughout Russia, production continues on quasi- Fordist principles of mass production and scientific management, which is virtually extinct in the West.

On the journey from Moscow's busy airport to the centre of town one passes a multitude of advertising boards offering Coca-Cola, Nestle and Adidas sportswear (a victory for Western marketing?). Intermittently, at the side of the road, numerous traders have erected stalls and sell everything from vegetables, cleaning materials, tools of all kinds to cassettes and videotapes. Along the Tverskaya Ulitsa, opposite the Kremlin are the fashionable and expensive shops, displaying jewellery and furs. These are similar to the upmarket shops in Bond Street or Regent Street in London.

In the Red Square itself, opposite Lenin's Mausoleum, the shopping arcade of GUM (pronounced 'Goom' which stands for 'State Department Store') appears as imposing as any major Parisian store. On the ground floor of the building, the window displays advertise the goods of Christian Dior, Channel and Calvin Klein. Inside, the shops house many of the world's leading fashion labels.

The leap from the shortages in the Soviet era to the abundance of consumer goods and services disguises the economic difficulties that continue to plague Russia. Many of the high-ticket goods had been available in the special shops during the Soviet era. Only high ranking government officials, Party members and the *Nomenklatura* would have been able to gain access to the extras that made Soviet life pleasurable. In the post-Soviet condition the Nomenklatura can be recognised as the top five per cent of Russian society: the new bourgeoisie of the Nomenklatura, made rich by the privatisation of state industry, a range of dubious economic relations, and the hoarding and disposal of assets of the state, particularly in the oil and gas sectors. The stunted transition is close to the claim that the:

> changes that have taken place since then, the collapse of the Soviet Empire, the demise of the Communist Party, and the moves to reform the economy bare all the hallmarks of revolution, without the overthrow of the old elite and their replacement with a new, revolutionary elite.[3]

The paradoxes of contemporary Russian life throw light on the processors that contributed to the decline of the cohesiveness of the Soviet system. The victims who were cheated by the sudden change continue to be the weakest and most vulnerable members of society.

> In the Metro nearest the Kremlin, Okhotniy Ryad (Hunter's Row) one encounters some of the hustlers, the dis-enfranchised and the desperate. One only has to take a brief trip on Moscow's Metro to have a surface impression of the social problems affecting Russia. The tunnels and platforms are lined with elderly citizens, chanting protestations of despair; the disabled, many ex-servicemen injured in Afghanistan and Chechnya subsist by vocal appeals to their fellow Russians by recalling guilt of association and abandonment; the venerable army of migrants and gypsies, from as afar as Moldovia jostle, under the 'protective' guise of the local Mafia, who take a commission of the roubles and dollars handed out by passers-by.[4]

Whilst a strong argument can be constructed to infer the activities of unofficial rock music and its pervasive operation of wider coded dissent damaged the ideology of Soviet communism, the *Nomenklatura* and the Russian Mafia were crucial actors in manipulating the changes in the political and economic spheres. It is worth noting that in the chaos of the Soviet change process that various components of the Russian Mafia were extremely well organised. Recognition of its role is important in making clear which aspect of decline in the system was related to which actor.

A Planned Economy?

It has been stated that during the economic turbulence of the 1970s, Fordist methods of production were revolutionised and led, along with the internationalisation of finance, to a structural change in the world economy. The market-centred reform, which rejected a strategy of national wealth creation and welfare provision founded on the Keynesian model, became accepted business and state practise in the West. In the process, it:

abandoned its steel mills and coal mines and moved into the post-modern age (once it passed over, in Jean Baudrillard's apt aphorism, from metallurgy to semiurgy. Stuck at the metallurgy stage, Soviet communism, as if to cast out its devils, spent its energy on fighting wide trousers, long hair, rock music and any other manifestations of semiurgical initiative).[5]

The structural devastation of Soviet economies went relatively unobserved by Soviet planners and Western analysts. Whilst difficulties were obvious, the reluctance of the Party-State elite to take responsibility for the economic disparities, in favour of mystifying them through reference to falsified statistical reports, disguised the extent of the structural difficulties plaguing the Soviet system. This appears to have misled Soviet analysts in the West.

In the advanced stages of the communist project:

> The giant steel mills (the more gigantic the better) and the grandiose irrigation schemes (the vaster the better) were still accepted [in the West] as the credible index of a well-managed society, on the way to fulfilment of its mission: the satisfaction of the needs of its members.[6]

What was not so apparent, along with the prevalent practise of corruption at all levels in the organisation and operation of the economy, was the increasing sophistication of psychological dissent: the desire to experience an exit from the prevailing reality. The rhetoric of the communist ideology had promised a material nirvana not actual poverty: the experience of shortages and the abandonment of quality in a range of goods and services could not be concealed. The failure of the command economy to meet the demand accelerating within it, and the lack of a viable program to meet and repeal global competitiveness, other than the re-articulated and refashioned rhetoric, hastened disillusion. It gave authority to the discourse of Soviet reformism and broadened the view that urgent change needed to be initiated to halt the decline.

The fundamental structural characteristics of the Soviet economy were its 'extreme qualitative heterogeneity' and deliberately engineered sectional imbalances, stemming primarily from the militarization of production.[7] The intention may originally have been to construct an egalitarian economy, but only the pretence of it prevailed. The 'special shops', although concealed behind the drab veil of respectability, highlight the material disparities and distance between members of the Nomenklatura and ordinary citizens.

In the 80s, the collapse of the economic situation was becoming obvious. It was becoming more and more a divided society. You know that we are equal but some are more equal than the others, that was the reality. The people had become fed up with the lies that justified the situation.[8]

In a contentious piece, written during Gorbachev's ascent to the leadership of the Soviet monolith, John Wilheim in *The Soviet Union has an administrated, not a planned economy*, explored whether it would be more accurate to define the Soviet economy as centrally 'managed' rather than centrally planned. Developing the work of Zaleski, Wilheim examined the anomalies inherent in an 'ever changing process of administrative corrections of "the plan" actually characterising economic activity'.[9] The author concluded that 'the optimal combination of planning, routinised adjustments and *ad hoc* responses in Soviet economic operations went far beyond the capabilities of any plan to control'.[10] For example, the management of a nexus of exchange relations through the mechanism of countertrade, offset and variants of barter that took place between industry and labour had become too complex to regulate effectively from a centralised location. It was so imbued with corruption and incompetence that the theoretical confines of an overarching plan, regardless of its sophistication, was useless in overcoming the logistical demands required to maintain a level of performance expected by the system, and in particular the hierarchy that functioned within it.

The vast network of barter and countertrade exchanges with the socialist bloc and its alliances throughout the world was necessary to sustain industry within the region. The increasingly complex nexus of trade relations between various units within the system became more cumbersome and difficult to effectively manage, with the scarcity and poor nature of resources being an on-going problem.

Informal contracts, corruption and theft proliferated in all sectors of the economy. Plans were regularly amended in both the Soviet Union and in the satellites. Despite the appetite for planning it was found 'to be a relatively weak technique for directing resources towards the highest yield uses',[11] but in regards to the political commitment to it, it was continued in Eastern Europe until it became financially impossible to do so.

Quotas of various kinds were met through a total disregard for quality. The additional costs associated with replacing defective components added to the difficulties of meeting the fundamental aims of the plan. The intention had been to limit waste and build a successful rational economy, but through incompetence and a prevailing resistance to change the objectives had become an anachronism before the implementation of restructuring. The effort required to rescue the system from collapse was greeted with suspicion and cynicism. Soviet indoctrination had successfully instilled a suspicion of change in the consciousness of its most dogmatic members. The solutions introduced by the regime added to the problems. In all areas of Soviet life, the communist system came to be widely perceived as adding to the problem.

The official policy of directing resources toward specific militarily dominated industries and applying rigid scientific principles in the management and organisation of the official sectors of the economy led to the illusion of order and stability.

On the one hand it:

> produced an economy with low rates of registered unemployed and achievement in those sectors of the economy (like the military complex and city Metros) that enjoyed high priority and produced measurable outputs. Major problems arose elsewhere, however, made worse by the concentration of resources on high priority sectors: repressed inflation, hidden unemployment low rates of technical growth, and above, all, low average living standards.[12]

In the military sector, the developments in military hardware and software inflated the costs. New kit required the training of skilled personnel to operate and maintain sophisticated equipment. In this light, the occupation of Eastern Europe by a large number of redundant red army units was increasingly viewed by the reforming fraction of the leadership as a burden that produced limited material and strategic benefits.

Despite some successes in the Soviet economy, it remained a fact that 'as a result of the leadership's single minded concentration on the arms race, the Soviet Union missed the third great technological revolution that [had] taken place in the past quarter century'.[13] The 'developed stagnation', as Elena Zoubkova from the Moscow International Higher Business School put it, was prevalent throughout the former Soviet Union at the end of the Brezhnev era. The difficulties in the domestic economy had begun to effect *all classes of the classless society*. This led to an atmosphere conducive to changing the mechanism by which the system functioned.

Cold War Propaganda and Manipulation

It was believed in the Kremlin that public opinion in the West would support a reduction in nuclear weapons. The reduction in the need for extensive defensive or offensive measures requiring the incorporation of new and expensive technology would allow valuable time to restructure the economy. Despite resistance from the military and conservatives within the Party, restructuring was required to redirect resources to other areas of the economy, which had repeatedly suffered a chronic shortage of investment. The reforms that were envisaged did not signify the fallacy of the Soviet project – on the contrary it was a tactical initiative expected to strengthen the fundamental principles of it.

The investment in the vast military complexes, encompassing secret cities with populations of over one million people, mostly occupied in arms production, had been considered by the Stalinist inspired members of the Communist Party as the foundation of the nation's strength in international affairs. The threat to it, from within the system, was an anathema to the conservative faction which could not easily be understood. The military issue in particular appears to have directly led to a reaction against the discourse of reform.

The difficulty in the re-direction of resources and the prevalence of censorship contributed directly to the stagnation in creativity and innovation, which unbalanced the domestic economy and rendered it virtually impossible to reform in the manner that its exponents desired. Material standards had declined 'with few exceptions, Soviet products [were] at least a generation and often several generations behind the technical and consumer standards of comparable products in other countries'.[14] Students at the various scientific and engineering institutions were not being trained on modern equipment and instructed in modern management techniques to make efficient use of the production process. This stalling on the acquisition of new equipment and training, and the widespread inaccessibility to the methods that underpinned the scientific and technological revolution allowed the 'electronics industry in the industrialised countries [to make] great strides during the past several decades'.[15]

The consequences of not introducing the management and technical principles that were restructuring business practise and industry in the world economy was particularly damaging to the effectiveness of the Soviet Union to compete with and provide products that could be internationally competitive. The Soviet Union's key exports – oil, gas and agricultural production – without investment and upgrading, rapidly lost value in the international markets. Whilst elements of the Nomenklatura attempted to canvass political support to overcome the intransigence in industry, there were comrades of a similar ilk intent on resisting change, perceiving it to be a threat to their authority and privilege.

In the domestic economy, the majority of ordinary people experienced shortages and the poor quality of goods and services but despite evidence to the contrary; it appears that there had been an improvement in the standard of living, although this was not being sustained. It has been shown that the memories of shared accommodation had become exactly that, a memory. The access to education had, despite difficulties with its higher levels, become widely available. The methods for treating a range of medical complaints and physical ailments had developed in sophistication, although the nation's damaging relationship with vodka had not been resolved (despite unpopular Government intervention, which invariably made matters worse).

Luxuries that would have previously been unimaginable to the majority of ordinary people become attainable and those who were less well off were compensated by virtually free provision of gas, electricity and water. In the cities however food shortages repeatedly occurred. But in the country, those with access to close arable land could sustain themselves without extreme difficulty.

> Living in the countryside, life in the countryside was much easier than in the cities. There were shortages in shops, and people were generally dependent on what was in the shops. But never on the scale seen nowadays in the former Soviet Union and in Romania, there was always something in the shops. Later on in the late 70s and 80s, the economies appeared to pick up a little bit. There was more in the shops. The social system, although it was imperfect, was fine. The old people had enough pensions to live on, everything was heavily subsidised and travelling was very cheap. OK, you had to constantly queue for food but it was just a part of your life. You never…you knew nothing else so there was no problem at all.[16]

In the attempt to overcome the shortages throughout the economy the semi-official facility of *blat* and the unofficial informal economy grew extensively throughout the 1970s. In many respects these sub-systems, by releasing tension and overcoming contradictions within the Soviet economy allowed the official economy to function albeit in an dysfunctional form. *Blat* was prevalent in Soviet society from the 1950s but it had functioned in various forms since the institutionalisation of Soviet life. The informal economy, which is present in all societies in varying degrees, was in the extensive throughout the socialist bloc and overlapped with official economic activity. This factor led to the embedded nature of corruption in the system and explained its distinctive variance from the fraud and theft common in modern Western economies.

Blat, as a form of exchange, 'aimed at acquiring desired commodities, arranging jobs and the outcome of decisions, as well as solving all kinds of everyday problems – became a pervasive feature of public life'.[17] It was not illegal, although it could lead to misunderstandings and difficulties with the authorities.

> The phenomenon of *blat* implies both 'explicit rules' and limits that invert them, both institutional restrictions and personal ways of circumventing them. The structural conditions do not only restrict but also enable and organise the practices.[18]

The recourse to *blat* and its insertion parallel to the official economy systematically assisted state planning in that it functioned to beat life into what could otherwise be a static and difficult mechanism, one that required repeated interventions at all levels of its operation. Despite its value in the short term, it concealed the shortcomings of state planning. The flaws in the system were not addressed but became part of the Soviet culture that allowed difficulties of all kinds to be ignored. The reliance on a form of social networking, resulted in, in regards to addressing the embedded structural difficulties, a considered amnesia. The problems that were not met with solutions were duplicated, a condition requiring further trickery in the selection, interpretation and presentation of statistical data. The model, which had been constructed on scientific principles, was abandoned through incompetence, empirical delusions and greed. To the degree that 'practices, in turn, penetrate, transform and thus shape the system'[19] the Soviet economy resembled not a scientifically regulated mechanism, but a comprehensive bazaar disguised only by the non-explicit official recognition of it.

The exponential rise of the black market in the 1960s further distorted the strength of the official economy. Other than the pronouncements in the official press, the state did not attempt to seriously curtail the dynamism and base entrepreneuralism that facilitated the substantial growth of illegal activity. Whilst the rhetoric of the Party admonished association with it, and token arrests were made to limit the incentive to engage with it, it expanded allowing corruption to transgress unofficial and official networks, and include all levels of Soviet life in its operation.

Everyone used the black market to buy luxuries. On special trips to Prague or Budapest (gold rings were obtained in Russia) – with an official in tow – people would buy goods in dollars and sneak the goods back into Poland. It was dangerous but common. If one was caught one could generally bribe the guard.[20]

The authorities attempted to limit the movement of groups visiting families and neighbours in adjacent towns and states, but the operation was difficult to monitor and people made the trip regardless of the dangers. Unless the citizen was a member of the Communist Party and had a good personal record travel was restricted. Despite the difficulties associated with travel, people used the official channels to try to obtain the necessary papers to leave the country. This procedure could take years to process and it was rare that an application would be successful.

Within the communist system, however, some citizens either through family contacts or informal links with officials had more ability to travel throughout the bloc.

From my point of view it was quite an easy life. I was able to travel every month from Czechoslovakia to Germany. East Germany at that time was quite well off. The shops had things that were not available in Czechoslovakia, especially clothes and things, which when as a teenager is all you want. So I would buy all my clothes and things from there. In some ways I was a little bit more privileged. Yes, you could get the basics there. As I've said, if you didn't know anything else it was all right. I had a pen friend, a Russian and we wrote occasionally. I remember his father came to visit the spa town. I certainly had no animosity towards him; I was quite pleased to see him. I think people just took him as a good down to earth Russian, even though he must have been in a good position to be able to travel to Czechoslovakia, to come here on a visit to a spa. You see Russians on the whole are very friendly, very hospitable people. He was very, very generous. We all got a little badge with a picture of Lenin on it. It was very pleasant. At the time, we didn't know that much about Russia. People who went away on holiday went to the resorts. It was reasonably OK to travel there. We were not allowed to travel to the towns and obviously the dissidents of any kind were kept very far away from visiting foreigners.[21]

Romania had tighter controls over its citizens than other East European states. People were regularly stopped and had their papers checked.

Visits by Romanians to other East European states were made in-groups and supervised. You couldn't just get into your car and drive to Budapest say from

Bucharest. When Hungary and East Germany began to let East Germans into the West, travel to those countries was stopped.[22]

Limits to travel could be overcome with bribes. It was a method familiar to the soldiers and the police although they would be careful not to attract attention and would usually only operate alone. The black market could be easily accessed, and it would be relatively well known which figures could supply what.

> Cassettes, Records and later videos were available on the black market – they were all illegal – however it was the authorities who often supplied the illegal goods. Video machines couldn't easily be obtained by official means, but on the black market there was a steady supply. Books were always in demand. Boris Pasternak's *Doctor Zhivago* and George Orwell's *Animal Farm* were particular favourites. Western records and tapes had been in demand earlier, particularly the Beatles. Operating within the black market, ordinary people and officials alike allowed one to make a reasonable living. Even if you got caught, unless there was a particular crack down, which was being monitored, you could usually bribe your way out of trouble.[23]

The influx of Western tourists to Bulgaria and Yugoslavia that increased from the late seventies and early 1980s brought with it wider access to Western clothes, music tapes and watches. Everything was in demand and brisk trade could be observed outside hotels, even on the ski-slopes someone would be doing good business buying jeans or exchanging currency, probably the most dangerous activity.

> Bus drivers who had contact with foreigners were changed daily so that they didn't become too familiar with tourists and those making regular trips between the East European states. There were only so many bus drivers, and they knew all the tricks.[24]

It was accepted that 'any surpluses above their quota that were produced by the collective farms could be sold in collective farm markets (street markets) in the towns. In addition, the workers on collective farms were allowed to own small private plots of land, and they too could sell their produce in the collective farm markets'[25] – goods produced through the activities of 'unofficial jobs' found a ready demand in the active 'underground economy'.

Unofficial exchanges took place throughout the economy distorting the development and application of centralised planning. 'At the level of industrial concerns, managers would exploit connections to obtain goods and services to meet production targets. At the individual level, people would use the same process of exchange and barter for their own personal benefit.'[26] These exchanges would not be recorded and would further undermine the interpretation of already skewed political collation of economic data.

The operation and recourse to the black market made an increasing number rich by Soviet standards. 'The black market boomed, accounting for up to 30% of all services in the late 1980s, with 100,000 or more underground millionaires.'[27] It was increasingly obvious that social disparities were widening. This situation had been allowed to deepen under Brezhnev. Ordinary people had to regularly queue for hours in the harsh winter conditions for low quality goods, whilst apparatchiks passed by in foreign cars on the way to the special shops that stocked the best quality goods and Western products.

The disparities between the material conditions within the former Soviet Union and between the Western developed states became increasingly obvious with the revolution in the various global media. Whilst recession, unemployment, and crime in the West was repeatedly presented to the Soviet people through news bulletins on television, it was shops well stocked with food and the latest fashions which captured the imagination of the ordinary Soviet citizen. The startling increase in mass communications among citizens within a nation and between them and the outside world ha[d] reduced pluralistic ignorance and atomisation. As communist societies became increasingly dependent on mass media of consumption and citizens could no longer be shut off from kinds of news and knowledge from which the regime wished to shield them, the Arendt model no longer applied.[28]

The totalitarian regime had been able through its rhetoric and monopoly of power over all aspects of social and political life to atomise and sap the strength of civil society. The implosion of cultural forms such as unofficial Soviet rock music emerged to undermine the social control and contributed to a form of sociability that made ridiculous the forced and false sense of camaraderie encouraged by the regime. In this context,

> what Hannah Arendt and most of us had failed to realise was that the atomisation model ceased to explain Soviet events once Soviet Citizens could no longer be insulated from contacts with the rest of the world and once individuals found ways of escape from the enforced isolation that had them in its grips during the Stalin years.[29]

The associations that developed from a pregnant civil society added to its increasing confidence to demand change. Aware of the threat to the longevity of the Soviet system, Soviet culture and its ideological surveillance teams attempted to reintroduce the control that had been temporarily relaxed in the desire to facilitate restructuring. From initially seeking to harness civil society in the interests of Soviet change process, Gorbachev recognised its intent to end communist rule, and sought to repair the damage that had resulted from the necessity of reform and the social accidents resulting from it.

Developed Chaos

It is argued in this investigation that the arrival of Mikhail Sergreyevich Gorbachev as the General Secretary of the Communist Party in 1985, and as President of the USSR in 1988 was not the catalyst of change. Gorbachev was merely a facilitator of reform in the political economy of the Soviet region.

> Gorbachev began his tenure as general secretary with what appeared to be a campaign to revitalise the Party, to shake it from "stagnation", and to make it carry through *perestroika* – a vaguely defined process and goal. In some ways his actions were highly traditional. He carried out the largest number turnover of cadres in the Party, state, and military since Stalin's purges of the 1930s.[30]

In the economy, the reforms benefited elements of the industrial Nomenklatura, who recognised the opportunities that could be gleaned from the move towards privatisation, and many well connected entrepreneurs, such as Boris Berezovsky. Gorbachev's *perestroika* accelerated the relations between traders and apparatchiks, who formed alliances to glean riches from the widespread decay in state industry. The *liberalisation* in trade from 1986 however led to:

> a series of legal changes in Russia that altered the ownership and employment relations within which production took place, and by 1989 specifically capitalist forms of enterprise had effectively been legalised, and the joint stock company became a feature of the Soviet system (Pomorski 1991). Concerns and associations were permitted to determine their production in relation to direct orders, and they were required to compete for these orders. Wage levels were to be determined according to the profitability of the concern.[31]

Despite the general support for reform the distance between the rhetoric and the policies that were implemented, monitored and reviewed was substantial. This appears to have been the result of the resistance to reform elsewhere in the system, and the culture of non-compliance which had developed in both subtle and excessive degrees in all areas and at all levels of the economy. It was not an economic revolution, but an implosion of material and structural standards resulting from the introduction of a flawed policy of political and economic restructuring and the clear lack of accountability and responsibility throughout the Soviet system.

The tensions between the traditional and reforming communists resulted in the eventual rejection of both. The shift in the industrial Nomenklatura to support more popular political voices, Yeltsin in Moscow for example, was paradoxically calculated to restrain the untrammelled move to capitalism, which was perceived as a threat to the stability of the economic order that benefited the elites in the Soviet system. The action signalled the end of the political and economic designs favoured by the reformers in the Kremlin.

Many of the discussions that led to the introduction of Gorbachev's policies had been televised. In particular, following the difficulties in reforming the Party, Gorbachev's creation of the Council of Deputies and its televising on national television, (re) introduced millions in the Soviet Union to the vagaries of Party and state politics, and the power struggles held therein. The impact of television on Soviet politics had not been thoroughly assessed or understood by the authorities, a mistake and opportunity alternative/counter-culture would exploit. It had been intended to convey a modicum of transparency in political affairs, but ultimately it removed the mystique and importance associated with the politicians themselves and undermined the respect they could tenuously claim. The transmission of 23 August 1991 included the famous exchange between Yeltsin and Gorbachev and signalled the Party's loss of control over the monopoly of the media and the Soviet Union. Yeltsin had shaken a presidential order and called for Gorbachev to sign a decree suspending the activity of the Russian communist party, an act that would earlier have led to an immediate arrest and severe punishment.

The debates, interjections, and rhetoric occurring within the Congress rapidly became more daring, heated and controversial, being critical of both the Party and the leadership. The split between Ligachev and Yeltsin, an enthralling drama between political rivals and ideas, but not diametrically opposed on key issues, despite claims to the contrary, focused the opposition. The transmission of political debate allowed the *ordinary* citizen to glean an insight into the performance of the General Secretary. It has been suggested that the capabilities of Gorbachev were far from extraordinary. In the past the characteristics and the limitations of the General Secretary would be known only to a select few – now suddenly a wide audience had a facility to assess and judge the man they were being led by.

The combination of forces, present in turbulent periods was impossible to contain without the introduction of widespread force and social repression, a strategy that could result in civil war. The social and economic situation deteriorated to incomprehensibility. The General Secretary of the second most powerful nation in the world was to be humiliated and rendered superfluous to the vortex inherent within the change process.

In the confusion that circulated throughout the former Soviet Union, intellectuals, political prisoners, unofficial Soviet rock bands, poets, entrepreneurs, gangsters, window cleaners, the vast range of alternative/counter-culture won and lost in a chaotic see-saw of fortunes power and privilege, despair and destitution. The institutional collapse of communism was not achieved through a set of calculated decisions taken at the highest level. The pressure that had accumulated in response to putrefying banality of the unceasing decrees, proclamations, detailed regulations notifications, plastered in the consciousness of the ordinary people as well as on the walls of every town and village, which could not be fulfilled. The evidence of failure was everywhere. The weight of negativity shattered the illusion and the hold exercised by the authorities. In a brief tumultuous moment, Soviet history was swept aside; its institutions vanished into thin air.

It is not a neat picture that presents itself and it should not be dramatised as such. Nonetheless, the role of alternative/counter-culture should not be underestimated. In the change process Soviet rock fans were generally in favour of the democratic process and sought directly to end the manipulation associated with the hierarchy of the Soviet regime in organising their lives. Did they, however, fall behind the democratic parties such as Popular Front in Moscow or were they suspicious of all political parties?

The latter would be closer to the truth. But that is not to say that they were indifferent. The negation of communism was prevalent. But the active support of the democratic movement was minimal. Emancipation of rock culture was seen by the rock generation as a definite gain in the struggle against totalitarian communist ideology so of course the democratic movement and the rock movement were closely associated in the minds of the youth. But as to a direct collaboration there wasn't much. At the same time one should mention the growth of a very strong pro-Communist anti-Western rock movement in the early 1990s. Egor Letov (an equally radical communism fighter in the 1980s) with his Grazhdanskaya Oborona is the main exponent.[32]

The desire to construct the means of escape from the established mode of social control transformed the regularities of everyday life into concrete political strategies. The wide opposition to the Soviet regime was initiated from a variety of starting points. Were musicians and rock fans in the unofficial Soviet rock movement interested in the potential of a political alternative?

> Well, first of all I can't divide people into "rock fans" and "the rest" when talking about politics. The division is more a generation thing: older people were generally more interested in politics while the younger generation (born in the sixties and later) were politically inactive. I recall a short period when politics was an issue: from the 19th (?) Communist Party Conference in 1988 (Yeltsin's case and everything after) to the Soviet Union's split up in 1991. Everybody seemed to be concerned about politics in those times. The crucial point was the August coup in 1991 – that was a time of big hopes in some "future". But, after August, people's anxiety about politics was lowering quickly, as there was virtually no signs of improvement, but people of my age and younger seem disillusioned. The reality is, that in Russian political life nothing depends on the people's choice, and all the political groups – no matter how they call themselves – are more or less the same.[33]

The bottle-neck of dissent that had accumulated from a variety of sources had broken the vestiges of an abandoned ideology and shattered the illusion of its perceived power. The various cultures that sought retribution from the Soviet corpse overwhelmed the regime and made public their divided interests. Without other than superficial economic and political reform and the relative democratisation of Soviet life, the wave of disillusionment in the system could not be contained without a widespread purge of the change culture.

Pressure Points

Gorbachev deepened and broadened his power base within the Party. Despite this, however, he failed to keep control of the countervailing forces either within or outside the Party. Alexander Rahr claims that the 'alternative power base of the presidency [was] not yet strong enough to sustain him'.[34] This resulted in various factions accelerating the change process through calculated and opportunistic episodic gains.

It has been argued that Gorbachev preferred diplomacy instead of an expensive arms race with the United States. In a CIA document entitled "Soviet SDI Options: The Resource Dilemma", dated 1 November 1987, the content suggests that the Soviet Union would not attempt to match SDI because associated costs would cripple the Kremlin's effort of modernisation.[35] Each attempt to reform the official economy was frustrated by the degree of illegal activity and corruption embedded within the system itself.

The elements within the Nomenklatura that required a form of managed capitalism, opposed either the return of a form of Leninist ideology or an extensive capitulation to untrammelled capitalism, which could lead to action against them. The authorities in their various clichés attempted to scramble and grasp what opportunities remained.

The twin pillars of the Soviet authority and control, the Communist Party of the Soviet Union and the Soviet state superstructure were transformed between 1985-91. The former, as both an institution, and mechanism of policy and ideological direction, was rendered defunct. Under Stalin, the CPSU had lost its power to the ambitious and harsh dictator. Following Stalin's death, and particularly with Khrushchev's manoeuvrings, it had re-established its influence and re-affirmed its control of both policy and ideological direction. The sudden institutional abandonment of communism following the putsch of August 19 1991 disguised its embedded weaknesses (a condition that the book has sought to expose through making explicit the link between counter-culture and reform).

The reform process, to which Gorbachev had been but a part, had for Soviet communism been an unmitigated disaster, resulting in complete systemic loss to the processes that challenged the pervasive monopoly of power. The (re) emergence of nationalist and republican passions, long believed subsumed under the omnipotent and omnipresent influence of Soviet ideology and culture, led to greater legal demands to de-centralise control over the mechanisms of state power. The Soviet State apparatus had been in the service of the Party. When the Party collapsed, it [the Soviet Union] became the subject of a disputed ownership. A crop of independent states replaced the monolith that had ruled over the multi-ethnic peoples of the former Soviet Union; the roof above them collapsed with never met promises.

The identification of counter-culture dispersed with the disintegration of communism into a nexus of diametrically scattered interests, fragmenting the tenuous harmony of opposition that had operated during the Soviet era. To the astonishment of the soldier and the student, the alternative view, which had provided the opposition to the legitimacy and longevity of the Soviet regime, dispersed, along with the certainties of the past.

Notes

[1] Chris Rojek (1995:130), *Decentring Leisure.*
[2] Boris Kagarlitsky (1998) Interviewed (April 1998).
[3] McAllister and White (1995:233), *The legacy of the Nomenklatura.*
[4] Sheeran (1998), *Diary notes.*
[5] Bauman (1991:187), *Communism: a post-mortem.*
[6] *Ibid* (1991:187).
[7] Iaremenko (1991:6).
[8] Anna Nirmadlendran (1997) Interviewed (8 December 1997).
[9] Wilheim (1985:119), *The Soviet Union has a administered not a planned economy.*
[10] *Ibid* (1985:129).
[11] Filatotchev (1992:506), *Privatisation and entrepenueralism.*
[12] *Ibid* (1992:506).
[13] Flaherty (1993:3), *Privatisation and the Soviet Economy.*
[14] Volkov (1991:91), Peretroikia, education and the Soviet economy.
[15] *Ibid* (1991: 91,92).
[16] Anna Nirmalendov (1987) Interviewed (8 December 1997).
[17] Ledeneva (1998:3), *Russian economy of favours.*
[18] *Ibid* (1998:7).
[19] Giddens (1984:21).
[20] Joanna Eccles (1998) Interviewed (8 February 1998).
[21] Nirmalendran (1997).
[22] A. Aszabo (1998) Interviewed (8 February 1998).
[23] *Ibid*, Aszabo.
[24] *Op cit*, Eccles.
[25] Sloman (1991:19), *Economics.*
[26] *Op cit* (1995:227).
[27] White (1994:11).
[28] Coser (1990:182), *The intellectual and Soviet reform.*
[29] *Ibid* (1990:182).
[30] Odom (1992:83), *Soviet Politics and after.*
[31] *Op cit*, Garnham.
[32] Alex Kan (1999) On-line e-mail (29 May 1999).
[33] Pantsirev (1999) On-line e-mail (28 May 1999).
[34] See Rahr (1991), *The CPSU in the 1980s: Changes in* the Party *Apparatus.*
[35] Tully, A. (2001), 'Russia: CIA Analyses Give Insight On U.S. Cold War Intelligence'.

10 The Politics of Unreason

It is not intended that this book should describe in depth the cultural mix that was subsumed under the one-dimensional appearance of official Soviet culture. The book has, however, demonstrated that in assessing the nature of the Soviet change process, the presence of dissent cannot be ignored. Under repressive conditions, deviance is rarely conducive to a neat categorisation. Imbued with indigenous positions, foreign interventions, ambiguities and discontinuities, it necessitates a caution in censorship that if ignored produce outcomes that undermine the authenticity of social and political representations.

The Ground Beneath Her Feet (A Global Phenomenon?)

The claim that dissent had disappeared in the former Soviet Union through the efforts of the regime, particularly during the Stalin era and in the late Brezhnev years, has been discredited. Civil society continued throughout the Soviet era to exercise the methods of coded criticism: modestly deviating from the system. The 'double-think' or presence of an alternative view was not the result of an organised political program within its ranks. The various elements that contributed to the denial of the dictates of CPSU were multifarious, encapsulating a range of social comment originating in a range of unconnected cultural sites.

It has been made explicit that the industrial *Nomenklatura* responded in part to the structural changes that took place in the West, but it is not accurate to suggest that purely technological factors and material developments in the international arena led directly to the disintegration of the Soviet Union. The Nomenklatura neither orchestrated a revolution from above nor resisted change in a systematic and coherent form, but it did respond to opportunities and threats that were unevenly presented to it.

Without a recognisable political opposition, facilitated through the establishment and development of political parties representing a range of interests, counter-culture utilised forms such as unofficial Soviet rock to popularise and comment on an alternative view and return confidence to personal opinion. A hybrid of cultures, without unity other than a

171

standpoint of opposition, generated pressure that directly led to political reform and the dismantling of the Soviet system.

Unofficial Soviet rock music was a unique tool in re-vitalising dissidence. It has been shown that it functioned to undermine the authority of the State and the ideology of the CPSU on various social and psychological levels. It was crucial in making clear the degree of corruption and incompetence that prevailed throughout the Soviet system. The extensive intertextual links between Soviet rock, Russian literature and poetry, all the way back to Puskin, were deeply influential in raising both the subconscious and explicit need for dissent, to the level of direct political opposition. This form of coded criticism played a fundamental part in ending the social straightjacket imposed by the CPSU.

In retrospect, the nature of unofficial Soviet rock and its relation to poetry, literature and philosophy, coupled with its intuitive function, attracted specific acts that contravened the safeguards imposed by the omnipotent and omnipresent Soviet system. The vehicle for public protest was invariably both mundane and creative, each receiving measured retribution. It was not only the material and structural difficulties that forced the acceleration of the change process, it was also the implicit ideological challenge, originating within Soviet society that went unnoticed by the adherents of an unproblematic form of structural realism.

Western rock music contributed to the popular conception within the Soviet Union of a mythical Western utopia. The appearance of Western cultural products had a significant influence on the emergence of an unofficial economy that operated throughout the Soviet Union, an influence producing a range of largely unmapped consequences. It is however clear that the Soviet system failed to isolate itself from global culture. The broadcaster Seva Novgorodsev and his weekly rock show was particularly influential in both popularising Western 'popular' music and prompting Soviet citizens through humour and satire to reflect on their relationship with the Soviet regime (the import of it adding to the existing disillusion). It seems that Western rock music did not cause direct political difficulties, but it did contribute to a range of social and economic demands, which could not, without fundamental and extensive reform, be met or regulated with acceptable force.

The failure of International Relations to understand the nature of the Soviet change process stemmed from its pervasive conservatism and deep reluctance to consider phenomena other than the overtly political relations between states and the systems that *house* them. In considering the Soviet change process, the internal forces that functioned within the system along with the subtle external interventions that contributed to the formulation and development of them were alien to theories that prevailed in the discipline of International Relations. Therefore, in the absence of any recognition of the effect of specific social forces, the failure to consider a range of possibilities and outcomes relating to the change process was due to a dispassionate observation, which was flawed in its limitations. The adoption of a form of pluralism that recognises the limitations of a one-dimensional version of human affairs and organisation unlocks the rigid dichotomies present in International Relations and questions the methods that prolong the rigid application of them (the appraisal of a messy IR as a conceptual framework is not a descent into methodological anarchy, but a view that recognises the benefits of a tolerant epistemological process that seeks to make clear content often presumed inactive).

The ability to undermine the rigours of social programming through various acts that range from open defiance to the nuances of a lyric, a joke or the exchange of a grumble (circulated and *amplified*) is explicitly the idea of cultural politics – the politics of unreason.

It has been demonstrated that International Relations as a discipline failed to adequately conceptualise the nuances of globalization. The communication of ideas and the transport of materials (technology transfers, credits, various goods and services) that occurred between the former Soviet Union and the West were significant. The wider effect produced through these exchanges contributed to a fluid change that could not be contained within the confines of a rigid social plan, irrespective of its sophistication.

The Body Electric

The State remains the significant actor in International Relations (the foreign policy of a United States influenced by the leadership George W. Bush – supports the observation). It must however be recognised that indigenous culture[s], is and are, an important force in shaping and being modelled by a range of institutions. The unbalancing of expectations generates disruption; a condition arrived at through experience and communication. It is this 'eclectic' exchange, which perpetrates borders and contributes to change within various social groups.

The intention of this investigation has been to draw attention to the narrowness of an often-perceived macho discipline. Although examples exist elsewhere (South Africa and the demise of the institutions that regulated and 'managed' apartheid), reference to the Soviet change process fundamentally highlights the limitations of International Relations in recognising the importance of culture. Institutions that impact on culture generate resistance through interference that is communicated beyond the location of intervention. What 'goes on' within states has relevance to relations between them.

A purpose generated by Cultural Politics in International Relations might be to stimulate a re-evaluation of the ideas and tools that have attempted to make clear the propensity for change in established systems. The collapse of the Soviet system suggests that the change process is not discernible purely from knowledge of the system within which it takes place. Without a thorough acknowledgement and assessment of the historical and cultural tensions present in the development and denial of the system, the results gleaned from a structural analysis will be disappointing. The range of possibilities, the endless trajectories and relationships produced by social contact, cannot be subdued by systems indefinitely. Preferences and aspirations arising in human life are proverbially the content of life itself. Contrary to appearances, mundane everyday life is not separate from the system nor is it without influence on it.

Bibliography

Anon (1933), *Out of the deep: Letters from Soviet Timber Camps*, London: Geoffrey Bles Publishers.

Anon (1988), 'Cities: the same the world over', *Chartered Surveyor Monthly*, Volume 8, Number 1, 30-31.

Alexeyeva, L. (1987 [1985]) *Soviet Dissent*, Middletown, Connecticut: Wesleyan University Press.

Alexeyeva, L. and Goldberg, P. (1990), *The Thaw Generation*, Boston Toronto London: Little, Brown and Co.

Ali, T. (1988), *Revolution from Above: Where is the Revolution Going?*, London: Hutchinson.

Amin, S. (1992), 'Thirty Years of Critique of the Soviet System', *MonthlyReview*, Volume 44, 43-50.

Appadurai, A. (1986), *The Social Life of Things*, Cambridge, Cambridge University Press.

Appadurai, A. (1990), 'Disjuncture and Difference in the Global Cultural Economy' in M. Featherstone (ed.), *Global Culture*, London: Sage in Association with Theory, Culture and Society.

Arendt, H. (1986), *The Origins of Totalitarianism*, London: Deutch.

Arndt, W. (1972), *Pushkin Threefold: Narrative, Lyric, Polemic, and Ribald Verse*, London: George Allen and Unwin Ltd.

Ashley, R.K. (1986), 'The Poverty of Neo-Realism' in Keohane, R. (ed.) *Neorealism and its Critics*, New York: Columbia University Press.

Ashley, R.K. and Walker, R.B.J. (1990), 'Speaking the Language of Exile: Dissident Thought in International Studies', *International Studies Quarterly*, Volume 34, Number 3, September 259-268.

Baker, G. (1998), '*The changing idea of civil society: models from the Polish democratic opposition*', Journal of Political Ideologies, Volume 3, Number 2.

Bakhtin, M. M. (1984), *Rabelais and His World* (trans. H. Iswolsky), Bloomington Ind: Indiana University Press.

Barabash, Y. (1977), *Aesthetics and Poetics*, Moscow: Progress Publishers.

Barghoon, F.C. (1973), '*Fractional, Sectorial, and Subversive Opposition in Soviet Politics*' in Dahl, R.A. (ed.), *Regimes and Oppositions*, Yale University Press.

Bauman, Z. (1991), '*Communism: A Post-Mortem*', Praxis International, 10: 3,4, 185-192.

Beamish, T. and Hadley, G. (1979), *The Kremlin's Dilemma*, London: Collins and Harvill Press.

Beck, U. (1997), *The Reinvention of Politics*, Great Britain: Polity Press.

Benjamin, W. (1986[1926]), *Moscow Diary*, Cambridge, Massachusetts and London, England: Harvard University Press.

Berlin, I. (1979), 'The Counter Enlightenment' in *Against the Current: Essays in the History of Ideas*, London: The Hogarth Press.

Betts, R. K. (1997), 'Should Strategic Studies Survive?', *World Politics – A Quarterly Journal of International Relations*, Fiftieth Anniversary Special Issue, Volume 50, Number 1, 7-33.

Blick, R. (1993, 1995), *The Seeds of Evil*, London: Steyne Publications.

Bonnell, V. E. (1989), 'Moscow: A view from Below', *Dissent*, Volume 36, Part 3, 311-317.

Bottomore, T. (1983, 1997), *A Dictionary of Marxist Thought*, Great Britain: Blackwell.

Bourdieu, P. (1977), *Outline of a Theory of Practise*, Cambridge: Cambridge University Press.

Boym, S. (1994), *Common Places: Mythologies of Everyday Life in Russia*, Cambridge and London: Harvard University Press.

Brezhnev, L.I. (1967), *Great October*, Moscow: Novostri Press Agency.

Bromley, V. Yu. (1988), 'Ethnographic Studies of Contemporary Soviet Life', *Nature, Society and Thought*, Volume 1, Part 3, 445-451.

Brown, Archie (1996), *The Gorbachev Factor*, Oxford: Oxford University Press.

Bukovsky, V. (1978), *To Build a Castle*, London: Deutsch.

Bukovsky, V. (1987), *To Choose Freedom*, Hoover Press Publication.

Bukovsky, V., Hook, S. and Hollander, P. (1987), *Soviet Hypocrisy and Western Gullibility*, The Ethics and Public Policy Centre.

Bulavka, L (1998), 'From the Cultural Revolution of 1917 to the Counter Revolution of the Present', *Counter-Hegemony*, Special Issue Zero, 8-15.

Bulgakov, M. (1974 [1938]), *The Master and Margarita*, London: Fontana.

Burlatsky, F. (1990), 'From the other shore', *New Left Review*.

Buszynski, Leszek (1995), 'Russia and the West: Towards Renewed Geopolitical Rivalry?', *Survival*, Volume 37, Number 3, 104-25.

Buzan, B. (1991), *People, States and Fear*, New York London: Harvester Wheatsheaf.

Cafruny, A.W. (1990), 'A Gramscian Concept of Declining Hegemony: Stages of U.S. Power and the Evolution of International Economic Relations' in Rapkin, D. (ed.), *World Leadership and Hegemony*, London: Lynne Reinner Publications.

Callinicos, Alex (1995), *Theories and Narratives: Reflections on the Philosophy of History*, Cambridge: Polity Press.

Calvoccoressi, P. (1991), *World Politics since 1945*, London New York: Longman.

Carr, E.H. (1981 [1939]), *The Twenty Years' Crisis*, London: Papermac.

Castells, M. (1998), *End of Millennium*, Great Britain: Blackwell Publishers.

Chan, S. (1993), 'Culture and Absent Epistemologies in the International Relations Discipline', *Theoria*, 33-45.

Clake, S. (1992), 'Privatisation and the Development of Capitalism in Russia', *New Left Review*, November/December, 3-27.

Clark, I. (1998), 'Beyond the Great Divide: globalization and the theory of international relations', Review of International Studies, 24, 479-498.

Cohn, N. (1989), *Ball the Wall*, London: Picador.

Corson, W.R. and Crowley, R.T. (1985), *The New KGB: Engine of Soviet Power*, Great Britain: The Harvester Press.

Coser, L.A. (1990), 'The Intellectuals and Soviet Reform', *Dissent*, Volume 37, Part 2, 181-183.

Cox, M. (1994), 'The end of the USSR and the collapse of the Soviet Union', *Coexistence*, 31, 89-104.

Cox, M. (1998), *Rethinking the Soviet Collapse*, London and New York: Pinter.

Cox, R. (1996), *Approaches to world order*, Cambridge: Cambridge University Press.

Cox, R. (1989), 'Production, the State and Change in World Order' in Rosenau and Czempiel, *Global Changes and theoretical challenges: approaches to world politics in the 1990s*, Lexington, Mass: Lexington Books.

Cushman, T. (1993), 'Glasnost, Perestroika, and the management of oppositional popular culture in the Soviet Union, 1985-1991', *Social Theory*, Volume 13, 25-67.

Cushman, T. (1995), *Notes from the Underground*, Albany, United States of America: State University of New York Press.

Cutler, R.M. (1980), 'Soviet Dissent Under Khrushchev', Comparative Politics, Volume 13, Number 1, 15-36.

Daniels, R.V. (1993), *The end of the communist revolution*, London: Routledge.

Denselow, R. (1989), *When The Music is Over: The Story of Political Pop*, London Boston: Faber and Faber.

Derian, J.D. and Shapiro, M.J. (1989), *International/Intertextual Relations*, New York: Lexington Books.

Devetak, R. (1996), 'Postmodernism' in Burchhill, S. and Linklater, A. *Theories of International Relations*, Hampshire: Macmillan Press Ltd.

Dewey, J. (1994), 'The Development of American Pragmatism' in Moser, P. and Mulder, D. (ed.), *Contemporary Approaches to Philosophy*, New York: Macmillan Publishing Company.

Dostoyevsky, F. (1953 trans), *The Devils*, London: The Penguin Classics.

Dunayevskaya, Raya (1973), *Philosophy and Revolution*, Brighton: Harvester Press.

Dunham, Vera S. (1990 [1976]), *In Stalin's Time*, Durham and London: Duke University Press.

Falk, R. (1993), 'Book reviews: International Relations', *American Political Science Review*, Volume 87, Number 2, 544.

Filatotchev, I. *et al.* (1992), 'Privatisation and Entrepreneurism in the Break-up of the USSR', *World Economy*, Volume 15, Part 4, 505-24.

Fisher, D.H. (1996), *The Great Wave*, New York: Oxford University Press Inc.

Fisher-Galati, S. (1967), *The New Rumania: From People's Democracy to Socialist Republic*, The M.I.T. Press.

Flaherty, P. (1992), 'Privatisation and the Soviet Economy', *Monthly Review*, Volume 43, Part 8, 1-14.

Foucault, M. (1966), *The Order of Things*, London: Tavistock Publications.

Frankel, J. (1969), *International Politics: Conflict and Harmony*, London: Allen Lane The Penguin Press.

Fukuyama, F. (1989), 'The End of History?', *The National Interest*, Summer.

Fukuyama, F. (1992), *The End of History and the Last Man*, London: Penguin Books.

Gaddis, J.L. (1978), *Russia, The Soviet Union and the United States: An Interpretative History*, New York: John Wiley and Sons, Inc.

Gaddis, J.L. (1992), 'International Relations Theory and the End of the Cold War', *International Security* (Winter) 5-58.

Garrard, G. (1997), 'The Counter-Enlightenment Liberalism of Isaiah Berlin', *Journal of Political Ideologies*, 2 (3), 281:296.

Geldon, J.V. (1996), 'Russian Rock and Soul: Seeing History from the Inside', *Radical History Review*, 66, 229-237.

George, J. (1994), *Discourses of Global Politics: A Critical (Re)introduction to International Relations*, Boulder, Colorado: Lynne Rienner Publications.

Gersham, G. (1984), 'Psychiatric Abuse in the Soviet Union', *Society*, Volume 21, Number 5, July/August 1984, Whole Number 151, 54-59.

Gibbs, P. (1921), 'Famine in Russia' in Carey, J. (ed.) (1987), *The Faber Book of Reportage*, London Boston: Faber and Faber.

Gill, S. and Law, D. (1988), *The Global Political Economy*, New York London: Harvester Wheatsheaf.

Gilpin, R. (1987), *The Political Economy of International Relations*, Princeton, New Jersey: Princeton University Press.

Gorbachev, M. (1986), *Political Report of the CPSU Central Committee to the 27th Party Congress*, Moscow: Novosti Press Agency Publishing House.

Gorbachev, M. (1987), *Perestroika: New Thinking For Our Country and the World*, London: William Collins and Sons.

Gramsci, A. (1977), *Selection from Political Writing 1910-1920*, London: Lawrence and Wishart.

Gramsci, A. (1978), *Selections from Political Writings 1921-1926*, London: Lawrence and Wishart.

Grant, B. (1995), *In the Soviet House of Culture*, Princeton, N.J.: Chichester: Princeton University Press.

Grant, N. (1964), *Soviet Education*, London: Penguin Books.

Gray, D.J. (1994), 'Russian Sociology: The Second Coming of August Comte: American Journal of Economics and Sociology', Volume 53, 163-174.

Gray, J. (1998), *False Dawn*, London: Gratna Books.

Gregg, Robert W. (1998), *International Relations on Film*, Lynne Rienner Publishers.

Halliday, F. (1994), *Rethinking International Relations*, London: Macmillan.

Halliday, F. (1995), 'Revolutions and the International', *Millennium: Journal of International Studies*, Volume 24, Number 2, 279-287.

Hammond, G.T. (1990), *Countertrade, Offsets and Barter: An International Political Economy*, London: Pinter Publishers.

Havel, V. *et al.* (1985), *The Power of the Powerless*, London: Hutchinson Education.

Held, D. (1996), *Models of Democracy*, London: Polity Press.

Heldman, D.C. (1977), 'Soviet Labour Relations', *Journal of Social and Political Studies*, Volume 2, Part 3, 191-203.

Helleiner, E. (1994), 'From Bretton Woods to Global Finance: A world turned upside down' in Stubbs, R. and Underhill, G.R.D. (eds) *Political Economy and the Changing Global Order*, London: Macmillan.

Heller, A. and Feher, F. (1988), '*Khrushchev and Gorbachev: A Contrast*', Dissent, Volume 35, Winter, 6-10.

Heller, M. and Nekrich, A. (1986), *Utopia in Power*, London: Hutchinson.

Hepbrun, R.W.H. (1995), 'Poetry' in Hondrich, T. (ed.), *The Oxford Companion to Philosophy*, Oxford New York: Oxford University Press.

Herrick, J. (1996), 'Freedom of Speech as a Universal Human Right', *New Humanist*, Volume 111, Part 1, 11-13.

Hewitt, E. and Winston, V.H. (1991), *Milestones in Glasnost and Perestroyka*, Washington: The Brookings Institution.

Heymann, H. (1945), *Can We Do Business with Russia*, Chicago New York: Ziff Davis Publishing Company.

Hill, R.J. (1988), 'Gorbachev and the CPSU', *The Journal of Communist Studies*, Volume 4.

Hirst, P. (1991), 'The state, civil society and the collapse of Soviet communism', *Economy and Society*, Volume 20, Number 2, 217-241.

Hobbes, T. (1651 [1985]), *Leviathan*, London: Penguin Books.

Hogan, M.J. (1992), *The End of the Cold War*, Cambridge: Cambridge University Press.

Hook, S. (1987), *The Paradoxes of Freedom*, Prometheus Books.

Hosking, G. (1990), *The Awakening of the Soviet Union*, London: William Heinemann.

Hosking, G. et al (1992), *The Road to Post-Communism: Independent Political Movements in the Soviet Union 1985-1991*, London: Pinter Publishers.

Hunt, R.N.C. (1950), *The theory and practice of Communism*, London: A Pelican book.

Isaak, R.A. (1995 [1991]), *Managing World Economic Change: International Political Economy*, London: Prentice Hall International Editions.

Jameson, F. (1984), 'Periodizing the 1960s' in Sahnya Sayres (ed.), *The 1960s Without Apology*, University of Minnesota Press.

Jones, R.J.B. and Willetts, P. ed. (1984), *Interdependence on Trial: Studies in the Theory and Reality of Contemporary Interdependence*, London: Pinter.

Kagarlitsky, B. (1988), *The Thinking Reed: Intellectuals and the Soviet State*, London New York: Verso.

Kagarlitsky, B. (1990), *The Dialectics of Change*, London New York: Verso.

Kagarlitsky, B. (1990), *Farewell Perestroika*, London New York: Verso.

Kagarlitsky, B. (1992), *The Disintegration of the Monolith*, London New York: Verso.

Kagarlitsky, B (1997), 'The Unfinished Revolution', *New Left Review*, Number 226, 155-159.

Kaldor, M., Holden, G. and Falk, R. (1989), *The New Détente: Rethinking East-West Relations*, London: Verso.

Kellnet, J. (1999), 'Poland's scramble for modernisation', *Chartered Surveyors Monthly*, Volume 8, Number 10, 28-29.

Keohane, R. (1986), *Neorealism and Its Critics*, New York: Columbia University Press.

Kissinger, H. (1994), *Diplomacy*, London: Simon and Schuster.

Kohn, H. (1957), *Basic History of Modern Russia*, Princeton, New Jersey: An Anvil Original.

Kotz, David with Fred Weir (1997), *Revolution From Above: The demise of the Soviet System*, London: Routledge.

Kryshtanovskaya, O. (1992), 'The New Business Elite' in Lane, D. (ed.), *Russia in Flux*, Edward Elgar.

Kumar, K. (1992), 'The 1989 Revolutions and the Idea of Europe', *Political Studies*, XL, 439-461.

Kundera, M. (1984), *The Unbearable Lightness of Being*, London Boston: Faber and Faber.

Lane, D. (1988) (ed.), *Elites and Political Power in the USSR*, Aldershot: Edward Elgar.

Lane, D. (1992), *Russia in Flux*, Aldershot: Edward Elgar.

Lane, D. (1997), 'Transition under Eltsin: the Nomenklatura and Political Elite Circulation', *Political Studies*, Volume XLV, 855-874.

Lawton, A. (1989), 'Toward a New Openness' in Golding, D.J. (ed.), *Post-New Wave Cinema in the Soviet Union and Eastern Europe*, Indiana University Press.

Ledeneva, A.V. (1998), *Russia's Economy of Favours: Blat, Networking and Informal Exchange*, Cambridge: Cambridge University Press.

Lenin, V.I. (1947, 1978), *What is to be done?*, Moscow: Progress Publishers.

Leonard, R.A. (1956), *The History of Russian Music*, London: Jarrolds.

Leontief, W. et al. (1983), 'Prospects for the Soviet Economy to the year

2000', *Journal of Policy Modelling*, 5(1): 1-18.

Levinson, C. (1978), *Vodka-Cola*, London: Gordon and Cremonesi.

Lichtheim, G. (1972), *Europe in the Twentieth Century*, London: Weidenfeld and Nicolson.

Lipsitz, G. (1994), *Dangerous Crossroads: Popular Music, Postmodernism and the Politics of Place*, London New York: Verso.

Little, R. (1996), 'The growing relevance of Pluralism?' in Smith, S., Booth, K. and Zalewski (eds) *International Theory: positivism and beyond*, Cambridge: University Press.

Lovell, S. (1998), 'Bulgakov as Soviet Culture', *Slavonic and East European Review*, Volume 76, Part 1, 28-48.

Lowy, M. (1991), 'Twelve Theses on the Crisis of "Really Existing Socialism"', *Monthly Review*, Volume 43, Part 1, 33-40.

Lupher, Mark (1992), 'Power restructuring in China and the Soviet Union', *Theory and Society*, 21: 665-701.

Macdonald, I. (1994), *Revolution in the Head*, London: Pimlico.

Maclean, R. (1992), *Stalin's Nose: Across the face of Europe*, London: Harper Collins.

Maier, C.H. (1991), 'The Collapse of communism: approaches for a future history', *History Workshop Journal*.

Marcuse, H. (1969), *An Essay on Liberation*, London Australia: A Pelican Book.

Marsh, D. and Stoker, G. (1995), *Theory and Methods in Political Science*, London: Macmillan.

Matustik, I. (1993), *Postnational Identity: Critical Theory and Existential Philosophy in Habermas, Kierkegaard, and Havel*, New York and London: Guilford Press.

Mazrui, A. (1988), *Culture of World Politics: North South relations in a Global Perspective*, London: Curry.

McAllister, I. and White, S. (1995), 'The legacy of the *Nomenklatura*: Economic privilege in the post-communist Russia', *Coexistence*, 32: 217-239.

Medvedev, R. (1982), *Khrushchev*, Oxford: Basil Blackwell.

Medvedev, R. (1983), 'Brezhnev: A Bureaucrat's Profile', *Dissent*, Volume 30, Part 2, 224-233.

Medvedev, R. (1983), *Andropov*, Oxford: Basil Blackwell.

Medvedev, R. (1986), *Gorbachev*, Oxford: Basil Blackwell.

Medvedev, Zh. (1998), 'What caused the Collapse of the USSR', *International Affairs: A Journal of World Politics, Diplomacy and International Relations*, Volume 44, Number 2, 84-91.

Middleton, R. (1990), *Studying popular music*, Milton Keynes Philadelphia: Open University Press.

Milner-Gulland, R. (1997), *The Russians*, Oxford: Blackwell Publishers.

Misztal, B.A. (1993), 'Understanding Political Change in Eastern Europe: A Sociological Approach', *Sociology*, Volume 27, Number 3, 451-470.

Morganthau, H. (1993[1948]), *Politics Among Nations: The Struggle for Power and Peace* (Brief Edition), New York: McGraw-Hill.

Morris, P. ed. (1994), *The Bakhtin Reader: Selected Writings of Bakhtin, Medvedev, Voloshinov*, London New York: Edward Arnold.

Mouffe, C. (ed.) (1979), *Gramsci and Marxist Theory*, London: Routledge and Paul Kegan.

Moynahan, B. (1994), *The Russian Century*, London: Pimlico.

Norlander, D. (1993), 'Khrushchev's Image in the Light of Glasnost and Perestroika', *The Russian Review*, Volume 52, 248-64.

Odom, W.E. (1992), 'Soviet politics and after: old and new concepts', *World Politics*, Volume 45, Number 1.

Oleszczuk, T. (1995), 'An Analysis of Bias in Samizdat Sources: A Lithuanian Case Study', *Soviet Studies*, Volume XXXVII, Number 1, 131-137.

Olson, W.C and Groom, A.J.R. (1991), *International Relations Then and Now: Origins and Trends in Interpretation*, London and New York: Routledge.

Pasternak, B. (1958, 1971), *Doctor Zhivago*, Great Britain: Fontana Modern Novels.

Perakh, M. (1978), 'Contemporary dissent in Russia', *Partisan Review*, Volume 45, 248-264.

Phillips, D.C. (1987), *Philosophy, Science and Social Inquiry*, Oxford New York: Pergamon Press.

Pilkington, H. (1994), *Russia's Youth and its Culture*, London and New York: Routledge.

Plato (1974 Second Edition Revised), *The Republic*, London: Penguin Classics.

Plyushch, L. (1979), *History's Carnival*, London: William Collins.

Popper, K.R. (1965 [1989]), *Conjectures and Refutations*, London and New York, Routledge.

Powell, B. (1998), 'Red Flag Redux', *Newsweek,* Part 16, 20-23.

Raeff, M. (1978), *Russian Intellectual History*, Atlantic Highlands, N.J. Humanities Press: Brighton: Harvester Press.

Rahr, A. (1991), 'The CPSU in the 1980s: Changes in the Party apparatus', *The Journal of Communist Studies*, Number 2, Volume 7, 161-169.

Rahr, A. (1992), 'The top leadership: from Soviet Elite to Republican Leadership' in Lane, D. (ed.), *Russia in Flux*, Aldershot: Edward Elgar.

Ramet, S.R. (1995), *Social Currents in Eastern Europe*, Durham and New York: Duke University Press.

Reavey, G. (1968), *The New Russian Poets 1953-68*, London: Calder and Boyers Ltd.

Reed, J. (1918, 1977), *Ten Days that Shook the World*, London: Penguin.

Richardson, D. (1995), *Moscow*, London: The Penguin Group.

Rigby, T.H. (1988), '*Staffing USSR incorporated: the origins of the Nomenklatura system*', Soviet Studies, Volume XL, Number 4, October. 523-537.

Riordan, J. (1989), 'Soviet Youth: Pioneers of Change', *Soviet Studies*, Volume 40, Number 4 (October).

Riordan, J. (1992), 'Soviet Youth' in Lane, D. (ed.), *Russia in Flux*, Aldershot: Edward Elgar.

Rosenau, J. (1990), *Turbulence in World Politics*, New York London: Harvester Wheatsheaf.

Rupert, M. (1995), *Producing hegemony: the politics of mass production and American global power*, Cambridge: University Press.

Rutland, P. (1994), 'Privatisation in Russia: One step forward: two steps back?', *Europe-Asia Studies*, Volume 46, Number 7, 1109-1131.

Rutland, P. (1998), 'Who Got it Right and Who Got it Wrong' in Michael Cox (ed.), *Rethinking the Soviet Collapse*, London and New York: Pinter.

Ryback, T.W. (1990), *Rock around the Bloc: A History of Rock Music in Eastern Europe and the Soviet Union*, Oxford: Oxford University Press.

Sacks, O. (1985), *The man who mistook his wife for a hat*, London: Picador.

Sakharov, A. (1974), *Sakharov Speaks*, Great Britain United States: Collins and Harvell Press.

Sakwa, R. (1989), 'Commune Democracy and Gorbachev's Reforms', *Political Studies*, Number 2, 224-243.

Sakwa, R. (1990), *Gorbachev and his Reforms 1985-1990*, Hemel Hempstead: Philip Allen.

Sakwa, R. (1993), *Russian Politics and Society*, London: Routledge.

Sanders, G. (ed.) (1974) *Samizdat: Voices of the Soviet Opposition*, Anchor Foundation.

Scholte, J.A. (1993), *International Relations of Social Change*, Buckingham Philadelphia: Open University Press.

Seilder, V.J. (1994), *Recovering the Self: Morality and Social Theory*,

London and New York: Routledge.

Shafarevich, I. (1976), 'Socialism in our past and future' in Solzhenitsyn, A. (ed.), *From Under the Rubble*, Great Britain: Fontana Books, William Collins and Sons.

Shelly, L.I. (1996), 'Post Soviet Organised Crime', Transnational Organised Crime, Volume 2, 122-38.

Sherman, H.J. (1990), 'The Second Soviet Revolution or the Transition from Statism to Socialism', *Monthly Review*, Volume 41, Part 10, 14-22.

Sherman, P. (1997), 'Gorbachev and the End of The Cold War', *Millennium: Journal of International Studies*, Volume 26, Number 1, 125-123.

Shutt, H. (1998), *The Trouble with Capitalism*, London New York: Zed Books.

Simirenko, A. (1975), 'A New Type of Resistance?', *Trans-action/Class Society*, Volume 13, Part 1, 35-37.

Sloman, J. (1991), *Economics*, New York London: Harvester Wheatsheaf.

Smith, H. (1976), *The Russians*, Times books.

Smith, S. (1994), 'Writing the History of the Russian Revolution after the Fall of Communism', *East-Asia Studies*, Volume 46, Number 4, 563-578.

Smith, S. (1995), 'The Self-Images of a Discipline' in Booth, K. and Smith, S., *International Relations Theory Today*, Polity Press.

Smith, S., Booth, K. and Zalewski, M. (eds) (1996), *International theory: positivism and beyond*, Great Britain: Cambridge University Press.

Solzhenitsyn, A. (1975), *Lenin in Zurich*, London Sydney: The Bodley Head.

Solzhenitsyn, A. (ed.) (1974) *From under the Rubble*, London: Fontana Paperback.

Soper, K. (1990), *Troubled Pleasures*, London New York: Verso.

Sorell, T. (1990), 'Hobbes's Persuasive civil science', *The Philosophical Quarterly*, Volume 40, Number 3.

Standing, Guy (1998), 'Societal Impoverishment: The Challenge for Russian Social Policy', *Journal of European Social Policy*, Volume 8, Sage Publications, 23-41.

Stenzl, J. (1991), 'York Holler's 'The Master and Margarita': A German Opera', *Tempo* (December), 8-15.

Struve, G. (1961), *Russian Stories*, A Bantam Duel-Language Book.

Suganami, H. (1997), 'Narratives of War Origins and Endings: A Note on the End of the Cold War', *Millennium: Journal of International Studies*,

Volume 26, Number 3, 631-649.

Teague, E. (1992), 'Manual Workers and Workforce' in Lane, D. (ed.), *Russia in Flux*, Aldershot: Edward Elgar.

Thayer, C.W. (1960), *Russia*, Times Inc.

Thucydides (1993 edition), *History of The Peloponnesian War*, London: Everman.

Tibbetts, P. (1977), 'Feyerabend's "Against Method": The Case for Methodological Pluralism', *Philosophy of Social Science*, Volume 7, 265-75.

Tökès, R.L. ed. (1975), *Dissent in the USSR: politics, ideology and people*, Baltimore and London: The John Hopkins University Press.

Tökès, R.L. (ed.) (1979), *Opposition in Eastern Europe*, London and Basingstoke: The Macmillan Press.

Tolstoy, N. (1981), *Stalin's Secret War*, London: Jonathan Cape.

Troitsky, A. (1987), *Back in the USSR: The true story of Rock in Russia*, London/New York/Sydney/Cologne: Omnibus Press.

Tully, A. (2001), 'Russia: CIA Analyses Give Insight on U.S. Cold War Intelligence', Radio Free Europe/Radio Free Liberty article.

Udovicki, J. (1987), 'the liberal model and the public realm in the u.s.s.r', *Philosophy and Social Criticism*, Volume 13, Part 3, 243-263.

Underhill, G.R.D. (1994), 'Conceptualising the Changing Global Order' in Stubbs, R. and Underhill, G. (eds), *Political Economy and the Changing Global Order*, London: Macmillan.

Vaughan James, C. (1973), *Soviet Socialist Realism*, Macmillan Press.

Volkov, Y.E. (1991), 'Perestroika, Education, and the Soviet Economy', *Forum for the Applied Research and Public Policy*, Spring, 90-97.

Volkov, Y.E. (1991), 'Perestroika, Education, and the Soviet Economy', *Forum for Applied Research and Public Policy, Spring*, Volume 6, Part 1, 90:97.

Voslensky, M. (1953), *Nomenklatura: Anatomy of the Soviet Ruling Class*, London Sydney: The Bodley Head.

Walker, E. W. (1993), 'Sovietology and Perestroika' in Gross Solomon, S. (ed.), *Beyond Sovietology*, M.E. Sharpe.

Walker, R.B.J. (1993), *Inside/Outside: International Relations as Political Theory*, Cambridge: Cambridge Studies in International Relations.

Wallerstein, I. (1991), *Geopolitics and Geoculture Essays on the Changing World System*, Cambridge: Cambridge University Press.

Waltz, K. (1979), *Theory of International Politics*, New York: Random House: Addison-Wesley Publishing co.

Wendt, A. (1997), 'The agent-structure problem in international relations theory', *International Organization*, 41, 3, Summer.

White, S. (1994), 'The decline and fall of the USSR', *Modern History Review*, Volume 6, Part 2, 8-11.

Wicke, P. and Shepard, J. (1993), 'The Cabaret is Dead: Rock Culture as State Enterprise – The Political Organisation of Rock in East Germany' in (eds) Tony Bennet et al, *Rock and Popular Music: Politics, Policies, Institutions*, London and New York: Routledge.

Wilheim, J.H. (1985), 'The Soviet Union has an administered not a planned economy', *Soviet Studies*, Volume XXXVII, Number 1, 118-130.

Williams, A. (1992), *Trading with the Bolsheviks: The Politics of East-West Trade*, Manchester: Manchester University Press.

Williams, R. (1988 [1976]), *Keywords: A vocabulary of culture and society*, London: Fontana Press.

Wimbush, S.E. (1989), *Glasnost and Empire: National Aspirations in the USSR* in RFE/RL Studies, Munich: Radio Free Europe/Radio Liberty, London Distributed by University Press of America.

Winn, J.A. (1984), 'The Beatles as Artists', *Michigan Quarterly Review*, Volume 24, Winter, 1-20.

Wolfe, T. (1975), 'The electric cool aid acid test' in Wolfe, T. and Johnson, E.W. (ed.), *The New Journalism*, Great Britain: Picador.

Woodcock, G. (1962), *Anarchism*, London: A Pelican Book.

Zaitsev, I. (ed.) (1990), *Soviet Rock: 25 years in the Underground, 5 years of Freedom*, Moscow: Progress Publishers.

Zaleski, E. (1980), *Stalinist planning for economic growth*, Chapell Hill: The University of North Carolina Press.

Index

References from Notes indicated by 'n' after page reference